THE USES OF
SCRIPTURE IN
RECENT THEOLOGY

The Uses of Scripture in Recent Theology

by

DAVID H. KELSEY

FORTRESS PRESS   Philadelphia

Library of Congress Catalog Card Number 74-26344

ISBN 0-8006-1374-0

First paperback edition 1979

7716E79   Printed in the United States of America   1-1374

In memory of my father
and my brother.

Contents

vii

Preface

For some time now my private title for this book has been *Text, Con-text, and Pre-text*. It was more than a little cute, and in any case suggested a sharper polemical tone than the book actually has, so it is probably wise that it was abandoned for the more bland but accurate title it now bears. Nevertheless, it did serve to identify three concerns that shape the essay. The hyphens in "con-text" and "pre-text" are important: When a theologian takes biblical texts as scripture authoritative for theology, what decisions does he make about these texts? What decisions does he make about the setting in which the texts will be used? And what decisions does he make before ever turning to the texts at all?

This essay has changed and grown over a longish period of time during which I have incurred an uncommonly large number of debts to critical readers. Sections of Part I began in a series of seminars on theology and scripture in which I learned a great deal from W. Sibley Towner with whom I co-taught the course. I got clearer on a number of points thanks to critical reactions by students, both in these seminars and in a graduate seminar that read a much later version of the manuscript. I must also thank in particular Hans W. Frei, George A. Lindbeck, Wayne A. Meeks, Charles W. Powers, and John H. Schutz who read final recensions of the essay and offered pointed, helpful, but not always heeded advice. And I am indebted to George Hunsinger for his meticulous work in preparing the index.

Chapter 1

"Proving Doctrine"

It has been more than a century since Benjamin Jowett pointed out with gentle irony that it is not "easy to say what is the meaning of 'proving a doctrine from Scripture'."[1] For almost a half century now Protestant theology has been dominated by various kinds of neo-reformation theologies that took the principle of scriptural authority with a ferocity that would surely have alarmed Jowett's sweet reasonableness. Virtually every contemporary Protestant theologian along the entire spectrum of opinion from the "neo-evangelicals" through Karl Barth, Emil Brunner, to Anders Nygren, Rudolf Bultmann, Paul Tillich and even Fritz Buri, has acknowledged that any Christian theology worthy of the name "Christian" must, in *some* sense of the phrase, be done "in accord with scripture." They wrote a staggering and sharply polemical literature developing subtle and complex doctrines about the Bible. Quite recently the reversal has come. Respected voices in both American and British theological circles have expressed a sharp sense of crisis about biblical authority. A radically new situation has developed, it is claimed, in which scripture does not, and indeed, some add, cannot serve as authority for theology.[2]

However, neither long and vigorous exercise in trying to use the principle of scriptural authority, nor searching analyses of why it cannot be used any more, has made it any clearer than it ever was just what might be meant by "proving a doctrine from scripture." That is what this essay is about. I want to demonstrate both positive and negative theses. Negatively, I hope to show that there is

1

no one, and certainly no one "standard" or "normative" meaning
of "authority." Moreover, I hope to show that most doctrines about
"the authority of scripture" are very misleading about the sense in
which scripture is "authority" precisely *for theology*. Positively, I
hope to map several related but importantly different concepts of
"the authority of scripture for theology." My procedure in support
of these theses will be to examine comparatively a variety of ways
in which theologians have construed and used scripture in the
course of their actual practice of theology in order to help authorize
their theological proposals. In addition, in order to be able to compare and contrast these uses of scripture without subtly and implicitly favoring one or another, it will be necessary to develop some
common diagnostic questions to put to every case studied and
some "theological position neutral" technical terms in which to state
contrasting positions fairly.

A ROADMAP

It may be useful at this point to sketch the general pattern of the
rest of this study. There are three Parts, each of which develops a
thesis about the notion of biblical authority.

In Part I, we shall try to identify a range of decisions theologians
make about how to *construe* the scripture they actually use to help
authorize theological proposals. Our thesis in this Part is that there
is in actual theological practice no one standard concept "scripture."
"Scripture" is not something objective that different theologians
simply use differently. In actual practice it is concretely construed
in irreducibly different ways.

We shall try to make our case for this thesis through seven case
studies of particular theological proposals made "on the basis of"
particular biblical writings. The cases are drawn from the writings
of seven quite diverse Protestant theologians who, with one exception, were active chiefly between the 1920s and 1960s: Karl Barth,
Hans-Werner Bartsch, Rudolf Bultmann, L. S. Thornton, Paul Tillich, B. B. Warfield (the one chronological anomaly; he was active
at the turn of the century), and G. E. Wright. We shall ask the
same set of four questions of each of these cases:

1) What aspect(s) of scripture is (are) taken to be authoritative?
2) What is it about this aspect of scripture that makes it authoritative?

3) What sort of logical force is ascribed to the scripture to which appeal is made?

4) How is the scripture that is cited brought to bear on theological proposals so as to authorize them? *(Part II)*

The seven cases are selected because they represent significantly different ways of construing scripture, not because they are necessarily representative of the work of the theologians from whom they are taken. This is in no way an effort to make a comprehensive examination either of all the ways in which any one of these theologians construes scripture, nor of the entire range of logically possible ways in which to construe scripture. What is important about these cases for our purposes is the options they illuminate, not the theologies they represent.

In Part II we shall try to identify a range of decisions theologians make about how to *use* scripture to help authorize their theological proposals. Our thesis is that there are a variety of such uses, each of which brings with it a different concept of "authority." It simply means something different when scripture is said to be "authority" for a theological proposal in that it is used in one of these ways than when it is said to be "authority" in that it is used in another of these ways. This brings with it a challenge to the familiar supposition that there is some one normative meaning of "authority," what it "really means," which could be used in critical assessment of a "theological position": "It doesn't *really* use scripture as authority."

Our device in this section will be to suppose that theologians use scripture in the *context* of an argument in support of a theological proposal. Hence attention to the structure of such arguments can help us factor out the various ways in which scripture might be put to work to authorize a proposal. The premise here, of course, is that an appeal to scripture is part of an effort to make a case for a theological proposal whose acceptability is actually or potentially in dispute. This, of course, does not mean that theology is usually written in the form of an argument, or even that theologians understand themselves to be arguing. The suggestion is only that it can be illuminating to take certain sections of theological writing *as* arguments in order to bring out some of the diversity and complexity in the ways scripture is in fact used.

On what basis do theologians make the decision to appeal to

scripture at all to help authorize their proposals? And when they do, on what basis do they decide how to construe and use the scripture to which they appeal? And in particular, what role does close study of biblical texts play in deciding such questions? In the first two chapters of Part III we explore the implications of the foregoing analyses for these questions. In a final chapter we draw some morals from this essay for theological doctrines about scripture.

THEOLOGIANS' METHODS AND
THEOLOGICAL METHODOLOGY

This is to be a descriptive study of some of the methods some theologians employ in doing theology. It might have been illuminating to contrast what those theologians have *said* about the authority of scripture with what they *do* with scripture in the actual practice of their craft; but that would be an exceedingly long undertaking and perhaps not very edifying. This is a much more modest enterprise. It is confined to a narrow range of topics in the hope that in the long run such concentration will open up a wide range of problems. It is limited to the way scripture has been brought to bear on specifically *doctrinal* proposals. It will not examine how scripture might bear on the formulating of church creeds, confessional statements, liturgies, sermons, or moral judgements and ethical principles. It may be that the practical meaning of "the authority of scripture" is substantially the same in all these cases. But then again, it may not be, and we ought not to beg that question.

At the same time, for all the narrowness of its range of topics, it addresses itself to a situation that is theologically open and characterized by rich theological pluralism. The cases we study are drawn from a large number of "theological positions" all claiming in some way or another to be "in accord with scripture." "Theological position" is deliberately vague here. It names a large class of writings that includes Schleiermacher's *The Christian Faith* and Calvin's *Institutes of the Christian Religion*, St. Thomas's *Summae* and Luther's *Works*, the three volumes of Tillich's *Systematic Theology* and all the volumes of Barth's *Church Dogmatics*, the sum total of Bultmann's brief essays on individual theological topics, or Brunner's longer essays, or St. Augustine's even longer ones. That is, the class "theological position" includes any elaborated complex of theological proposals concerning the major traditional topics or *loci* in Christian theology. If there is an important distinction to be drawn between "systematic theology" and "dogmatics," it is ignored here. Nor is the class defined by any normative principles specifying what counts as "Christian." Although we shall confine ourselves to Protestant theologies, any complex of theological proposals that chooses to identify itself as "Christian" may count as a member of the class. Comprehensiveness in regard to traditional *loci* is more important for our purposes than Christian correctness. It is no part of our purpose to set up standards by which to decide when a "theological position" *really* is in accord with scripture. On the contrary, part of our thesis is that any question put that way is meaningless. Rather, it is our concern to find ways in which to state what it *means* in each case to say that scripture is "authority" for this theological position.

Is this, then, a study in theological methodology? Perhaps it is, in some sense. But in order to save the reader serious misunderstandings of its intent, and correspondingly misguided expectations, it is important to distinguish this exercise from another quite different sort of enterprise that currently is called "theological methodology." Perhaps the most important essay in this more usual sort of study of theological methodology by a Protestant theologian is Langdon Gilkey's *Naming the Whirlwind*.[3] It may be useful to contrast what Gilkey undertakes with what is intended in this essay.

Gilkey defines the "problem of method" as the problem about the "sources, content, and criteria of theology as a form of thought."[4] The problem is created by modern secularity, whose "heart" is the view "that human experience, secular or religious, is devoid of relation beyond itself to any ground or order, and that there is no form of human thought that can by speculation come to know of such a ground or order."[5] This raises the basic problem about the "sources, content, and criteria of theology": "Is the general language game of religious discourse, of which Christian God-language is a particular example, applicable in secular existence; does it have any use there; do its symbols relevantly fit and so thematize our ordinary secular life?"[6]

The way Gilkey goes about answering that question has two steps. He first challenges the secular spirit "in terms of the essential characteristics of secular life itself."[7] He sets out to show that the central "elements of the secular spirit," i.e., its sense of contingency, relativity, temporality, and affirmation of autonomy, raise questions "on the level of felt existence . . . with which secular symbols cannot fruitfully deal."[8] He then, secondly, tries to show that religious symbols like "God" in fact "thematize"[9] a "hidden or forgotten dimension of ultimacy that . . . appears significantly in our experiences of our contingency, relativity, temporality, and autonomy," i.e., in secularity itself.[10] These two steps are carried out in Part II of *Naming the Whirlwind* and together constitute Gilkey's solution to the "problem of methodology."

That sort of "theological methodology" is at once part of Christian theology and yet logically prior to systematic theology. It is, to be sure, an apologetic enterprise, designed to show the skeptic that the Christian "language game" is a significant use of language and not just an idling of our language motors. But it is also an inescapable part of Christian thought because Christians themselves share in the secular spirit whether they like it or not.[11] Accordingly, the problem of theological method "is the meaninglessness and unreality of that language for ourselves as churchmen and theologians."[12] Nevertheless, solving this problem is logically prior to and independent of systematic theology. "Such an analysis can at best be only a prolegomenon to systematic theology as a whole, establishing the meaningfulness of the general language game of theology, but not a direct part of systematic theology; it is, if you will, anthropology and not yet theology."[13] In this and many other respects, Gilkey's essay on theological method is an exercise in what contemporary Roman Catholic theology calls "fundamental theology," at once part of and yet prior to "dogmatic theology":

> Fundamental theology today . . . seeks to take the place of that part of systematic theology (dogmatic theology) where it tries to take stock of itself in a "formal and fundamental" way and thus explicitly become part of dogmatic theology itself, so far as the latter . . . must, as a science seek to explain and substantiate itself; yet in method it remains separate, because the "material" enquiry of dogmatic theology into what is concretely contained in Revelation can . . . be distinguished from the enquiry of formal and fundamental theology into the "formal modes" of revelation.[14]

There are two major differences between the sort of enterprise in which Gilkey is engaged and the sort of enterprise this essay represents. They differ in the logical relation that obtains between each of them, on one side, and actual theological positions on the other. And they differ in that one is heavily theory-laden and the other is not.

For Gilkey, "theological methodology" is something a theologian does to solve a problem he faces in getting started at doing theology. It is quite correctly called a "prolegomenon" to theology. It must (logical "must") be done before systematic theology proper can begin. It is as though "methodology" were to systematic theology what aesthetics is to creative writing, and further, as though there were some problems in aesthetics (say: "Is it possible to write a novel in the present cultural situation?", a question sometimes debated in knowledgable circles with great seriousness) that have to be resolved before anyone can actually write a novel. The present essay, on the other hand, consists only of a series of notes and observations about what theologians are actually doing as they pursue their craft. It presupposes that theological positions are being written quite independently of its comments, instead of seeing itself as presupposed by the writing of any adequate theological position. It is as though this essay on theological method is to actual theological positions as literary critical essays are to the bodies of fiction on which they comment. My intent in this essay, then, is not to help make theology possible once again but rather to help prompt fresh insight into theological positions that have come to be anyway. It is a study of theologians' methods, not an exercise in "theological methodology."

This essay differs from essays in theological methodology in a second way. Essays like Gilkey's necessarily involve the development of a *theory* about what theology is. Gilkey's very way of stating the "problem of method" is already theory-laden. Theology, he says, is " *a* form of thought." It turns out to be one form of thought among many. Its distinguishing feature is that it is critical reflection on a set of mental and linguistic phenomena: "religious symbols" in which man consciously "thematizes" pre-articulate, pre-conscious, pre-thematic modes of awareness. As Gilkey rightly points out, the basis of his theory about the nature of theology as "a form of

thought" is a more general theory about the nature of man, i.e.,
an anthropology.

In this essay I shall try to comment on how theologians go about
their business without relying on any theory about the nature of
theology as a "form of thought." To do otherwise would be to beg
at least two kinds of questions.

For one thing, to employ such a theory is to assume that theology
is but *one* form of thought and has but *one* proper method. But
is it true that Christian theological positions have generally been
instances of some one "form of thought"? If that is the case historically, is Gilkey's theoretical account of it adequate to all the
instances? Or does his theory not rather serve as normative proposal: "This is what Christian theologies ought to be"? To use such
a theory in a normative way obviously runs the risk of distorting
one's understanding of theological positions that do not conform to
the norm. More than a decade ago Gustaf Wingren argued that "talk
about *the* theological method obscures the situation." He went on,
"When the theological procedure is conceived of correctly and real-
istically, it becomes entirely relative, adapted to a specific situation
when certain problems are the object of discussion, . . ."[15] The questions Wingren's thesis raises are open and ought not to be begged.
That is one reason why I have tried in this essay to devise a way
of commenting on quite different theological procedures without
relying on a general theory about the nature of theology.

A second matter: A theory about the nature of Christian theology
inevitably entails a judgment about the nature of "Christianity."
Wingren pointed out that the most basic decision a theologian makes
is his answer to the question, "What is the essence of Christianity?"[16] In Part III I hope to show that a theologian's answer to that
question, and the way he makes that decision, is decisive for the
way he construes scripture and for the ways in which he uses scripture in the course of making his own theological proposals. If this
essay were grounded in a particular theory about the nature of
Christian theology, it would also take as normative one particular
answer to the question about the essence of Christianity. Clearly, to
do so would risk serious distortion in understanding theological
positions to which quite another answer to that question was central. That would obscure insight into how different judgments about

the essence of Christianity lead to different ways of bringing scripture authoritatively to bear on theological proposals.

It ought to be clear from these remarks that this essay is no more a "programmatic essay" than it is an exercise in "theological methodology." It is not a proposal about how to revive something called "biblical theology," though it implies no criticism of efforts to do that. So too, unlike James Barr's important new study, *The Bible in the Modern World*,[17] it is not even implicitly a sketch of a new doctrine about the Bible and its authority for Christian theology. Programmatic essays seem more often than not theological millstones more efficient at sinking theologians than polishing doctrine. Strictly speaking, I suppose, this is not a theological essay at all; it is *about* theologies. It does not make theological proposals to the Christian community as such. Rather, it makes recommendations to anyone interested in the matter, about fruitful questions to put to the intellectual structures Christians build, about fairer ways to compare them and analyze them.

This has important bearing on the sorts of criticism this essay invites. It would be a sign of misunderstanding to object to any part of the following that it is historically in error; it makes no historical claims, not even any exegetical ones. It would be equally inappropriate to object at any point, "But you make the theological error here of thus-and-such." The essay makes no Christian theological proposals. Objections that are appropriate would take the form, "The way you put your questions is misleading or unfair in regard to this theologian for the following reasons . . ." or "The terms you use to represent and contrast these theologians' views distort this man's position or that man's in the following respects . . ."

"Theological positions" are, among other things, fascinating works of the imagination. Like literary works of the imagination, they solicit sensitive and probing analysis. They generate a somewhat parasitic body of theological criticism analogous to works in literary criticism. This essay is intended, not so much as a contribution to the resolution of theological problems properly speaking, as a contribution to theological criticism that focuses on the *structure* of theological positions. To be sure, along the way our remarks do tend to show that there is no good reason for declaring the very concept "authority" meaningless or inherently inappropriate in Christian thought, though there may be forceful reasons for not using the concept based on other grounds than the concept itself. But before questions about a theological position's "adequacy" can be addressed, or even its "truth" Christianly speaking, it is necessary to make some judgments about the kind of intellectual enterprise it is, the way it is "put together." How does one go about making such judgments? Everything turns on the questions put to the "position." Which questions will prove most illuminating? What categories will prove the most useful tools both for taking the position apart and for taking it as a whole? In the studies that follow, I hope to illustrate the power of some fresh proposals about that.

NOTES

1. Benjamin Jowett, *The Interpretation of Scripture and Other Essays* (London: Routledge & Sons, n.d.), pp. 27–28.
2. The "25th Anniversary" issue of *Interpretation*, the one American scholarly journal devoted to the question of the relation of scripture to theology, was devoted to this issue, with articles both lamenting and apparently celebrating the evaporation of scripture's effective authority; vol. XXV (Jan. 1971). At a consultation at Boldern, near Zurich, on October 21-26, 1968, the Commission on Faith and Order of the World Council of Churches inaugurated a fresh study of the problem of the authority of the Bible, giving as one of the reasons for doing so the fact that "there appears to be a general crisis of authority at the present time, or at least the notion of authority is different." James Barr drafted "A Study Outline" based on that consultation, to which have been appended "Four Preliminary Considerations of the Concept of Authority" by Eberhard Jüngel, Gerhard Krodel, Rene Marle, and John D. Zizioulas respectively; *V. The Ecumenical Review*, XXI (April, 1969), pp. 135–166. James D. Smart has lamented the loss of effective biblical authority in American church life and proposed ways to counteract it: *The Strange Silence of the Bible in the Church* (Philadelphia: Westminster Press, 1970). By way of sharp contrast, Robin Scroggs, in his inaugural address as Professor of New Testament at Chicago Theological Seminary, notes precisely the same signs of the absence of effective biblical authority, but as a sign of a new cultural situation which—on theological grounds—is to be embraced, not resisted: "Tradition, Freedom, and the Abyss," *New Theology #8*, ed. D. Peerman and M. Marty (New York: Macmillan Co., 1971), pp. 84–104. See also D. E. Nineham's objections to the "dogma of normativeness" in the "The Use of the Bible in Modern Theology," *Bulletin of the John Rylands Library*, Vol. 52 (Autumn, 1969), pp. 178–199, and Christopher Evans, *Is "Holy Scripture" Christian?* (SCM, 1971.)
  For studies of some of the neo-orthodox literature, *v.* Robert Bryant, *The*

Bible's Authority Today (Minneapolis: Augsburg Publ. House, 1968); Robert C. Johnson, *Authority in Protestant Theology* (Philadelphia: Westminster Press, 1959); and, in regard to the Old Testament, John Bright, *The Authority of the Old Testament* (Nashville: Abingdon Press, 1967).

3. Indianapolis: The Bobbs-Merrill Co., 1969. Hereafter cited as "Gilkey."
4. Gilkey, p. 121.
5. Gilkey, p. 188.
6. Gilkey, p. 231.
7. Gilkey, p. 249.
8. Gilkey, p. 250.
9. *V.* Gilkey, p. 201, 209, 250.
10. Gilkey, p. 243.
11. Gilkey, p. 231.
12. Gilkey, p. 181.
13. Gilkey, p. 261; *cf.* p. 301.
14. Karl Rahner and Herbert Vorgrimler, *Theological Dictionary* (New York: Herder and Herder, 1965), pp. 181–182.
15. Gustaf Wingren, *Theology in Conflict*, (Philadelphia: Muhlenberg, 1959), p. 80.
16. Wingren, p. 163.
17. London: SCM, 1973.

PART I:

CONSTRUING THE TEXT

Chapter 2

Doctrine and Concept

When Jowett's essay "On the Interpretation of Scripture" appeared a century ago in *Essays and Reviews* it caused a furor because it proposed to a British public largely innocent of continental biblical higher criticism that scripture ought to be interpreted in the same way as any other ancient book. To Jowett that seemed the only way to take the Bible seriously as the court of final appeal in theological disputes. Medieval theologians had "translated" scripture all too freely into their own theological proposals by relying on the method of "four-fold interpretation." But that, Jowett complained, proved "an instrument . . . of such subtlety and pliability as to make Scripture mean anything—'*Gallus in campanili*' as the Waldensians described it; 'the weathercock on the church tower' which is turned hither and thither by every wind of doctrine."[1]

After a century of subjecting the Bible to the same rigorous scholarly standards and methods of interpretation as are applied to any other ancient document, there is still reason to share Jowett's concern. That is partly because the proposal raised unrealistic expectations in the first place. Close examination of theologians' actual uses of scripture in the course of doing theology shows that they do not appeal to some objective text-in-itself but rather to a text construed *as* a certain kind of whole having a certain kind of logical force. To call each different way of construing the text "scripture" is to use "scripture" in importantly different ways. In short, the suggestion that scripture might serve as a final court of appeals for theological disputes is misleading because there is no one, normative

14

concept "scripture." Instead, there seems to be a family of related but importantly different concepts "scripture." That, at any rate, is the thesis I hope to develop in Part I.

FOUR QUESTIONS

This chapter and the next two are devoted to seven case studies of theologians' construals of the scripture they choose to use to help authorize specific theological proposals. Our general aim in this study is to identify the major decisions they have to make in construing scripture. To that end it will be useful to put four leading questions to each of the cases we study:

1. What aspect(s) of scripture is (are) taken to be authoritative? Is it the concepts in scripture, or the doctrines, or the historical reports, or the liturgical utterances, or the "symbols," or some combination of these, or something else?

2. What is it about this aspect of scripture that makes it authoritative?

3. What sort of logical force seems to be ascribed to the scripture to which appeal is made? Has it the force of a descriptive report, of an injunction, of an emotive ejaculation; is it self-involving?

4. How is the scripture that is cited brought to bear on theological proposals so as to authorize them?

The first question provides the principle by which material from seven theologians is organized into three chapters. Each chapter deals with one major way to answer the question. The authoritative aspect of biblical writing is sometimes its doctrinal or conceptual content (Chapter 2), sometimes its recital or narrative (Chapter 3), sometimes its mythic, symbolic, or imagistic expression of a saving event (Chapter 4). In the course of each chapter the other three questions are also asked of each case.

There is a temptation to take these three chapters together as constituting a typology of ways in which scripture may be construed as authoritative for theology. That would be a mistake. The range of ways of taking scripture exhibited here is probably not exhaustive of all the logical possibilities. Since a fairly brief passage by a single theologian is used to illustrate each of these possibilities, the discussion certainly does not exhaust all that could be said about any one of these theologians' actual use of scripture. A full and candid disclosure of Karl Barth's use of scripture, for example, would prob-

ably show him using all of the ways of construing scripture sketched
here—and more! It is important to remember that what is presented
here is not a typology nor is it exhaustive. It is simply a series of
illustrations of the diverse ways in which biblical writings can be
construed when taken as authority for theological proposals.

"CONTENT" AS AUTHORITY

What is it in scripture, what aspect of it, that is authoritative? At
first glance the question fairly begs for a "put-down": "What do
you mean, 'aspect of scripture'? Its *content* is what's authoritative,
obviously! What it *says* is what's important." This is the common-
sensical answer, and the traditional one. In this chapter we shall
trace how that view controls the use of scripture in writings of two
theologians, the traditional Calvinist, B. B. Warfield, and the contemporary Lutheran, Hans-Werner Bartsch. Warfield, *the* Princeton
theologian, was far and away the ablest mind defending Calvinist
orthodoxy in the United States in the 1880s and 1890s. We shall
examine his use of scripture to authorize his conclusions in some
essays defending the divine inspiration of scripture. Bartsch is a
German theologian probably best known in the English-speaking
world as the editor of the several volumes of *Kerygma and Myth*,
which collects the major documents in the debate over Rudolf Bultmann's project of "demythologizing" the New Testament. We shall
examine his use of scripture to authorize his proposals about the
Christian understanding of international peace. This discussion is
found in an unpublished paper Bartsch wrote for the World Council
of Churches.[2]

Neither of these men has been selected because he was in some
middle-of-the-road way "representative" of a larger school of theologians. On the contrary, each is quite distinctive in the originality
and flair with which he develops his themes. Rather, we pick their
essays because they highlight certain consequences of one answer to
our first question: What aspect of scripture is taken to be authoritative? Those consequences show up as we go on to ask the other two
questions: What is it about this aspect of scripture that makes it
authoritative? And: What sort of logical force is ascribed to the
scripture that is used? In brief, what these two share is the view
that the authoritative element in scripture is its doctrinal or con-

ceptual *content*, which is important because it is divinely inspired, is to be used to frame descriptions of the true Christian view of things, and, hence, is simply and directly to be restated in contemporary idiom by modern theology.

DOCTRINE AS CONTENT

B. B. Warfield is probably best known for his vigorous defense of the doctrine of the plenary verbal inspiration of the scriptures of the Old and New Testaments. In his paper on "The Church Doctrine of Inspiration" he explained "the doctrine of the plenary inspiration of the Bible" as "the doctrine that the Bible is inspired not *in part* but *fully*, in all its elements alike,—things discoverable by reason as well as mysteries, matters of history and science as well as of faith and practice, words as well as thoughts."[3] So understood, the Bible is not simply a record of revelation; it is rather revelation itself.[4] It is the very Word of God itself, "a Word of God in which God speaks directly to each of our souls."[5] Let us examine the arguments Warfield advances in support of this view. We will concentrate, not on the validity of the argument or the cogency of its conclusions, but on the way he uses scripture to authorize his proposals about the authority of the very scripture he is already using as authority.

Warfield offers several different kinds of reasons for adopting his view of the Bible's plenary inspiration. We shall deal with two of these. The first is a claim about how the Bible has functioned in the Christian's life. As used in the church the Bible is a *holy or numinous object* so that members of the community unquestioningly "receive its statements of fact, bow before its enunciations of duty, tremble before its threatenings and rest on its promises."[6] This claim is made in the course of an argument about the history of Christian doctrine. He contends that the doctrine of plenary inspiration has been the common teaching of the church universal, "the assured persuasion of the people of God from the first planting until today."[7] This involves an appeal to the common *experience* of men trying to live the Christian life. We register the following rather lengthy passage in full because it so effectively evokes a sense for that experience:

> . . . our memory will easily recall those happier days when we stood as a child at our Christian mother's knee, with lisping lips following the

words which her slow finger traced upon this open page,—words
which were her support in every trial and, as she fondly trusted, were
to be our guide throughout life. Mother church was speaking to us
in that maternal voice, commending to us her vital faith in the Word
of God. How often since then has it been our own lot, in our turn, to
speak to others all the words of this life. As we sit in the midst of our
pupils in the Sabbath-school, or in the center of our circle at home, or
perchance at some bedside of sickness or death; or as we meet our
fellow-man amid the busy work of the world, hemmed in by temptation or weighed down by care, and would fain put beneath him some
firm support and stay: in what spirit do we then turn to this Bible
then? With what confidence do we commend its every word to those
whom we would make partakers of its comfort or of its strength? In
scenes such as these is revealed the vital faith of the people of God in
the surety and trustworthiness of the Word of God.[8]

In the corporate *experience* of the Christian community the Bible
is received as an aweful and holy object and is used in a variety of
ways: instructing the young, comforting the ill and dying, guiding
the tempted. All these uses of the Bible taken together seem to
presuppose its plenary inspiration, for only so dare one use it in
such a variety of circumstances without any reservations or qualifications. Thus in the essay from which these passages are drawn
Warfield is making two points. First he is arguing the historical
claim that the doctrine of the plenary verbal inspiration of the Bible
has always been the church's doctrine. But in and with that argument he is also giving a reason for accepting the doctrine of plenary
verbal inspiration: No other view on the part of the church could
make sense of her numinous experience when she uses it in these
various ways.

A second sort of reason Warfield gives for holding the doctrine
of plenary inspiration is that the Bible itself teaches it. ". . . The
church doctrine of inspiration was the Bible doctrine before it was
the church doctrine; and the church doctrine only because it was the
Bible doctrine."[9] This is the sort of argument in which it will be
instructive to analyze how Warfield himself uses scripture.

Warfield begins his essay on the "Biblical Idea of Inspiration"
with short studies of three texts:

All Scripture is inspired by God and is profitable for teaching, for
reproof, for correction, and for training in righteousness. 2 Tim. 3:16

R.S.V. (Warfield acknowledges that it might also be translated: Every Scripture inspired by God is also profitable for teaching, etc.)

And we have this prophetic word made more sure. You will do well to pay attention to this as to a lamp shining in a dark place, until the day dawns and the morning star arises in your hearts. First of all you must understand this, that no prophecy of Scripture is a matter of one's own interpretation, because no prophecy ever came by the impulse of man, but men moved by the Holy Spirit spoke from God. 2 Peter 1: 19–21, R.S.V.

Jesus answered them, Is it not written in your law, "I said you are gods"? If he called them gods to whom the Word of God came (and Scripture cannot be broken), do you say of him whom the Father consecrated and sent into the world, "You are blaspheming" because I said, "I am the Son of God"? John 10:34 ff., R.S.V.

In each case Warfield does three things.

He tries to show that in context each passage clearly refers to the whole of scripture, Old Testament as well as New. There are some fascinating arguments here. The passage from 2 Timothy clearly refers to the Old Testament, since that is what would count as "scripture" for Jewish Christians like Paul and Timothy. *But* in 1 Timothy Paul had no compunctions about combining a passage from the Old Testament with one from the New Testament and crediting both to scripture. In 1 Tim. 5:18, St. Paul writes: "For Scripture saith, Thou shalt not muzzle the ox when he treadeth out corn" (which is from Deuteronomy), and "the laborer is worthy of his hire" (and that is from Luke). So who is to say, when Paul tells Timothy in the *second* epistle that all scripture is inspired, that he does not have Luke in mind as well as the Old Testament, and along with Luke "whatever other books he classified with the old under the name of Scripture"?[10]

Although the 2 Peter passage refers explicitly only to prophecy, Warfield argues that "inasmuch as the entirety of scripture is elsewhere conceived of and spoken of as prophetic," it is probable that all scripture is meant here too.

Although the passage from John 10 refers explicitly only to law, the Old Testament passage actually quoted ("I said, you are gods") is from a psalm. Hence Jesus is ascribing legal authority to the entirety of scripture, "in accordance with a conception common enough among the Jews."[11] The conclusion, then, is that "these three terms, law, prophecy, scripture, were indeed, materially, strict synonyms . . ."[12] Hence the three passages make the same claim: *All* scripture is inspired.

Warfield also stresses that the basic intent of each passage is to claim that all scripture issues directly from a divine origin. God is the direct cause of their writing. That is what creates scripture's numinous quality or, as Warfield calls it, its "spiritual power."[13] Warfield extends this point a bit by some word studies which add together as one doctrine. The 2 Timothy passage contains the notorious word *theopneustos*, which is usually translated "inspired by God." Warfield points out that this is an imprecise translation. The term has "nothing to say of *in*spiring or *in*spiration; it speaks only of a 'spiring' or 'spiration.' What it says of scripture is, not that it is breathed into by God or is the product of the Divine 'inbreathing' into the human authors, but that it is breathed out by God, 'God breathed,' the product of the creative breath of God."[14] Warfield's point is that the passage is simply concerned to assert that God did create scripture by his almighty power, and does not give any indication of *how* God operated to produce it.

To this, however, must be added a second step in building the doctrine. The force of a word in the 2 Peter passage is crucial. There it is claimed in the King James translation that "no prophecy ever came (margin: was brought) by the will of man, but it was borne by the Holy Spirit . . ." Warfield insists that the term "borne" has a very specific meaning here. It is not the same as "guiding," or "directing," or "controlling." "What is 'borne' is taken up by the 'bearer,' and conveyed by the bearer's power, not its own, to the bearer's goal, not its own."[15] In short, it specifically stresses that the human authors of scripture are used by God as *instruments* in such a way that their humanity is not violated, but in no way affects the content of what is written.

Finally, a third point must be added to finish the doctrine. Starting with Jesus' use of the Old Testament in the John 10 passage, Warfield moves on to other places in the New Testament to show how Jesus, and then Paul, interchangeably refer to what "God says" and what "Scripture says." This shows how closely both of them assimilated scripture's words to God's word. In short, they saw scripture "as a compact mass of words of God. . ."[16]

Taken all together, then, these passages of scripture teach a doctrine about scripture in its entirety: scripture was directly created by the power of God, using men as his instruments, to produce a book consisting quite literally of the words or oracles of God uttered directly to us. This is the biblical doctrine of inspiration.

Now notice what Warfield has been doing with scripture. His answer to our first question is already explicit: What is the authoritative aspect of scripture? The *doctrines* it teaches. This fits with his view of the nature of saving faith. Saving faith necessarily includes belief that certain doctrines are true. Since it is important that the belief be utterly confident, the truths must be utterly trustworthy. That creates the need for an utterly trustworthy authority determining what those doctrines are. And scripture is, for the Protestant, that authority.

The answer to our second question is clear, at least in principle: What is it about biblical doctrine that makes it authoritative? The fact that it is inspired. This claim has a peculiarly sensitive status in Warfield's theology. The doctrine of inspiration is *methodologically indispensable* for doing theology Warfield's way, but *logically dispensable* so far as the explication and defense of other doctrines is concerned.

On the one hand, no other doctrines hang on the doctrine of inspiration. It is logically dispensable. As Warfield put it in a striking passage:

> Let it not be said that thus we found the whole Christian system upon the doctrine of plenary inspiration. We found the whole Christian system on the doctrine of plenary inspiration as little as we found it upon the doctrine of angelic existences. Were there no such thing as inspiration, Christianity would be true, and all its essential doctrines would be credibly witnessed to us in the general trustworthy reports of the teaching of our Lord and of his authoritative agents in founding the Church, preserved in the writings of the apostles and their first followers . . . Inspiration is not the most fundamental of Christian doctrines . . .[17]

If inspiration were dropped out, no other doctrine would go. It is logically dispensable.

On the other hand, given that it *is* a doctrine taught by scripture, as a matter of positive fact, it must become the basic rule governing our use of scripture. It is a rule, and not an empirical generalization about biblical texts. The rule is that scripture is *inerrant*.

That claim might have been advanced as an empirical generalization. That is, having tested all the truth claims in the biblical texts and found them all true, we might conclude to the empirical generalization that the Bible as a collection of texts is inerrant. Then we might infer that it is inspired. But for Warfield this procedure would be just backwards. It would violate a distinction that seems implicit in Warfield's writings between two different kinds of status biblical texts can have: as texts and as scripture. Scholarly study of the *texts* can show, he believes, "the authenticity, credibility and general trustworthiness of the New Testament writings."[18] Of itself, that would not prove the inerrancy of *all* biblical texts. However, the biblical texts do teach the inerrancy of scripture and, indeed, that Jesus taught the same. If one takes the texts as *scripture*, (i.e., if one takes Jesus and the biblical writers as religiously and not just historically authoritative) then one would accept their teachings, including the teaching about the plenary verbal inspiration of scripture. And from belief in scripture's inspiredness one would then infer its inerrancy. Inerrancy follows inspiration, not the other way around. Thus the doctrine of inspiration provides us with a rule: Always suppose that scripture is inspired and therefore inerrant. The rule instructs us *a priori* to treat apparent errors or inconsistencies in the Bible as being merely apparent and not real. As Warfield puts it, "all objections brought against" the doctrine of inerrancy "pass out of the category of objections to its truth into the category of difficulties to be adjusted to it."[19]

To put it another way, the doctrine of inspiration is a vast hypothesis functioning methodologically like the Copernican theory or the theory of evolution.[20] Anyone who relies on the hypothesis has the confidence that any conflicts that appear between facts and the hypothesis can be explained within the framework of the hypothesis. It would take an enormous number of conflicts to raise serious doubt about the adequacy of the hypothesis. Thus, while it is logically dispensable, the doctrine of inspiration is methodologically basic to Warfield's entire biblical-theological method.

This leads immediately to our fourth question: How is the authoritative aspect of scripture to be brought to bear on theological proposals so as to authorize them? Very directly indeed. The metaphor of "translation" is especially apt for Warfield's view of theology's relation to scripture. Apparently the theologian's task, for Warfield, is to define what the biblical doctrines are and then systematically to interrelate them. The complexity of the task varies from doctrine to doctrine. As Warfield himself points out, "some doctrines are stated with explicit precision that leaves little to systematic theology in its efforts to define the truth on all sides, except to repeat the words which the biblical writers have used to teach it."[21] Evidently the doctrine of the inspiration of scripture is one of these. "Others are not formulated in Scripture at all, but are taught only in their elements which the systematician must collect and combine and so arrive finally at the doctrine. . ." In every such case, however, the theologian proceeds inferentially. Doctrine is inferred, not from isolated verses, but from teachings stated or implied in various passages.[22]

Warfield expressly rejects a proof-texting method and aligns himself with the most unlikely of allies: Friedrich Schleiermacher, who taught us "to build our systematic theology . . . on the basis, not of the occasional dogmatic statements of Scripture alone, taken separately, and, as it were, in shreds, but on the basis of the theologies of the Scripture—to reproduce first the theological thought of each writer or group of writers and then to combine these several theologies (each according to its due historical place) into the one consistent system . . ."[23] Warfield calls this "biblical theology." It clearly is a kind of biblical positivism.

Despite this positivism, the reference to Schleiermacher is not totally out of place. The positivism rises out of the "hypothesis" about inspiration. The hypothesis is validated in a number of ways. As we saw, one way is to demonstrate that what the texts *report* is generally reliable, from which Warfield infers that they are also reliable when they *teach* their own "inspiration." But another way seems (to return to the first point we made about Warfield) to consist in an appeal to a particular form of Christian *experience*. The doctrine of plenary inspiration is one of the doctrines in the system of doctrines constituting the authoritative content of scripture. It differs from the other doctrines in being self-reflexive: It teaches that even the doctrine of inspiration is inspired. One believes the doctrine of plenary inspiration because it is taught in scripture. It is logically dispensable, but in fact it is taught there. But why does one believe what scripture teaches on this point? Because scripture is authoritative. But why is scripture authoritative? Surely, the answer cannot be, "Because the doctrine of plenary inspiration so teaches." That would beg the issue. Nor, as we have already noted, is belief in scripture's authority based on its verifiable inerrancy. To hold to the biblical texts' inspiration is, we saw, more like holding to a rule governing all interpretation of the Bible than it is like believing an empirical generalization. It is to take the texts as "scripture." And one basic reason for a Christian's holding the Bible to be authoritative scripture is simply that it does as a matter of fact function in his life as a holy object. Biblical texts, construed as containing a system of doctrine, strike with numinous power so that one's initial responses, as Warfield reports it, are awe, trembling, and submission. He takes them as "scripture." Thus much of the force of the second kind of reason Warfield advances for holding the doctrine of plenary inspiration, viz., that it is taught by scripture itself, depends on the first kind of argument, viz., that it is experienced as a holy object.

CONCEPTS AS CONTENT

Compare this way of construing and using scripture with a much more recent version of "biblical theology." Let us call it "biblical concept theology." In this kind of theology the chief aim is to lay out the distinctively biblical concepts of one thing and another. These concepts then serve as the basis for proposals about how Christians should think today. A "biblical" concept is often sharply contrasted with non-biblical, especially Greek, concepts with which it is said to be confused by the careless. The "biblical" concept is isolated and defined by extensive word studies of key biblical terms. From the 1930s into the 1950s, especially in Great Britain and the United States, there were a number of theological proposals "authorized" by appeal to "biblical concepts" specified in this manner.[24] In more recent years this sort of approach has been followed in studies of the Christian's responsibility in and for the world.[25]

For example, the Ecumenical Institute at Bossey, Switzerland, was the setting in 1965 of a conference on the theme "God's

Reconciling Work Among the Nations Today" for which Professor
Hans-Werner Bartsch prepared a paper entitled "The Concept of
Reconciliation in the New Testament—The Biblical Message of
Peace."[26] It is a moving discussion, skillfully argued. Although, so
far as I have been able to determine, the paper has never been published, we shall discuss it with some care precisely because it moves
from study of biblical concepts to contemporary theological proposals in an uncommonly deft way. Once again, it is important to stress
our caution that his paper is not necessarily "representative" or
"typical" of all "biblical concept theology," nor does analysis of
this paper exhaust all that might be said of the works that belong
to that family of theology. It is, however, very instructive about
one way in which scripture can be construed and then used to
authorize theological proposals.

Bartsch's central thesis is that in the New Testament the event of
reconciliation is understood most basically in terms of the concept
"peace" rather than "salvation," and that "peace" is a highly distinctive, not to say specialized, concept: (a) Peace is not just the
absence of hostilities, but a dynamic relation that obtains between
parties. (b) In the Old Testament this relation obtains primarily
between whole peoples, and then only for that reason between individuals too. (c) Peace obtains between peoples and individuals precisely in their public experience and not simply in the private or
inward side of life. (d) This peace is a humanly unattainable eschatological reality. (e) Men are not commanded by the Bible to establish peace, but to let an already given peace become manifest to the
eyes of un-faith through acts of reconciliation with one's neighbor.
What appear to be biblical admonitions to us to establish peace are
not moral imperatives but calls to bring the hidden reality of peace
into public manifestation.

These are some of his theses; now we must note how he defends
them. He seems to establish them in two ways. First, he sometimes
traces the history of the use of a term. For example, he argues that
the concept "peace" in the New Testament has its historical roots in
the Old Testament concept "shalom," and therefore the New Testament concept of "peace" carries with it all the implications of the
concept "covenant" with which "shalom" is always related in the
Old Testament. Similarly, he claims that the Old Testament concept

of "peace" has its historical roots in the fact of God's promises that
Israel would find in the promised land "peace among the peoples."
Therefore, the Old Testament concept "peace" and the New Testament concept rooted in it both include the sense that peace designates a political situation and not just an inward state of love.

Secondly, Bartsch sometimes supports his theses simply by exhibiting patterns of juxtaposition among concepts. For example, he
contends that in the New Testament the concept "peace" is regularly paired with the concept "life." Therefore, he argues, "peace"
is as comprehensive a concept as "life" and hence more comprehensive than "reconciliation" which is only occasionally put into
parallel with "peace" and "life."

With this account of the core biblical concept of peace in hand,
Bartsch moves to some proposals about how Christians today ought
to think about peace. (a) Christians should understand that they
are to let peace become manifest through the way they relate to
their neighbors (i.e., through reconciliation with their neighbors);
this is simply to repeat the biblical call. (b) The fact that peace is
a relation between peoples in their public life implies that the Christian is to understand his call as a call to manifest peace through the
way he relates his own people to other nations in concrete political
activity. (c) The fact that peace is an eschatological gift implies that
it cannot be won through any human political party or under the
guidance of any ideology. Hence the call to manifest peace through
political activity is not to be understood as a call to identify Christian obedience with the program of any one political party or movement. (d) The fact that peace is an eschatological gift implies that
the Christian must respond to his call to manifest peace neither with
an optimism based on the alleged progress of evolutionary forces
immanent in history nor with a pessimism grounded in fears of self-
destructive forces immanent in man.

There are some troubling difficulties with Bartsch's way of using
scripture to authorize theological proposals. We can use our four
diagnostic questions to help bring them into focus. If we ask what
Bartsch has decided is the authoritative aspect of scripture, the
answer quite clearly is "biblical concepts." But his way of specifying just what they are trades on some dubious notions about concepts and how to discover their meaning. Bartsch seems to assume

that if one concept, *p* (say, the New Testament concept "peace") has a historical relation to concept *s* (say, the Old Testament concept "shalom"), then *p* always and everywhere in the Bible includes the full meaning of *s*. Or, if *p* is usually juxtaposed to concept *l* (say, the New Testament concept "life"), then *p* always includes the meaning of *l* everywhere it occurs in the New Testament, even if *l* happens in some cases in fact to be missing.

That is, Bartsch proceeds as though a concept, biblical or otherwise, were (a) a kind of container that lugs the selfsame meaning-content into every context, and (b) a kind of onion that accumulates layers of meaning from its several contexts of use in the past, interrelates them systematically, and thereafter bears them in all contexts whatsoever, so that all uses of the concept are present when any one is explicitly used. Accordingly, he can set out, as he himself puts it at the outset of his essay, to describe the *structure* of *the* concept of reconciliation in the Bible. That seems immediately to beg the question whether there is in fact any *one* concept "reconciliation" in the Bible. Furthermore, it suggests the view, without defending it, that a concept consists in some kind of ordered set of relationships that fall into a "structure." But relationships among what? The assumption seems to be that they are relationships among various "levels of meaning" of the term. There is no need to develop them here, but very troubling objections to this entire procedure have been advanced by James Barr in *The Semantics of Biblical Language*,[27] both in regard to its implicit notions about how concepts mean, and in its methods of discovering the meaning of biblical terms.

If, to move to our third question, we ask what logical force Bartsch seems in his paper to allow to the authoritative content of scripture, we turn up another set of troubling problems. Given Bartsch's apparent views of how biblical concepts mean, then it must be the case that the Bible is tacitly treated as a system of *technical* concepts. In ordinary discourse, surely, a word does not have one structure of systematically interrelated senses that goes with the word in every context of use. Rather, the meaning of a word used in ordinary talk is learned by attending to the way it is used in some particular context. The different uses that a single word may have in various contexts have at most, as Wittgenstein has taught us to see, a family resemblance to one another. However, for special purposes, for example in framing theories in physics and metaphysics, it is possible to stipulate that a given word will have a single highly specified meaning in every place in which it used. A whole network of such terms may be developed. It constitutes an artificial language useful for special purposes.[28] If biblical concepts have the properties that Bartsch seems to assume they have, then they would be technical terms and in their mutual relationships would constitute a systematic network of concepts. If that is the case, then the canon is being construed as though it were constructed so calculatingly that its most prominent concepts are technical terms. It might be objected that the implausibility of such a view hardly needs comment.

What is it that makes scripture authoritative for Christian life and thought? The answer to this question now seems clear: Scripture is authoritative because of one of its intrinsic *properties,* viz., the distinctiveness of its quasi-technical concepts. No other faith centers on just these concepts; these are what make Christian faith specifically Christian. This is a watershed decision. As we shall show, other ways of relating scripture to theology take scripture to be authoritative only in so far as it *functions* in certain ways in Christian living and thinking.

Finally, how is theology to be related to scripture such that the scripture authorizes the theological proposals? In Bartsch's practice the relation is very direct indeed. His theological proposals are "based on" biblical concepts in that they simply repeat biblical concepts and draw out their implications. It is this view of what the theologian is to do that leads to construing the Bible as a lexicon containing a system of quasi-technical terms. The systematic interrelationships among biblical concepts established the basic internal coherence of that dimension of scripture that is authoritative, i.e., the concepts. This coherence is of principal importance because it is the basis of the coherence of the theology "based on" these concepts. It is only because the biblical concepts hang together that the theological proposals directly authorized by them can be shown to hang together too.

Before drawing back to make some general remarks about the differences between the ways of construing scripture illustrated by these essays from Warfield and Bartsch, it is important to remember again how narrow these case studies are. None of the question marks set against Bartsch's apparent assumptions and methods in his paper count as an assessment of his theological proposals as such. His discussion is exciting and eminently relevant to major social crises of our time. Nor can they be supposed to throw a shadow over his theological work as a whole, for there is no claim here that the particular essay under discussion is representative of his work. Indeed, they may not even be decisive in regard to this one paper. We mention them, not to endorse them, nor to assess the cogency of Bartsch's argument, but simply to indicate where its critics might begin to question it. We selected this one paper solely because it illustrates so effectively some ways of construing and using scripture in theology that one finds frequently in the writings of many theologians.

AUTHORITY AND PROPERTIES OF SCRIPTURE

The similarities in the respective theological methods in these two essays are striking and important. Together they hold that the authoritative element in scripture is its stateable content. In one case the content is construed as doctrines and in the other as concepts, although in practice there seems only the thinnest line between a theological concept and a doctrine. Together they hold that this content falls into a systematic structure which constitutes the unity of scripture.

Where they may differ significantly is on the question, Why is scripture authoritative? Bartsch may not accept Warfield's doctrine of the plenary inspiration of the Bible or its comprehensive inerrancy. But this would not in fact be a decisive difference. Warfield himself admitted that the doctrine of inspiration is not logically central or necessary to Christian theology. At a formal level there is again a striking parallel between the two: Both hold that scripture is authoritative because of some intrinsic *property* of the text, viz., for Warfield, *inerrancy*, and, for Bartsch, the *distinctiveness* of the Bible's quasi-technical concepts. They suppose scripture to have this property because its important content simply *is* the content of revelation.

In this "biblical concept theology" stands classical Protestant orthodoxy, current "evangelical" theology,[29] and pre-Vatican II

Roman Catholic theology. By the same token it stands over against
the other theologies we shall examine here. The others all seem to
understand "authority" *functionally*, i.e., as a function of the role
played by biblical writings in the life of the church when it serves
as the means by which we are related to revelation. Indeed, we shall
see that one basic distinction to be made among different notions of
"authority" is the distinction between understanding authority functionally and understanding it as an intrinsic property of canonical
writings.

NOTES

1. Jowett, p. 29.
2. H. W. Bartsch, "Begriff der Versöhnung im Neuen Testament—Die biblische Botschaft vom Frieden," mimeographed, unpublished paper.
3. *The Inspiration and Authority of the Bible* (Philadelphia: The Presbyterian
and Reformed Publishing Co., 1948), p. 113: hereafter cited as "Warfield."
4. Warfield, p. 161.
5. Warfield, p. 125.
6. Warfield, p. 107.
7. Warfield, p. 106.
8. Warfield, p. 107.
9. Warfield, p. 114.
10. Warfield, p. 164.
11. Warfield, pp. 138–139.
12. Warfield, p. 139.
13. Warfield, p. 135.
14. Warfield, p. 133.
15. Warfield, p. 137.
16. Warfield, p. 147.
17. Warfield, p. 210.
18. Warfield, p. 212; cf. pp. 213, 174. Warfield, of course, would hold that
the results of scholarly study of biblical texts as texts themselves give good
reasons for taking the texts as scripture. He would hold that showing the
"general trustworthiness" of New Testament writers also shows that their
writers are "trustworthy as doctrinal guides" (p. 174). That does not follow
self-evidently, since the writers of biblical texts might report in a trustworthy
way what Jesus taught and what they believed, and still be untrustworthy doctrinal guides. The merits of Warfield's arguments in support of the claim that
it does follow even though it is not self-evident fall outside the scope of this
discussion. However, it is fair to note that it raises the question whether the
transition from taking the biblical texts as sources in which one has faith to
taking them as sources in which one has *saving* faith, from taking them as
texts that are trustworthy reports to taking them as *scripture* that are trustworthy doctrinal guides, can rest on *any* amount of historical research.

19. Warfield, p. 174.
20. The "logic" by which such an hypothesis is accepted and by which it might be given up would seem to have close parallels with that by which major hypotheses in the physical sciences are adopted and abandoned, as analyzed by Thomas Kuhn, *The Structure of Scientific Revolutions* (Chicago: University of Chicago Press, 1962), esp. Chs. 6–10.
21. Warfield, p. 209.
22. Warfield, p. 209.
23. Warfield, cf. pp. 198–199, 209.
24. E.g., Thorlief Boman, *Hebrew Thought Compared with Greek,* trans. Jules L. Moreau (London: SCM Press, 1960); Oscar Cullman, *Christ and Time,* trans. Floyd V. Filson (Philadelphia: Westminster, 1954); G. A. F. Knight, *A Biblical Approach to the Doctrine of the Trinity* (Edinburgh: Oliver & Boyd, 1957); John Marsh, *The Fullness of Time* (London: Nisbet, 1952); J. K. S. Reid, *The Biblical Doctrine of the Ministry* (Edinburgh: Oliver & Boyd, 1955); Alan Richardson, *The Biblical Doctrine of Work* (London: SCM Press, 1954); Thomas F. Torrance, *The Biblical Doctrine of Baptism* (Edinburgh: St. Andrews Press, 1958) and *Royal Priesthood* (Edinburgh: Oliver & Boyd, 1955); G. Ernest Wright, *The Biblical Doctrine of Man in Society* (London: SCM Press, 1954). For an account of the demise of "biblical theology," including what I have called "biblical concept theology," see Brevard S. Childs, *Biblical Theology in Crisis* (Philadelphia: Westminster Press, 1970), Chs. 1–4.
25. E.g., Harvey Cox, *The Secular City* (New York: Macmillan, 1965), esp. Ch. 1.
26. Bartsch's paper, "Begriff der Versöhnung im Neuen Testament," is included in mimeographed "Minutes of the Conference on God's Reconciling Work Among the Nations Today, 28th June-3rd July, 1965" from the Ecumenical Institute, Bossey, Switzerland.
27. James Barr, *The Semantics of Biblical Language* (London: Oxford University Press, 1961), esp. Chs. 6–8.
28. James M. Robinson, in his essay on "Theology as Translation," makes the astounding claim that "The language of theology is not a technical terminology, for what theology has to say is not technology but rather has to do with authentic life." (*Interpretation,* XX, p. 526). Whether or not the language of theology, or of the Bible for that matter, is a "technical terminology" or a "technical language" may be a debatable point, but it surely does not turn on the question whether theology or Bible talk about "technology"! A language is "technical" in contrast to "ordinary." What makes it "technical" is not its field of reference (e.g., "technology") but whether the rules employed for the use of language are stipulated, and thereby quite exact and clear, or learned in the ordinary course of life, and therefore likely to be rather more loose and ambiguous.
29. V. Carl F. H. Henry, ed., *Revelation and the Bible* (Grand Rapids: Baker Book House, 1958).
30. V. George Lindbeck, *The Future of Roman Catholic Theology* (Philadelphia: Fortress Press, 1970), esp. Ch. 5.

Chapter 3

Recital and Presence

Story-telling is at least as prominent in the Bible as doctrine-teaching. Indeed, there has been a wide-spread consensus in Protestant theology in the past four decades that the "revelation" to which scripture attests is a self-manifestation by God in historical events, and not information about God stated in divinely communicated doctrines or concepts. Scripture is said to be important because it preserves the content of revelation. That means that it narrates these revelatory events, not that it teaches the divinely sanctioned doctrines. The authoritative side of scripture, then, is its narrative and not its didactic aspect.

There is, however, more than one way to use biblical narrative to authorize theological proposals. In this chapter we shall contrast two of them. One way is to construe the narrative as historical recital, and the other is to see it as a story rendering an agent. For an illustration of the first we shall turn to a discussion by G. Ernest Wright of how God is known. The second will be illustrated by a passage from Karl Barth's discussion of the humanity of Jesus Christ. Throughout Part I we need to keep in mind that these seven diverse ways of construing and using scripture in theology are not necessarily incompatible with each other. Some or all of them may turn up in different places in the writings of any particular theologian. Although our case studies necessarily have to come from the writings of particular theologians, we are not typologizing theologians; we are trying to sort out different typical ways of construing scripture and using it to authorize theological claims.

SCRIPTURE AS RECITAL

In his widely influential book *God Who Acts*[1] G. Ernest Wright
explicitly takes the view that the authoritative aspect of scripture
is narrative, and that narrative is to be construed as confessional
recital. Moreover, he grounds this on the view that the revelation
to which the Bible witnesses consists in a series of historical events.
"God is . . . known by what he has done."[2] Accordingly, "The Bible
is not primarily the Word of God, but the record of the Acts of
God, together with the human response thereto."[3] Wright draws a
sharp line between construing the Bible as a collection of doctrines
and construing it as recital: "The Bible does not present us with
doctrine . . . and the attempt to make it do so is to misuse it."[4] It is,
instead, "recital, in which Biblical man confesses his faith by reciting
the formative events of his history as the redemptive handiwork of
God."[5] Because that is the basic "logical force" of biblical writings,
"No system of propositions can deal adequately with the inner
dynamics of Biblical faith."[6] To be sure, Wright acknowledges that
there are propositions taught in scripture too. However, the biblical
writers' "knowledge of God was an inference from what actually
happened in human history."[7] The biblical doctrine is inferred from
the historical recital. The clear implication is that the recital is theologically more basic and important than the doctrine. Consequently,
while it is true that one cannot discuss scripture "without dealing
with the *ideas* of which it is composed," still, "to conceive of it primarily as a series of ideas which we must arrange either systematically or according to their historical development is to miss the point
of it all. It is fundamentally an interpretation of history, a confessional recital of historical events as the acts of God . . ."[8]

Wright's central thesis is that "God is . . . known by what he has
done. The so-called 'attributes' of God are inferences drawn from
the way he has acted,"[9] not from a grasp of his being and essence.
And when God's attributes are understood in terms of his acts rather
than in terms of his being, the very concept of God undergoes
important changes.

In his argument for this thesis Wright makes three revealing
moves.

First, he stresses the *uniqueness* of the biblical understanding of
God's relation to history. Other ancient Near Eastern religions

understood man "as embedded in society and society was embedded in the rhythm and balance of nature which was the realm of the gods. The whole aim of existence was thus to fit into the rhythm and integration of the cosmic society of nature."[10] For Israel, by contrast, the problem was how to live in history in accord with the will and purpose of God. When other cultures did declare the acts of their gods in history, it was always in connection with the individual exploits of kings and heroes. Israel concentrated instead on "the unity and meaningfulness of universal history" through which as a whole God acts.[11] This history was seen as "a meaningful process *en route* to a goal."[12] Thus God is to be understood in terms of his acts in history where "history" is understood in a unique way.

Second, Wright shows that there is a common structure to the way Old and New Testament theologies are organized. The contents of each testament are organized around a basic *kerygma* which consists of a simple recital of the most basic acts of God. Wright draws on von Rad's identification of several expressions of the basic Old Testament *kerygma*, of which Deut. 26:5–9 is perhaps the most striking.[13] All of these passages emphasize (1) God's election of Abraham, (2) his deliverance of Israel at Exodus; and (3) his gift of the land.[14] The central point is that "Around the theme of God's greatest acts in bringing the nation into being, early Israel collected all her traditions, including the various stories about the Patriarchal period and the covenant traditions of Sinai, Moab, and Schechem."[15] It seems that all other Old Testament material, Wisdom literature for example, is to be understood in terms of its relation to this *kerygma*. That is, it is to be understood as having the force of a recital of the kerygmatic narrative or as being a comment upon it.

At the heart of the New Testament too there is a *kerygma* in which is recited "the work of God in the life and death of a historical person."[17] Wright follows C. H. Dodd in tracing a Jerusalem *kerygma* consisting of six points, which is "the nerve center of the New Testament." Indeed, "the Gospels themselves represent the expansion of the *kerygma* from a number of sources of tradition."[18]

Now an important feature of the New Testament *kerygma* is that it includes the Old Testament *kerygma*. Its story characteristically begins, e.g., in Acts 13:16 ff., with the Patriarchs, moves to David, and then jumps to Jesus Christ. Wright takes pains to explain why

David is the shifting point from Old Testament *kerygma* to New Testament *kerygma*. The line from David to Jesus is marked by a pattern of continuity and discontinuity, of promise and fulfillment. The New Testament *kerygma* recites Jesus' story as the unbroken carrying through of the purposes of God expressed in the David story in the Old Testament *kerygma*. The election of David and his dynasty was representative of God's election of Israel, and embodied a promise of the eventual working out of God's intention through Israel to secure justice and security and to draw all men into a universal kingdom.[19] The New Testament *kerygma* recites the story of a Jesus who stands in that dynasty and so embodies the same election and hopes. Here is continuity. But the historical dynasty of David, and by extension Israel herself, failed to realize those promises. The promises embodied in the election of David and his dynasty were projected into the future and, for the Prophets, became the substance of eschatology.[20] The New Testament *kerygma* recites the story of Jesus who fulfills the promises, which is to say that he inaugurates the eschatological period. Here is the discontinuity between the two kerygmas.

In short, Wright shows that what unites the two testaments into a single whole is the one integral history of the acts of God. It runs from the Patriarchs to Paul and has a kind of center in Jesus Christ.[21] Thus the nature of God is to be inferred from a sub-set of events in world history and not from history as a whole. To be sure, the history of God's acts is set within the context of universal history,[22] and it promises future, as yet unrealized events as an ultimate goal.[23] But the history in which God is revealed and which scripture recites is only part of history, a *Heilsgeschichte*.

Third, Wright outlines the attributes of God that are to be inferred from this history by sketching the history of the development of the concept of God. Israel's doctrine of God arose initially, Wright contends, "from an attempt to explain the events which led to the establishment of the nation."[24] More exactly, the event to be explained was her "election," and Israel inferred from that a God of "grace."[25] From this a second inference was drawn concerning the elected people; they are a "covenant community" united to a God of law who governs communal life. By a third inference, God's Lordship is extended to nature,[26] but in such a way that God's control of nature is primarily a witness to his relation to history and human society.[27]

Thus the proper concept of God seems to involve three elements that are arranged in a definite, not to say systematic, order: God is the gracious, electing Lord, who *therefore* is said to be the rightful lawgiver for society, and *therefore* is seen as Lord of nature. The order of these points is both the order of their historical development in Israel's religious life and the order of their internal logic. God is not said to be the Lord of history (gracious elector) because he was first said to be the Lord of a people's life (guarantor of their laws and values); nor is he said to be the Lord of a people because before that he was known as the Lord of nature. No, this concept of God is such that the relations of logical dependence run in the opposite direction. The sense in which God is said to be Lord of society is dependent on the way in which he is understood to be Lord of history; and the sense in which he is said to be Lord of nature is dependent on the ways in which he is understood to be both Lord of history and Lord of society.

This is an ancient concept of God that arose in the history of the religion of ancient Israel. How should it bear on modern proposals about God? Very directly indeed. "Theology," Wright says, is "the discipline by which the church, carefully and with full knowledge of the risk, translates Biblical faith into the non-Biblical language of another age."[28] Theology today is simply to restate the biblical notions in language accessible to modern man. The basic categories Wright proposes using today are "act" and "history," rather than "being" or "substance" which were used in an earlier day to "translate" the biblical concept of God. Of course, "A tension will always exist between the Bible and our attempts to communicate its faith in rational language at a given historical period."[29] The tension Wright concentrates on is one created by the central concept "act of God in history." He contends that the notion must be taken quite straightforwardly. He attempts to refute what he takes to be Bultmann's view that talk about "acts of God in history" is myth.[30] On the contrary, he claims, talk about the "acts of God in history" is "history interpreted by faith."[31] It is a "projection of faith into facts which is then considered as the revelation of the true meaning of the facts."[32] The modern Christian must assert that the facts happened,

that the history occurred and that our understanding of God is to
be inferred from them. "If we cannot accept this as true, let us
frankly say so; but we should not misinterpret the Bible by making
timeless ethical and spiritual abstractions its core or kernel of
truth."[33]

There is a great irony about the way scripture has been used to
authorize this contention. The intent of the argument is to show
that a truly biblically based Christian understanding of God must
be cast in dynamic rather than substantialistic terms. God is to be
understood in terms of "history," not "being." The ground given
for this is the claim that the theologically authoritative aspect of the
biblical witness is its narrative aspect, construed as history. But consider how scripture was in fact used in the course of the argument.
The biblical narrative was used as the source of data from which
the central attributes of God were inferred, and in a complex way.
Some features of the right understanding of God are inferred from
the material implications of the judgments passed by the biblical
writers in the course of narrating the history. Others are inferred
from the history of the development of the narratives themselves.
And others are inferred from the way in which the narratives themselves are structured and organized.

But precisely the *narrative* mode of biblical literature plays no
role in shaping the theology. Once this is noted, Wright's initial
stress on the narrative features of scripture at the expense of its
openly didactic features seems quite misleading. The narrative *qua*
narrative does not authorize proposals about God. It simply gives
us the grounds for defining biblical concepts which the modern
Christian is to take over as his own and restate. The concepts are
what is authoritative for theological proposals today, and the narrative from which they are distilled is left behind. Despite what
originally looked like a clear and emphatic rejection of the ways of
construing and using scripture that we studied in the previous chapter, it seems, ironically, that Wright himself has brought us back to
biblical concept theology!

This is not to suggest that there are no important differences
between the way scripture is construed in Wright's discussion and
the ways it was construed in the essays we examined in chapter 2.
In Wright's essay the narrative aspect of scripture, not its doctrines

or concepts, is taken to be what is authoritative about the Bible. And biblical writings in their authoritative aspect are taken to have the logical force of confessional recitals of history, and not the force of a set of coherent doctrines or a system of technical concepts. These disagreements, however, are different answers to questions about whose formulation there is total agreement. First, it is agreed that scripture has a body of content that is "authoritative" for all Christian theology *in the sense that* it is the content which modern theology must simply restate. There is agreement, then, that scripture bears on theology very directly. Where the biblical content is easily understandable, it is to be repeated; where it is cast in terms obscure to modern men, it is to be stated in terms accessible to modern men, but with as little change in content as possible. Theology is related to scripture as a "translation" is to the original. Second, there is agreement among the ways of construing scripture illustrated by Wright, Warfield, and Bartsch, that scripture is authoritative in virtue of the fact that its authoritative content is identical with the content of divine revelation. Revelation in the past gave men a body of content. Scripture faithfully preserves that content, whether understood as a set of doctrines, concepts, or a historical account. Theology is to state it, though sometimes in more contemporary idiom. No question whatever is raised about the validity of the implicit distinction between "content" and "form" in scripture.

Incidentally, although analysis of doctrines of revelation is not part of the burden of this essay, one feature of talk about revelation in Wright's essay calls for comment. Wright argues that in the biblical view God reveals who he is and what he is like in acts in history. He glosses this by saying that man's understanding of God is *inferred* from historical events. That seems an odd use of "reveal." When Sherlock Holmes infers from the details of a skillfully concealed crime what the nature of its agent was, one hardly says that the culprit "revealed" himself by committing the criminal act. Surely one says rather that the Holmes "discovered" him or "found him out." Yet it seems odd to say that ancient Israelites "discovered" God or "found him out" in the things he did to the citizens of Ai, or to citizens of Jerusalem for that matter.

RENDERING AN AGENT
There is another way in which biblical narratives may be used to authorize theological proposals. It consists in construing the narratives as "identity descriptions." Narrative can "render" a character. A skillful storyteller can make a character "come alive" simply by his narration of events, "come alive" in a way that no number of straight-forward propositional descriptions of the same personality could accomplish. He can bring one to know the peculiar identity of this one unique person. Moreover, what one knows about the story's central agent is not known by "inference" from the story. On the contrary, he is known quite directly in and with the story, and recedes from cognitive grasp the more he is abstracted from the story. So too, biblical narrative can be taken as rendering an agent whose identity and actions theology is then to discuss.

This way of construing scripture is widely used in Karl Barth's *Church Dogmatics.* It is not the only way Barth construes and uses scripture. Indeed, one of the fascinating things about Barth's *Dogmatics* is the inventiveness and variety of the ways he uses the Bible. But this is one important way, and we shall rely on his discussion of the humanity of Jesus Christ to provide our case study.

Barth discusses the humanity of Jesus Christ in a section he entitles "The Royal Man." In the immediately preceding section, in which he reinterprets the classical description of Jesus in the Creeds, Barth insists that Jesus' "humanity" must be understood in terms of a "history" rather than in terms of a "nature."[34] To describe the humanity of precisely *this* man, one must describe, not the most general properties of "humanness as such," but the history of the acts in which this man has his identity. In "The Royal Man" Barth is concerned to make four additional points:

(a) The acts in which Jesus has his being are *his* acts. They are enactments of his most basic and abiding intentions, and are not simply things that happen to him. They *constitute* his identity and do not just *illustrate* it.

(b) His intentions and their enactments are two-sided. It was his intention to live in unbroken fellowship with God; and it was his intention to help man in his conflict "against the power of chaos and death which oppresses him."[35] The acts in which he enacts *both* sides of his intention constitute the concrete actualization of the Kingdom of God in history;[36] but they are also "one long summons to faith" in the

God of the Kingdom.[37] Jesus may thus be described as the one who totally invested himself in, or totally identified himself with this two-sided project.

(c) This is true of his life and death taken as a single integral whole. The crucifixion was the paradigmatic enactment of Jesus' two-sided intention. Otherwise all that had been so "royally" enacted in his life thereto would abruptly have been rendered very un-royally absurd by his death.

(d) Jesus' intentions were enacted in a "royal" way marked by a "sovereign freedom"[38] but in strict analogy with the mode of sovereign freedom God himself exhibits.

The movement of the discussion in "The Royal Man" virtually reverses the order in which the points have been made here. Barth spends the first two parts of the section making the fourth point, dealing with acts that merely *illustrate* who Jesus is. Only in the third part of the discussion does he identify acts that *constitute* Jesus' identity by enacting his intentions. And Barth saves until the last part of the discussion the point that is most central to his thesis: That the crucifixion is the act which most fully enacts Jesus' intentions and hence is of a piece with his life. We shall examine these four parts of Barth's discussion in reverse order.

In the fourth part of "The Royal Man" Barth appeals to the overall structure of the New Testament narratives about Jesus in order to warrant the claim that the crucifixion is coherent and continuous with the rest of the story. The story has a complex shape because it expresses two quite different perceptions that the disciples had of this history of Jesus' words and deeds. One of these perceptions is subordinated to the other.

From their standpoint in watching the history of Jesus unfold, the disciples perceived the story's basic movement going from one high point to another—"the revelation of Jesus as Israel's Messiah, the mount of transfiguration and the triumphant miracle at its foot, the promise of a heavenly reward which they themselves should share . . ."[39] Seen this way, there is "a glaring contrast between the beginning and content and meaning of the existence of Jesus and its outcome and end."[40] Such a story moves "in an intolerably abnormal and crooked direction" toward "an absurd future."[41]

However, from their standpoint as witnesses to the crucifixion and resurrection, the disciples retrospectively perceived that the story did not really have a "movement in an abnormal and crooked direction, but a movement from the high points, from the totality of the acts and words of Jesus, to their true depth and height, to their hidden glory . . . to the fulfillment of the Kingdom of God inaugurated and revealed with his appearance."[42] From this standpoint, Jesus' death is perceived, not as a "misfortune" that happens *to* Jesus, but as an act he himself accepted and willed.[43] In two exegetical sections Barth adduces evidence that the New Testament stories express the view by narrating Jesus' death as the act in which he finally achieved his intention to live in unbroken response to God's will.[44]

It is this second perception of Jesus' history that dominates the New Testament narratives. Barth points out in another exegetical passage that, for all their diversity in narrative detail, the Synoptic Gospels each introduce the same predictions of Jesus' death at precisely the same three points in their stories: Mk. 8:31 and par., immediately after the messianic confession; Mk. 9:30 f. and par., immediately after the accounts of the transfiguration; Mk. 10:32 f. and par., immediately after sayings of Jesus about the heavenly reward promised his disciples (in addition Mt. adds two more: 26:1 f. and 26:45, which is par. Mk. 14:41).[45] These predictions serve to integrate the death into the rest of the story by making the story explicitly refer forward, not to its apparent end, but to an unexpected end. They also provide an overall pattern or periodicity to the stories within which another perception of Jesus' history may be subordinated. In short, the story and its ending are related in an ironic way. The crucifixion is not at all the ending one is likely to expect of a narrative of a man who so perfectly trusts God as to actualize the kingdom of God in his own life and who so urgently exhorts others to the same trust. Yet seen retrospectively that ending seems oddly satisfying and appropriate. It is to this structure of the story as a whole that Barth appeals to authorize his claims about the integral unity of Jesus' life and death.

In the third part of "The Royal Man" Barth appeals to patterns of word usage and to characteristic structures in New Testament accounts of miracles to authorize the claim that Jesus' words and miracles constitute (and not just "illustrate") Jesus' identity by enacting his most basic and abiding intentions. In an intensive word-

study of *euaggelizesthai, didaskein,* and *kērussein,* the principal New
Testament terms for Jesus' speaking, Barth draws attention to patterns that occur regularly in the use of these terms. Jesus' "good
news," "teaching," or "proclamation" is always about faith in God
and his kingdom. But this is not something distinguishable from
Jesus himself. On the contrary, the kingdom has its actual advent
in the very act of Jesus' speaking.[46] Jesus' words are "performative":
They do not merely describe or predict the kingdom; they enact it.
In another place Barth undertakes a description of the recurrent
structure of miracle events narrated in the Synoptic Gospels. Regardless of differences in other details, they regularly are done to men
for whom things are going badly, they give sinful men a new future,
they are concrete enactments of God's covenant fellowship with
men, they show Jesus sharing men's suffering and resisting it with
them, and they are the acts of a man enabled to do them by divine
grace.[47] Thus Jesus' miracles are the concrete enactment then and
there of the "omnipotence of mercy."[48] Like his words, Jesus' miracles are the human acts (not divine acts only!) that enact the presence of the kingdom and summon men to faith in the God of the
kingdom. Indeed "words" and "miracles" are mutually inclusive
classes. The miracles were "cosmic actualizations of the *kerygma*"[49]
and the words were "an incomprehensible act" or miracle.[50] Together they *constitute* Jesus' "life-act,"[51] in contradistinction to his
"death," as his own act. They are the act in which Jesus has his
being because they enact his intention to live in covenant fellowship
with God (they enact the kingdom) and to be of help to his neighbors (they summon to faith).

In the first two parts of "The Royal Man" Barth abstracts generalizations about Jesus' characteristic way of relating to people
from a diverse collection of incidents in the Gospels. In the first
part he notes four aspects of "the way in which Jesus was present
as a man among the men of His time."[52] For example, the claim that
Jesus was present in such a way that men could not fail to see and
hear him is authorized by a collection of incidents like Mk. 1:27 f.
and Lk. 5:26 in which men are amazed by Jesus or led to say "We
have seen strange things today."[53] Or the claim that Jesus was present in a quite unforgettable way because of his "sovereign" freedom
is authorized by reference to incidents in the Gospels (like the Lk.

4:30 account of Jesus passing through a hostile crowd at Nazareth, or the Mk. 5:38 account of Jesus' behavior in the house of Jairus) which show this to be a major theme in the traditions about Jesus.[54] The claims that he was present in an irrevocable way and in a way demanding decision from men are authorized in similar fashion.[55] Taken together they describe a "royal" presence.

In the second part Barth notes four ways in which the acts constituting Jesus' existence are analogous to God's mode of existence among men. Barth does this, not as an argument for Christ's "divinity," but as a way of specifying in more detail how he fully enacted God's will for all men. Each of these is supported more by reference to Jesus' sayings than to his actions. Thus, the claim that Jesus' history is that of "one who is ignored and forgotten and despised and discounted by men,"[56] is authorized by a study of the parables of the kingdom which express the view that this "Royal man's" lordship is very hidden indeed. So too, the claim that Jesus' history is that of one who "ignored all who are high and mighty and wealthy in the world in favor of the weak and meek and lowly,"[57] is authorized by a study of the beatitudes in both Luke and Matthew. For all their diversity, they express the tradition's perception of a major reversal in Jesus' mission: It begins in and for elected Israel and becomes a mission for rejected gentiles.[58] Similar support is offered for the claims that Jesus' acts were revolutionary in relation to "the orders of life and value current in the world around Him,"[59] and that they were the acts of a man "for others."[60] Jesus' presence among men was "royal" in the same hidden, serving way that God is present among men as their "King."

Throughout the first and second parts of "The Royal Man" Barth seems to treat scripture as a source of anecdotes about what Jesus said or did which one would tell to show "what he was like." The anecdotes that fall together into a given group are interchangeable. Barth is not interested in them for themselves but for the *patterns* that recur in a number of them. The incidents the anecdotes recite serve to *illustrate* Jesus' personhood, not to constitute it.

Barth appeals to scripture in precisely the same way when he turns to explicate the "divinity" of Jesus Christ, and again when he undertakes to explain how Jesus Christ accomplishes the reconciliation of man with God. We may turn to his discussion of recon-

ciliation for a final illustration of this way of construing and using
scripture to authorize theological views.

Reconciliation, i.e., the restoration of covenant fellowship between man and God despite man's disruptive hostility, was the intention that superintended all Jesus' actions. It is revealed for all to
know in the resurrection. The resurrection, says Barth, was Jesus'
"self-declaration."[61] This is why the structure of New Testament
narratives clearly centers on the resurrection: it is the event in which
Jesus' identity was decisively manifested.

If the resurrection is taken as the intention-action that is centrally
characteristic of the identity of this person, then an adequate description of the identity of this person will have to be quite complex.
On one side there are the intentions enacted in the utterly *human*
actions that constitute the life of one who came before the resurrection and was crucified.[62] This is a pre-eminently human life, the
"true man."[63] It is for this reason that the synoptic accounts of his
earthly acts are essential for theology. They provide data for identity
descriptions of the one subsequently raised from the dead and pres-
ently living.[64] On the other side, the intention manifested in the
resurrection of Jesus is to be identified as God's intention from all
eternity to enter into covenant relationship with that which is other
than himself. Put another way, the acts constituting the identity of
this person collectively enact God's love.[65] They effect reconciliation
which is the fulfillment of God's covenant-intention.[66] If identity is
constituted by intention-action, then this person in all his humanity
is also *literally* Emmanuel, God with us. In short, an adequate description of the identity of this agent will, in its complexity, have
important parallels to traditional Chalcedonian "two-nature" Christology. However, instead of describing this agent in terms provided
by fifth-century metaphysics, it describes his identity in terms of the
intersection and coincidence of two kinds of intention-action sequences, two kinds of personal agency. To demonstrate the correctness of his characterizations of these sequences, Barth repeatedly
appeals to patterns in scripture that are taken as reflecting intention-
action sequences in the life of Jesus.

Notice what Barth has consistently been doing with scripture.
It is clear that narrative is the authoritative aspect of scripture.
Throughout the discussion of reconciliation and "The Royal Man,"

as Barth expressly and repeatedly points out, he authorizes his theological proposals by appeal to the New Testament narratives just as they stand in the received texts. He takes them as the expressions of a tradition having a particular point of view and not as the sources for historical reconstruction either of earlier traditions out of which the final tradition may have been fashioned or of "what really happened":

> . . . . . we have presupposed as the "New Testament"—not naively, but deliberately and consciously—a fixed form of the tradition denoted by this term; not a form which is hypothetical, but one which is as a whole well-known to us historically. We have thus refrained (again deliberately) from any critico-historical construction or reconstruction of this presupposition. In so doing we have consciously accepted what is surely obvious to any unprejudiced reader (not only of the Epistles but also of the Gospels), that the standpoint from which they saw Jesus and told us about Him lies beyond the temporal limits of His life; that they saw and attested Him in the context of events which took place after His death and which they described as His resurrection and ascension and the impartation of His Holy Spirit to the community. From this standpoint they saw and represented the totality of His life as that of a royal man, not with the intention of adding something to the truth of His historical existence, or in any way glossing it over, but with the intention of causing the one and only truth of His historical existence, as it later disclosed itself to them, to shine out in the only way which is at all commensurate with it. We have simply followed it in this.[67]

This tradition is a collection of stories. The stories are taken as having the logical force of identity-descriptions of Jesus. They give, Barth says, a "picture" of Jesus. The picture is not inferred from the details of the story. It *is* the stories. It "is only a fragmentary picture, and this in four different groupings of which it is difficult to grasp the continuity and inner coherence from a biographical standpoint . . ."[68] Nevertheless, Barth insists, there is an unmistakable unity to the picture which they drew of the activity of Jesus and it gives an "internal coherence" to the four Gospels.[69] This unity is precisely not the unity of a theological perspective projected onto historical facts as their "interpretation." Rather it is the unity of "the *story* . . . seen by them as a single whole."[70] Literally speaking, what gives the story unity is its structure and that is why Barth consistently appeals to the patterns that structure the story into an identity description of a single agent.

Indeed, Barth sometimes seems to argue that the unity of the Bible rests on the fact that all of it renders the one selfsame agent. In at least one place Barth tries to show that the history of Israel, not in individual detail, but in its totality exhibits patterns that closely parallel the patterns of action and intention characteristic of Jesus' life. The history of Israel enacts in a collective way the same intentions as are re-enacted in a concretely personal way in the history of Jesus. Hence it is possible to say that the history of Israel as a whole, though not necessarily the testimony of any individual prophet, prophesies or prefigures Jesus Christ as mediator.[71] The identity of the same agent is manifested through two sets of patterns. The whole canon thus renders the same subject.

This way of construing biblical stories as identity-descriptions is backed by a particular view of what a person is and how he is best described. Despite his Christocentrism, Barth's theological method rests at this point on some anthropological commitments.[72] He obscures this point somewhat by locating his analysis of what it is to be a person in the context of his discussion of the being of God. God alone, he insists, is a "person" in the proper and unqualified sense of the term. However, men may be called "persons" by analogical extension of the term.[73]

Barth's account of what it is to be a person is rather sketchy. However, it develops theses that have striking parallels, as Hans W. Frei has pointed out,[74] with some aspects of intention-action descriptions of personal identity worked out by philosophers like P. F. Strawson and Stuart Hampshire.[75] In intention-action descriptions, a person's "being" is said to be constituted and not just illustrated by the intentions he carries into action. Intention and action are dialectically related: An action has to be described as an enacted intention, and an intention as an implicit action. Contrary to every Cartesian dualism, intentions are not separate "mental" acts anterior to and parallel to "physical" events which they somehow mysteriously "cause." So, to describe a person one must recount characteristic patterns of intention-action. Accordingly, Barth holds that there is no non-material "essence" lying behind a person's actions and constituting his "real" being.[76] "The being of a person is being-in-act."[77] At the same time, a person is not to be resolved into his actions as though "person" were only the collective name for an arbitrary sequence of physical events. As Barth puts it, a person is lord of his acts; he intends them, and they are his.[78] Barth's view of the self is no more "behaviorist" than it is "substantialist." A particular agent's identity is constituted by his intentional acts. His acts are not simply the effects in the physical world caused (mysteriously) by his utterly hidden, mental, "real" self. Nor is his identity a culturally conditioned accidental modification of an underlying, ontologically prior and more "real" entity like a "soul." Rather, his identity, constituted by his acts, simply *is* his "being." His identity can be described only by recounting the characteristic patterns in his intention-action sequences. And those, in turn, are to be found only in narratives of his actions.

This view of what constitutes a person also underwrites Barth's answer to the question, Why is the narrative aspect of scripture authoritative? Barth is party to the consensus view that scripture is authoritative because it provides our normative link with God's self-disclosure. But Barth has his own version of it. God's self-revelation in Jesus Christ, says Barth, was an event in which God reveals himself and "speaks as *I* and addresses as *thou*."[79] God does not just communicate information about himself in this event; he makes his "person" to be present *to* men in something like an I-thou encounter. Scripture witnesses to this event, either in anticipation of it (in the Old Testament) or in memory of it (in the New Testament). That, Barth seems to believe, is exegetically demonstrable.

However, that is not what constitutes scripture's authority. Reading and, indeed, understanding a passage of scripture does not necessarily bring man into an encounter with God. But it may. Sometimes, when used in church as the basis of preaching and worship, the texts may provide the occasion on which the revelatory event occurs here and now and God "speaks as *I* and addresses as *thou*." On such occasions the stories "work." The agent they render is truly made present to the worshiper in a revelatory encounter.

Thus the authority of scripture is understood in *functional* terms. The texts are authoritative not in virtue of any inherent property they may have, such as being inerrant or inspired, but in virtue of a function they fill in the life of the Christian community. To say

that scripture is "inspired" is to say that God has promised[80] that
sometimes, at his gracious pleasure, the ordinary human words of
the biblical texts will become the Word of God, the occasion for
rendering an agent present to us in a Divine-human encounter.

When construed this way, how does scripture bear on theological
proposals so as to authorize them? In contrast to the three cases
we have studied up to now, Barth's answer is, "only indirectly." In
Barth's practice, the basic subject matter of theology is an agent in
action in history: The incarnate Lord. Of course, there are other
topics to be dealt with in theology too. The self-understanding a
man comes to have in existential relation to this person, sequences
of acts performed by this agent ("salvation history"), the reflection
of earlier Christians on this agent (as preserved in scripture and
tradition) are all to be explicated in theology. But they are done
correctly only when the identity of this person is first adequately
described. The central task of theology, then, is to reflect on this
person and say what must be said about him today.

How does scripture bear on this? We can answer only in relation
to the one use of scripture we have been examining here. Recall what
we have already seen: Narrative is taken to be the authoritative
aspect of scripture; it is authoritative in so far as it functions as the
occasion for encounter with an agent in history, viz., the Risen Lord.
Hence we may say that scripture is taken to have the logical force
of stories that render a character, that offer an identity description
of an agent. Scripture does this by means of certain formal features
of the writing, certain patterns in the narrated sequences of intentions and actions. It is to these patterns that the theologian appeals
to authorize his proposals. These are not (as in the illustration from
Bartsch) the patterns of logical connection among concepts, nor (as
in the illustration from Warfield) the patterns of a doctrinal argument, nor (as in the illustration from Wright) the patterns giving
the structure to a substantial stretch of world history. Rather, they
are like the patterns in a realistic novel or short story to which a
literary critic might draw attention when he tries to analyze "characterization." Indeed, it is as though Barth took scripture to be one
vast, loosely structured non-fictional novel—at least Barth takes it
to be non-fiction! The characteristic patterns in the narrative guide
what the theologian says about the agent/subject of the stories, in

much the way that patterns in a novel guide what a literary critic may say about the characters in the novel.

In the case of the biblical story, they are "non-psychological," i.e., they are not patterns characteristic of episodes in Jesus' emotional life, or the evanescent changes in the stream of his consciousness, or the passing oddities of his more or less unconscious wishes. Barth stresses that in its fragmentariness the tradition's picture of Jesus leaves out these patterns. That is why a biographical reconstruction of Jesus in the mode of a "character-sketch" is impossible.[81] The patterns are far more fixed or "objective," though nonetheless "personal." They are the patterns of Jesus' characteristic dispositions toward men, his abiding attitudes about them, his settled intentions concerning them.

These patterns serve to rule the things said today about the identity of that agent himself, about the world in the light of the fact that such an agent is found within it. For example: The Chalcedonian description of Jesus Christ, cast in terms of fifth-century metaphysics, is nearly unintelligible today. But a description of his identity can be given that has important formal parallels to the Chalcedonian description. This agent is constituted by a series of intention-action sequences that are utterly human. At the same time, his acts are acts of God's primordial intention to enter into covenant fellowship with all men, so Jesus can *literally* be described as Emmanuel, *God* with us. Another example: Barth has tried to show in his essay, "The Humanity of God," that when the world is described in the light of the fact that such an agent is found within it, a host of world-affirming judgments follow and with them a particular set of attitudes of hope and openness toward history and the future.[82] None of these theological proposals is found expressly in scripture or follows as a material inference from any statement in scripture. They are authorized only indirectly by the patterns in biblical narrative that render an agent and sometimes occasion an encounter with him.

It is difficult to see how this way of construing scripture can be assessed. It can in principle be neither confirmed nor disconfirmed by historical-critical exegesis of scripture. For it does not claim that every passage of scripture is self-evidently part of one vast rendering of one agent. It certainly does not claim that the human authors

of the several biblical books understood themselves to be engaged
in such an enterprise. It only supposes that it is possible to look at
or to take the canonical scriptures this way, without claiming that
there is any historical evidence justifying such a construction. It
amounts to an hypothesis that functions like Warfield's hypothesis
of plenary inspiration. The only reason to adopt Barth's hypothesis
would seem to be the fact—if it is a fact—that it describes the way
scripture actually does function in the experiences of members of
the Christian community. This has the advantage that it provides a
basis for taking the canon as a unity which is not vulnerable to ero-
sion by the results of biblical criticism.

"AUTHORITY" AND NARRATIVE

The two cases we have examined in this chapter implicitly agree
that the Bible is authoritative for theology to the extent that it can
be taken as recital or narrative. They also agree, at least formally,
as to why scripture is to be taken as authoritative: It provides our
one link with revelation. God makes himself to be known or, in
Wright, to be knowable, in historical events, and biblical narrative
represents those events. They disagree, however, over how to take
the narrative. In Wright's essay, biblical narrative seems to be construed to have the logical force of a recital of a continuous segment
of world history, namely, salvation history. The identification of
biblical narrative with *Heilsgeschichte* is expressly rejected by Barth,
however.[83] In his essay on "The Royal Man" it is instead construed
to have the logical force of stories rendering an agent. So too, they
disagree about how scripture, properly construed, is to be brought
to bear on the framing of theological proposals. It is brought to
bear on Wright's proposals very directly: Contemporary theological proposals simply restate the substance and material implications
of biblical narrative. Scripture is brought to bear on Barth's proposals indirectly: Formal patterns in the biblical narratives serve
as rules guiding what the theologian says today, but they do not
necessarily serve as the source of what he asserts materially.[84]

NOTES

1. London: SCM Press, 1952. Hereafter cited as "Wright."
2. Wright, p. 84.
3. Wright, p. 107.
4. Wright, p. 107.
5. Wright, p. 38.
6. Wright, p. 36.
7. Wright, p. 44; v. p. 84.
8. Wright, p. 57.
9. Wright, p. 84.
10. Wright, p. 20.
11. Wright, p. 39.
12. Wright, p. 40.
13. "Then you shall solemnly recite before the Lord your God: 'My father was a homeless Aramaean who went down to Egypt with a small company and lived there until they became a great, powerful, and numerous nation. But the Egyptians ill-treated us, humiliated us and imposed cruel slavery upon us. Then we cried to the Lord the God of our fathers for help, and he listened to us and saw our humiliation, our hardship and distress; and so the Lord brought us out of Egypt with a strong hand and outstretched arm, with terrifying deeds, and with signs and portents. He brought us to this place and gave us this land, a land flowing with milk and honey.' "
14. Wright, p. 72.
15. Wright, p. 72.
16. Wright, pp. 108; 115 fn. 1.
17. Wright, p. 67.
18. Wright, p. 68.
19. Wright, pp. 78–79.
20. Wright, p. 79.
21. V. Wright, pp. 29, 56.
22. Wright, p. 39.
23. Wright, p. 40.
24. Wright, p. 44.
25. V. Wright, p. 43; 50.
26. Wright, p. 46.
27. Wright, p. 48.
28. Wright, p. 108.
29. Wright, p. 109.
30. Wright, pp. 118–128.
31. Wright, p. 128.
32. Wright, p. 117.
33. Wright, p. 120.
34. V. Church Dogmatics, Vol. IV, Pt. 2, p. 26 on "nature." Hereafter Church Dogmatics cited as CD with appropriate volume and part numbers.
35. CD, Vol. IV, Pt. 2, p. 239.
36. CD, Vol. IV, Pt. 2, p. 210; v. pp. 28; 30.
37. CD, Vol. IV, Pt. 2, p. 238.

38. *V. CD*, Vol. IV, Pt. 2, pp. 219; 232.
39. *CD*, Vol. IV, Pt. 2, p. 254.
40. *CD*, Vol. IV, Pt. 2, p. 250.
41. *CD*, Vol. IV, Pt. 2, p. 254; *v.* pp. 250–251.
42. *CD*, Vol. IV, Pt. 2, p. 254.
43. *CD*, Vol. IV, Pt. 2, p. 249.
44. *V. CD*, Vol. IV, Pt. 2, pp. 258–259; 259–260.
45. *CD*, Vol. IV, Pt. 2, p. 253.
46. *V. CD*, Vol. IV, Pt. 2, pp. 196–204.
47. *V. CD*, Vol. IV, Pt. 2, pp. 221–223.
48. *CD*, Vol. IV, Pt. 2, p. 232.
49. *CD*, Vol. IV, Pt. 2, p. 217.
50. *CD*, Vol. IV, Pt. 2, p. 239.
51. *CD*, Vol. IV, Pt. 2, p. 194.
52. *CD*, Vol. IV, Pt. 2, p. 156.
53. *CD*, Vol. IV, Pt. 2, p. 157. Barth also cites Mt. 5:14, 15; 12:19; 13:17; 13:33; Mk. 13:17; Lk. 17:22.
54. *CD*, Vol. IV, Pt. 2, pp. 160–161. Barth also cites Mt. 3:11, 14; 11:11, 12; 17:3; Lk. 2:1, 29; 3:1; Jn. 1:20, 33; 18:28; 19.
55. *CD*, Vol. IV, Pt. 2, pp. 163–165; 157–159.
56. *CD*, Vol. IV, Pt. 2, p. 167.
57. *CD*, Vol. IV, Pt. 2, p. 168.
58. *CD*, Vol. IV, Pt. 2, pp. 169–171.
59. *CD*, Vol. IV, Pt. 2, p. 171.
60. *CD*, Vol. IV, Pt. 2, p. 180.
61. *CD*, Vol. IV, Pt. 3.1, pp. 296; 290–301, Vol. IV, Pt. 2, p. 301.
62. *CD*, Vol. IV, Pt. 3.1, p. 291.
63. *CD*, Vol. IV, Pt. 2, pp. 154–264.
64. *CD*, Vol. IV, Pt. 1, p. 320; Vol. IV, Pt. 2, p. 164.
65. *CD*, Vol. IV, Pt. 2, pp. 761–766.
66. *CD*, Vol. IV, Pt. 1, pp. 70–78.
67. *CD*, Vol. IV, Pt. 2, p. 248.
68. *CD*, Vol. IV, Pt. 2, p. 165; *v.* p. 193.
69. *CD*, Vol. IV, Pt. 2, p. 193.
70. *CD*, Vol. IV, Pt. 2, p. 251, emphasis added.
71. *CD*, Vol. IV, Pt. 3.1, pp. 53–55; 65.
72. Gustaf Wingren makes the same charge, although with an entirely different emphasis and to support a thesis that the present essay would not support. Wingren is concerned with the way Barth's anthropology is developed "independently" of scripture and hence forces interpretation of scripture into a procrustean bed. *V. Theology in Conflict*, Chs. 2 and 4.
73. *CD*, Vol. II, Pt. 1, p. 272.
74. Hans W. Frei, "Theological Reflections in the Gospels' Account of Jesus' Death and Resurrection," *The Christian Scholar*, XLIX, 4 (Winter, 1966), pp. 263–306. Frei's remarks are incidental to a constructive proposal of his own that develops this way of construing scripture in a more sophisticated and self-conscious way than does Barth. Frei's proposal has developed into a constructive essay in Christology, *The Identity of Jesus Christ* (Philadelphia: Fortress Press, 1975).

75. Stuart Hampshire, *Thought and Action* (New York: Viking, 1959); P. F. Strawson, *Individuals* (London: Methuen, 1959).
76. *CD*, Vol. II, Pt. 1, p. 300.
77. *CD*, Vol. II, Pt. 1, p. 271.
78. *CD*, Vol. II, Pt. 1, p. 331.
79. *CD*, Vol. I, Pt. 1, p. 352.
80. *CD*, Vol. I, Pt. 2, p. 514 ff.
81. *CD*, Vol. IV, Pt. 2, p. 165.
82. *The Humanity of God* (Richmond: John Knox, 1964), pp. 37–68.
83. *V*, e.g. *CD*, Vol. I, Pt. 2, p. 12.
84. There is an imaginative force to these two ways of taking biblical narrative seriously that has made them highly influential during the past twenty years. Variations on them seem to be fundamental to several recent theological proposals. For example, Wolfhart Pannenberg and Gordon Kaufman take biblical narrative to be the authoritative aspect of scripture because it provides the sources for reconstructing the history of God's acts wherein God is revealed. In this they are close to Wright, as we have seen. Kaufman is quite explicit: "Since the Bible has lost what authority it at one time had in its own right, and its principal significance for faith and theology is now its indispensability as the primary collection of reports of the acts of God, it is essential that it be dealt with as any other historical source and be subjected to careful critical scrutiny at every point. We are not concerned to recover simply 'What the Bible says'; we are seeking to find out 'What actually happened' in Israel and the early Christian church so that we will be in a position to assess the claim that God himself was active there, making himself known to all mankind through that particular historical development" ("What Shall We do With the Bible?" *Interpretation*. XXV, 1 [January, 1971], pp. 104–105).
Pannenberg differs sharply with Wright at two points at least. For Pannenberg, revelation takes place through history, but not in any event or sub-history of events. God is revealed only in history's end event, although from that perspective it is possible to see retrospectively that the "totality of history" brought to a completion in the eschaton has been, as a *totality*, God's becoming known (*Revelation as History* [New York: Macmillan, 1968], pp. 16. 131, 133), the core of the church's proclamation is that the revelatory end-event happened proleptically in the "fate of Jesus," i.e., the resurrection (*Revelation as History*, pp. 139–145).
Secondly, Pannenberg rejects the distinction between "facts" and "evaluations," which we saw seemed implicit in Wright's essay ("The Revelation of God in Jesus," *Theology as History*, James M. Robinson & John B. Cobb, Jr., eds. [New York: Harper & Row, 1967], p. 126), and also rejects the notion that revelation comes when historical events are interpreted by the "eyes of faith" ("The Revelation of God in Jesus," p. 137). Events do not need to be "interpreted." They carry their revelatory meaning with them (*Revelation as History*, p. 155) precisely because "events" always occur, always are just what they are, in the context of a "tradition" which thus is integral to the event (*Revelation as History*, pp. 145; 149; "Revelation of God in Jesus," p. 127). Despite these differences with Wright over what the "history" is in which God is to be known, and how that "history" is known, Pannenberg uses scripture in much the same way as Wright. Biblical narrative is not itself revela-

tion. It is rather "promise" before God's historical action, setting the tradition that is constituent in the revelatory events; or "forthtelling" of the moral and social implications of revelation, in which case it presupposes that God is already known and so is not itself revelatory; or "report," e.g., the *kerygma*, of revelatory events, in which case it is our sole source for reconstructing the events (including their constituent traditions) in which God was known (*Revelation as History*, pp. 152–155). For Pannenberg the one event that must be reconstructed that way is Jesus' resurrection, for it certifies Jesus' ministry as the eschatological event and therefore as the sole basis on which the totality of history may be read as revelation.

If Pannenberg and Kaufman in important respects stand with Wright in their way of construing and using scripture, Hans W. Frei and Jürgen Moltmann stand more with Barth. That claim, of course, does not entail any claims about any agreement on substantive theological matters between Frei and Moltmann, any more than it does in regard to Kaufman and Pannenberg. In a recent book, Frei combines an imaginative and fresh historical study of hermeneutics since the early eighteenth century with a thesis of his own designed to argue the importance for Christian theology of taking biblical narrative as authority precisely as *narrative*, and not either as source for historical reconstruction or as objectification of the inner existential history of its authors or its believing readers (*The Eclipse of Biblical Narrative*, Yale Press). For Moltmann too, biblical narrative is the authoritative aspect of scripture because, precisely as narrative, it gives an identity description of Jesus Christ in the only apposite way. Although often grouped with Pannenberg as a "theologian of hope," Moltmann differs radically from Pannenberg in regard to what it is we are to hope *in*. What we have hope in is not the outcome of something called the "totality of history" (Moltmann has obvious doubts about the intelligibility of that phrase), but rather the future of one agent in history: "Christian eschatology does not speak of the future as such . . . Christian eschatology speaks of Jesus and *his* future." (*Theology of Hope*, trans. James W. Leitch [London: SCM Press, 1967], p. 17). Consequently, the basic question is, Who is Jesus Christ? The answer can come only in the form of narrative. Moltmann stresses strongly the *promissory* character of the biblical narrative (cf. pp. 42–45; 102–106; 124–148). It renders the identity of Israel, first, as something unfinished, and then the identity of Jesus as something not yet fully realized. That is why scripture can only come in narrative form that combines report and proclamation (pp. 188–9). In particular, the dialectical relation between cross and resurrection in the Gospel narratives is the only way to give an identity description of Jesus: "the identity of Jesus can be understood only as an identity *in*, but not above and beyond, cross and resurrection. In that case the contradictions between the cross and the resurrection are an inherent part of his identity . . . It is formally a question of a dialectical identity which exists only through the contradiction, and of a dialectic which exists in the identity . . . The point of identification lies not in the person of Jesus, but *extra se* in the God who creates life and new being out of nothing." (p. 200, cf. pp. 219–220). This dialectic does not simply describe the identity that Jesus *was*. The resurrection of the *crucified* one describes the identity of one who *was*; but in as much as it is the *resurrection* of one crucified, it reveals him "as the Lord on the way to his coming lordship, and to that extent in differentiation from what he will be" (p. 87). His stress on the unfinishedness of Jesus' identity distinguishes Moltmann from Barth. It is "promissory" in regard to an identity not yet fully realized. At the same time, it describes the identity of an agent enacting *God's* intentions (p. 203). "Hence, to acknowledge the resurrection of Christ means to recognize in this event," not only the as yet unfulfilled future identity of this one agent in history, but also "the future of God for the world and the future which man finds in this God and his acts" (p. 194).

Chapter 4

Event and Expression

Theologians sometimes take the Bible on a "string-of-beads" or "muffin-full-of-berries" model. It is as though what is theologically important about scripture is a multitude of more or less discrete units, like so many beads or berries, which taken separately and together express the occurrence of a revelatory event. "Express" is the important and slippery term. The authoritative elements may be called "images" or "symbols" or "myths." Perhaps the most general, though vague, thing to say about them is that they "signal" the occurrence of the revelatory event. Revelation is said to be an event in which man is made new, in which he becomes a new creation. Men have verbally expressed their experience of that event in very concrete, iconic ways. Scripture is a collection of those expressions. The expressions may not state beliefs that brought about the change, nor need they describe the dynamics of the change, though, of course, they may do both. The analysis proper to them is more like the analysis given literary symbolism than like conceptual analysis. Since the revelatory-saving event took place in history, scripture's expressive witness to it usually takes a narrative form. But what is religiously important about the event is not any set of factors accessible to a historian. So scripture is not theologically important because it tells a story. Instead, by "expressing" the occurrence of the revealing and saving event, scripture somehow links us with that event.

We shall examine three illustrations of this way of construing scripture and using it to authorize theological proposals. They are drawn from the writings of L. S. Thornton, Paul Tillich, and Rudolf Bultmann.

IMAGE AND MYSTERY

L. S. Thornton's three-part work, *The Form of the Servant*, is the most remarkable attempt at once to be adequate to the modern mind and to use the ancient tradition of typological argument in theology. It is an immensely learned and subtle essay in Christology. Thornton's very compact way of arguing from scripture to his own theological proposals is probably unique in modern theology. We shall examine a passage from the second of the three volumes, *The Dominion of Christ*.[1]

The over-all theme of this volume is the "restoration of Adam's dominion in Christ, a restoration which takes the form of integration; that is to say a return of our nature to that wholeness of being for which we were designed."[2] We shall analyze Thornton's use of scripture in his discussion of the first part of that theme, how Christ restores Adam's dominion. The second part of the theme, how Christ's work affects us now, returning us to wholeness, is developed in terms of our participation in a new organic community, the body of Christ, where power creative of human wholeness is available;[3] but we shall not discuss Thornton's use of scripture in that connection.

Thornton contends that divine restoration of fallen man is best understood as an exercise of divine creativity and that Jesus Christ is paradigmatic of divine creativity. A study of redemption is also a study of creation, and both must be done in a christocentric way. Redemption is necessary because chaos has invaded creation. "If chaos invades creation, creativity in the person of the God-man can overcome chaos only by entering into it."[4] Now creativity "in the person of the God-man" is "creativity" in a special mode. There is a peculiarly Christian concept of "creativity." To get a grip on it, one must carefully examine "the form in which the Divine Victory is presented to us in Scripture."[5] In particular one must note the odd mix of glory and humiliation that characterizes divine creativity when it overcomes chaos.

Thornton authorizes his proposals on this subject in the last chapter of *The Dominion of Christ* by a close analysis of the Evangelists'

accounts of events leading from Peter's confession at Caesarea Phil-
lipi to Jesus' transfiguration. These accounts express an aspect of
the "form" of the Divine Victory over chaos. Thornton thinks the
significance of these accounts is seen only if one notes the various
ways in which they refer to, incorporate, echo other biblical passages
by using the same symbolic materials.

The basic significance of the transfiguration story is established
by the way it parallels the story of Passion Week and the story of
Easter. Thornton holds that this is true of all three Evangelists'
accounts of the story,[6] although he shows it only in Mark. Mark
underscores the parallel pointedly by including exact notes of time
only in these two stories out of his entire Gospel. In Ch. 9:2 he says
that the transfiguration occurred "six days later" than Peter's confession; in Chs. 11–16:8 he carefully divides the Passion Week into
a schedule of six days. "The parallel . . . is this: each of the two
weeks begins with an acknowledgment of Jesus as Messiah, passes
through a record of his humiliation and suffering, and ends with
his glorification. The principal difference . . . might be expressed by
saying that what is rehearsed in speech on the former occasion is
enacted in historical reality in the final week."[7] The transfiguration
story is a symbol for Holy Week and for Easter. Thornton subsequently draws attention, as we shall note below, to details in the
transfiguration story in Matthew that underscore certain peculiar
features of the "form" of the Divine Victory in Holy Week and
Easter.

Before turning to that, however, a second kind of significance
must be noted in the transfiguration story. Its six-day structure in
Mark relates it to a second major biblical passage: "Now in scripture as a whole there is one week which stands out as having special
significance for every Jew. It is the week of creation which was
spread over the six days of creative work followed by a sabbath
rest."[8] The six day structure thus begins to emerge as a symbol in
its own right. In this case, its use in the transfiguration story expresses the fact that the Divine Victory which it symbolizes is an
act of Divine creativity. But with a difference. The recreation of
men exhibits a pattern that is the reverse of the pattern of the creation of Adam. This is shown by drawing attention to images used
in the story as symbols. In the Marcan account Jesus is identified

with "Messiah" by Peter, and then Jesus promptly identifies himself with "Son of man" and says the "Son of man" must suffer. The equation of "Messiah" with "Son of man" is repeated in the Marcan story of Passion Week (Ch. 14: 61–64), with a direct reference to the use of "Son of man" in Daniel.

Earlier (Chapter III) Thornton had argued that the image "Son of man" in Daniel has Genesis as its background; "Son of man" is equated with "Son of unfallen Adam." Hence the equation of the image "Messiah" with "Son of man" means an "identification of the dominion of Jesus with a restored dominion of Adam." However, the remark that the "Son of man" must *suffer* lengthens the chain of equations among symbols. For it identifies both "Messiah" and "Son of Adam" with the image "Suffering Servant." The "Son of David is first identified as Son of Adam and then humbled to the Servant's destiny." To have the "Servant's destiny," Thornton has already argued in Chapter III, is to be identified with "the lot of the fallen sons of Adam." Accordingly, the Marcan account of the transfiguration story has Jesus identify "the messianic office with a vocation to accept the 'heavy yoke' which is 'upon the sons of Adam,' namely suffering and death." Starting with his full identification with the lot of fallen men, Jesus reverses the pattern of Adam's fall: tempted by Satan through Peter's lips, Jesus repudiates the temptation. He will not evade the price of identification with the fallen sons of Adam, viz., suffering and death. Thus, by the way it uses as symbols the images "six days," "Messiah," "Son of man," and "suffering," the Marcan account of the transfiguration expresses something of the *form* of the "Divine Victory": it is an act of divine creativity that begins not with a display of transcendent power but rather begins in the humiliation of suffering and death.[9]

Thornton elaborates this point in extraordinary detail on the basis of close reading of Matthew's account of the beginning of the transfiguration story in parallel with his account of the start of Holy Week. We can note only a few of the details here. Mt. 16 opens the transfiguration story by identifying Jesus with Jonah in his "descent" to the great fish; Mt. 21 starts Holy Week by assimilating Jesus to David and his "ascent" of Mt. Zion. Together they express the dialectic of humiliation and glory that characterize divine creativity in the person of the God-man.

Thornton takes Mt. 16 to be a single unit, so that the story of
the transfiguration begins with Jesus' remark that no sign will be
given to "this generation" except "the sign of Jonah." In Mt. 12:
38–41 Jesus is already identified with Jonah; so Ch. 16 makes Jesus
himself the sign that will be given. A few verses later in Ch. 16,
after his confession, Simon Peter is called "son of Jonah." Thus
"there is a double play upon the apostle's names, Bar-jonah and
Peter; and the two word plays hang together in one frame of
thought." The connection between the two is seen in the roots of
the symbols "rock" (Peter) and its parallel to the symbolic significance of "Jonah." In Ezek. 38:12 Israel is said to dwell "upon
the central summit of the earth." This probably meant that Israel
was geographically the center of the world. More particularly, cen-
trality was associated with the Temple. More precisely still, it was
identified with a stone protruding from the floor of the Holy of
Holies. A rabbinical saying refers to it as the "navel" of the world
"because from it the world was founded." "Rock" has a second,
related, symbolic significance. In the creation-myth, Thornton claims,
"the ocean-monster had to be overcome by God before chaos gave
place to an ordered universe" and so "God cast a stone into *tehom*,"
the watery deep flowing from the mouth of Sheol. The "rock" is
the center of the world because it blocks the opening through
which chaos pours. Here "rock" reverberates in the symbol "Jonah":
"For as the rock stopped the mouth of Sheol so Jonah stopped the
mouth of the 'ocean monster' when he calmed its raging for his
fellow travelers." Thornton wants to claim that in Mt. 16 "Jonah"
and "rock" are symbols for Jesus, and not just names for Simon,
though the justification for taking them this way is unclear.[10] The
point he wishes to make is clear enough: the symbolism of the
transfiguration story, expressing the *form* of the Divine Victory
over chaos, stresses that divine creativity is present in the mode of
a "descent" into the very source of chaos, the mouth of Sheol.[11]

The symbolism at the beginning of the story of Holy Week, the
story of precisely the same Victory, stresses an "ascent." In Ch. 21
Matthew depicts Jesus' entry into Jerusalem on Palm Sunday as a
"recapitulation of David's story in David's Son." David stormed the
stronghold of the Jebusites to build a temple there; Jesus cleanses
the temple that his people had allowed to become a "Jebusite"

stronghold again, i.e., a den of robbers. David took away the blind and lame with whom his enemies claimed they could hold the stronghold against him (2 Sam. 5: 6–9); Jesus healed the blind and lame as they came to him in the temple courts. Jesus' entry into Jerusalem is thus itself an image that gains symbolic power by echoing all that David's conquest of Mt. Zion has come to symbolize. Matthew's account of how Holy Week began expresses the fact that divine creativity was present in all its power. But paradoxically, Matthew's account stresses that creative power was present in meekness. Matthew alone of the Evangelists fully quotes Zechariah 9 with its reference to the "meekness" of the man who rides an ass. "The meek son of David enters the temple-courts in strange contrast to his great ancestor who stormed the stronghold of the Jebusites that he might build there a temple to the Lord."[12]

The images used at the start of the transfiguration story and the Holy Week story must be held together. Together they express the doubly dialectical *form* of the Divine Victory. Redemption is a continuation of creation; we have already seen how Marcan imagery symbolizes that. Transcendent creativity overcomes chaos only as it *descends* into the very presence of chaos in order to empower man to *ascend* to new wholeness of life; and divine creativity is present in power only as it is present in meekness. Thornton rightly points out that the same pattern recurs in Pauline writings.[13]

Clearly, Thornton takes biblical *images* to be the aspect of scripture that is authoritative for theology. He regularly appeals to images, or more exactly to the relationships between images,[14] to authorize his own theological proposals. He says that the "normal medium" in which scripture expresses revelation is "symbolic pictures, or events symbolically described" rather than formal statement. Even when scripture does seem to make straightforward statements, they are important because they "are charged with suggestive power by virtue of the pictorial images which they evoke."[15] Indeed, he seems to construe the Bible as a kind of album of pictures that all express a cosmic creative process. Because they all express different aspects of the same process, these images are tied into a complex network that gives the album an inner unity. The theme that gives the Bible its unity is "restoration."[16] Old and New Testament writings are integrated into a single whole in this network of images. Jesus Christ is the central revelation of this theme, and "the New Testament writers reassemble Old Testament images according to a new pattern given in Christ."[17] Moreover, because each image has its symbolic value only as it stands in a network of relationships with other images, the symbolic value of the whole is implicit in any image in the network taken alone.[18] This backs a hermeneutical rule that Thornton uses to warrant reading symbolic value into passages where that value is not explicitly evident.

Scriptural images symbolize the cosmic creative and recreative process only as it is revealed, however. That is what makes the images authoritative in the first place: they serve to link us with divine creativity where it reveals itself. Thornton calls these manifestations "mysteries." "In its theological meaning a mystery is something which throws light upon other things, . . . like a bright lamp showing clearly the relationship between the various objects that surround it. Our eyes, indeed, cannot bear to look directly at that light; yet its rays are the medium in which we can see all things clearly."[19] The incarnation of divine creativity in Jesus Christ is the central mystery because Jesus is the one link between the "human foreground" of history and its "cosmic background" in the creative process. What is manifested in Jesus Christ is a process that has been going on all along anyhow. "What happened at Calvary," for example, "is in principle that which has been happening in the historical foreground from the fall of man onwards, namely a turning away from light to darkness, a refusal of response to the Word."[20] So too, when divine "creativity in the person of the God-man" overcomes chaos by entering it, he overcomes it by following an *eternal law of the cosmos*, viz., that nature "dies to live."

> He fulfills that law as the faithful Servant of his Father's purpose, but also, and equally, as the Son "in whom all things were made." The law of dying to live is his own law; for he is the mould and archetype of creation's order. Consequently his self-committal to the Servant's mission is glorious; for therein he manifests what deity is and, further, shows what deity is in terms of what every child of Adam should be and may yet become.[21]

Thus the central Christian mystery, the historical life of Jesus, is revelatory precisely because it is a "foreground" instance, albeit the uniquely archetypal instance, of an eternal law of the "background" cosmic process. And biblical images are authoritative for theology because by symbolizing that mystery they put us in touch with the creative process it reveals.

How is scripture, construed in this way, to be brought to bear on theology? In the discussion we have examined, theological proposals were advanced that claimed to describe the victory of divine creativity over chaos and how that affects our lives now. Thornton seems to think there is double access to that process.

On the one hand, the process is symbolized by biblical images insofar as it is incarnated in Jesus Christ. Accordingly Thornton sets out to describe the Divine Victory by mapping the relations among these images and noting their subtly diverse symbolic significance. This is thoroughly Christocentric theology; it consists in an elucidation of christological symbolism in biblical writings. Done this way theology seems a species of literary criticism in which the critic, far from translating the image-rich text into a paraphrase, confines himself to identifying and sorting out the symbols and suggesting how they "work" in the text. The biblical images bear very directly on what the theologian says, just as a literary text directly dictates what the critic says. Sometimes, however, this seems to lead Thornton to require that modern Christians archaize themselves. On occasion he can point out that a key biblical image reflects a "primitive outlook"[22] and yet continue to insist that Christians ought to let their outlooks be shaped imaginatively by that image. It is as though he supposed men could by some kind of act of will decide to construe experience in terms of an image that is incoherent with the families of images currently vital in their own culture.

On the other hand, divine creativity can be described in metaphysical language. Thornton clearly thinks that the most appropriate technical metaphysical terminology is one in which "process" and "creativity" and "organism" are key terms. Done this way, theology is an attempt to give a view of the world as a whole. Biblical images bear on this enterprise only indirectly. At most they provide the basic institutions and root metaphors for this world view whose central abstract concepts are perhaps "suggested" by the concrete images. It is not obvious that a metaphysics whose key terms are concepts like "organic process" can do justice to the biblical images (e.g., "body of Christ") that allegedly suggest them. For, as existentialist theologians have been pointing out insistently for some time, biblical discourse characteristically stresses individual responsibility before God to make one's own decisions whether or not to trust, to love, and to hope. It is not clear that a process or organismic metaphysics can do justice to the dimensions of personal existence underscored by such calls to individuating decision.

Nor is it evident how these two ways of describing the victory of divine creativity are related to each other. Sometimes Thornton seems to want to keep them quite separate as though they were two quite different ways of talking about the same thing, each logically irreducible to the other. In that case biblical images might be said to symbolize concrete "mysteries," but ought not to be taken as pictorial expressions of abstract concepts. Other times Thornton writes as though the metaphysical account stated with abstract exactness what the biblical images symbolized more concretely but less precisely. In that case the biblical images may be said to symbolize concepts and to be open to reduction to propositional paraphrases.

SYMBOL AND MIRACLE

Paul Tillich agrees that the authoritative elements in scripture are the biblical images, only he calls them "symbols" and he has rather different notions about how they function and why they are authoritative. At one point late in his *Systematic Theology* he says that "The subject matter of theology . . . is the symbols given by the original revelatory experiences and by the traditions based on them."[23] The theologian is to show that Christian symbols contain the "answers" to existential "questions" men are asking today.[24] In order to see how this might be done in practice, we shall examine the use Tillich makes of scripture to authorize his own proposals about who Jesus of Nazareth was and why he has been religiously important to so many people. The appeal is almost entirely to the central Christian religious symbol, the "biblical picture of Jesus as the Christ."[25] It will be helpful before we turn to that, however, to give a brief sketch of what "religious symbols" are and why they are authoritative for theology.

What Tillich means by "religious symbols" can be understood, at least in part, in terms of the functions he says they play in revelatory events. A revelatory event is an event in which men receive power by which they are made new beings. It is at once a manifestation of that power and an occasion for healing, for salvation. Although men are estranged from themselves, their neighbors, and God, they come to know reconciliation and healing, albeit in a fragmentary and ambiguous way, when this power is mediated to them. As Tillich analyzes it, every revelatory event has two sides. There is a "giving" side or "miracle." It is a material object, or a person, or a natural phenomenon experienced as holy, i.e., as being at once fascinating and terrifying because through it is mediated a power that can both destroy and create new life. The other side is the "receiving" side or "ecstasy." It is the state of a thinking, feeling, imagining subject when he is grasped by this power of new being and made whole. Tillich insists that men stand on the "receiving" side of revelatory events only as they are united in groups; revelation always creates community. In the revelatory event that created the Christian community, Jesus of Nazareth was the miracle or giving side, and the faith of the disciples was the receiving side. This was the "final" revelatory event in that it is the standard by which every other such event is to be measured.

There are sets of revelatory events held together by common symbols. In each set there is an "original" revelatory event in which a new religion is founded. In an original revelation both the "giving" and the "receiving" sides are novel. For example, the events constituted by Jesus and his disciples, Buddha and his disciples, the Koran and the early Islamic community, or Mt. Sinai and a band of fugitive slaves from Egypt are all original revelatory events. Diverse ways of expressing the sheer occurrence of these events arise within the communities participating in the events. They may be non-verbal like pictures or carvings or ceremonial actions, or verbal things like poems or sayings or stories. Tillich covers them all with the umbrella "religious symbol."

In subsequent generations of these communities other revelatory events occur that are dependent on the original event. Tillich calls them "dependent" revelations. Their "receiving" side is always new because new generations of men come along who receive the power of new being afresh for themselves. But the giving side of dependent revelations is fairly constant. It consists in the religious symbols created in the revelatory event to express its occurrence and now serving as holy objects to occasion new revelatory events. Thus, religious symbols provide the continuity among a set of dependent revelatory events and link them all to the original event. In the case of Christianity, the disciples of Jesus created a verbal symbol, the "biblical picture of Jesus the Christ" which is cast in narrative form, to express the fact that the original revelatory event had occurred and that they personally had participated in it. This picture thereafter occasions dependent revelatory events as it is read or preached in church.[26]

In short, biblical religious symbols are authoritative because they fill two functions: They *express* the occurrence and content of the original revelation in Jesus as the Christ, and they *occasion* dependent revelatory events having precisely the same content as the original one. The continuity of content between the original and dependent events apparently hangs entirely on the fact that the same symbols function in them all. Thereby the symbols, and above all the "biblical picture," effectively link us with the healing power mediated to men by Jesus of Nazareth.

One of the central themes in Tillich's discussion of "The Reality of Jesus" is the paradoxical claim "that he who is supposed to overcome existential estrangement must participate in it and its self-destructive consequences."[27] To say that Jesus of Nazareth is the Christ is to say that New Being was present in this "personal life." That is a "paradox," in Tillich's sense of the term, not by being self-contradictory, for it is not, but because it goes against received wisdom that such events cannot happen. The "personal life" we know is always marked by the conditions of "existence," that is to say, by alienation from self, neighbor, and God, while "New Being" designates unbroken unity between God and man.[28] Yet Jesus managed to overcome the conditions of "existence" and preserve unbroken unity with God while nonetheless truly and fully participating in our common human life.

In an important essay outside the system Tillich outlines three things a theologian must do with religious symbols, and he does each of them as he appeals to scripture to authorize this claim. It will be useful to organize our analysis of his use of scripture around these three tasks. In "Theology and Symbolism"[29] he says that religious symbols must be "conceptualized," "explained," and "criticized."

To *conceptualize* religious symbols is to show "the relation of the symbols to each other and to the whole to which they belong." Tillich is adamant that it does *not* consist in trying to translate murky symbols into clear concepts.[30] Indeed, he distinguishes sharply between concepts and symbols as though neither were reducible to the other. Accordingly, he analyzes the biblical picture of Jesus as the Christ into two main component symbols, each of which is a story: the "Cross of Christ" and the "Resurrection of Christ." Together they express the central paradox in the "giving" or "miracle" side of the original revelatory event. The story of the crucifixion expresses Jesus' own participation in and subjection to the conditions under which all fallen men suffer: being utterly cut off by others, suffering, dying. The story of the resurrection expresses Jesus' unambiguous conquest of these existential conditions. Thus together in dialectical relationship they express the central paradox of the *way* in which the original revelatory event occurred: The power of New Being was mediated by one who at once shared with men the consequences of their estrangement and brokenness and yet was not himself estranged from God, man, or himself. The conqueror is victim; a weak victim is a strong conqueror.

It is important to note that this pair of symbols express something about Jesus, about the objective, giving side or original revelation, or "miracle" and not something about the disciples' subjective experience in the presence of Jesus. These two stories must be held together within the overall picture of Jesus. By standing side by side they create the tension at the heart of the biblical picture. Neither may be left out or reduced in significance or subordinated to the other. The *pattern* of their relationship gives the picture the basic pattern that reflects the paradoxical structure of the giving side of the original revelatory event. Without this pattern, the picture could not express the occurrence of that event adequately.[31]

Tillich proceeds to show how other stories in the New Testament contribute to the overall picture of Jesus as the Christ. One set of stories gains its significance through its relationship to the story of the crucifixion. Stories about Mary and Joseph's flight into Egypt, about political threats against Jesus, and about his agony in Gesthemane are all ranged around the symbol "Cross of Christ." Each functions as a religious symbol expressing one specific way or another in which Jesus shared man's common existential plight. Another set of stories, like those about the Virgin Birth, Jesus' pre-existence, or his deeds following death, has significance in virtue of their relationship to the story of the resurrection. Each expresses in one way or another the unbroken unity between Jesus and the power of being that he mediated.

A second thing Tillich does with the biblical picture is to show its relation to that to which it points. In "Theology and Symbolism" Tillich calls this *explaining* a symbol. The picture of Jesus as the Christ points to the power of being which can be mediated to broken and estranged men, sometimes through the picture itself, so that for them it is a power for *new* being. The traditional name for this power is "God."

Tillich seems to try two ways by which to show the relation between the picture and God, one by way of his analysis of the dynamics of revelatory events and the other by way of his ontology. As we have seen, an analysis of revelation can show how religious symbols like the biblical picture function in revelatory events to mediate the power of being to estranged men. In any situation in which they do so function, they "point to" that power by making it present and effective. By his ontology, on the other hand, Tillich tries to show how a finite thing like the man Jesus or the imagina-tively created picture *can* serve to mediate the power of being in such a way that it makes existentially broken men whole again.

Tillich does not attempt to mount an ontological argument prov-ing that the biblical picture does in fact express and occasion revelatory events. That cannot be demonstrated by any argument. Ontological analysis is useful only for the more modest tasks of showing that the relationship of finite realities like Jesus and the picture of Jesus to the power of being does make it *possible* for them to serve as holy objects mediating that power to men, and then showing that the ontological structure of men is such that they may come to need to have such power mediated to them. Accord-ingly, in his analysis of "being" Tillich tries to show how every actual finite reality is related to the power of being, how at least one class of finite actualities, viz., men, can simultaneously be es-tranged from that power, and how under certain circumstances certain finite actualities may serve to point to that power or make it manifest in power.[32]

The third thing Tillich does with the biblical picture is show how some symbols are more adequate to express the occurrence of original revelation than are others. He calls this *criticism* of religious symbols in "Theology and Symbolism." In the section of the *Systematic Theology* that we are taking as an illustration, Tillich is concerned to show how the biblical picture of Jesus as the Christ is uniquely adequate to express the Christ event. To make his point, Tillich draws our attention to certain formal properties of the picture and compares them with the formal characteristics of several styles of painting. It is an apt and accurate picture of *how* the original revelatory event took place, but not in the way "realistic" paintings are accurate. It does not even attempt to report in a photographic way surface details of Jesus' career or personality. Nor is it like a portrait in an "idealistic" style that might represent Jesus as embodying the highest aspirations and ideals of the first century men who created it. Instead, the picture deliberately distorts and exaggerates. In that respect, it is like a picture painted in the "expressionist" style.

According to Tillich, the expressionist style commonly involved exaggeration and distortion of the subject being painted. Instead of simply reproducing the subject's surface traits, the painter uses distortions of those traits to "express what the painter has experienced through his participation in the being of his subject."[33] Precisely in virtue of its formal distortions, the biblical picture bears *analogia imaginis* to the original revelatory event in Christ. The distortions themselves express the important thing going on through Jesus when he is received as the Christ: the mediation of the power of being. It is in that sense that the picture is uniquely adequate, indeed, apt as an expression of original revelation.

Throughout the section on "The Reality of Christ" Tillich has appealed to the religious symbols in the Bible, and especially the picture of Jesus as the Christ, as the authoritative element in scripture on the grounds that they link us with original revelation by aptly expressing just how it occurred. In doing so he assumes that the scripture he uses holds together as a whole in virtue of the network of *relations* among the symbols. Indeed, "conceptualizing" the picture of Jesus consists in nothing else than tracing out the formal structure of the picture in which two central component symbols, cross and resurrection, are coordinate with each other in a dialectical relation, and a host of other symbols are subordinated to one or the other of the central symbols. And "criticism" consists in nothing else than showing that it is precisely by being held together in this pattern that these component symbols constitute a whole which, as a whole, expresses most aptly the giving side of original revelation.

It is as though Tillich construed the New Testament materials as a kind of verbal equivalent of a very complex Byzantine mosaic. The mosaic might consist of a number of separate, highly stylized—indeed, "expressionistic"—images, whether of Old Testament figures or New, angels or saints, set in a formal pattern such that together they constitute one composite icon. The pattern among the component images might be fully as important as the content of any one of them, so far as the force of the whole taken as a single work is concerned. So too, apparently, with the biblical picture of Jesus as the Christ, taken as a single religious symbol.

The Old Testament is authoritative to the extent that it contains symbols used in the New Testament picture. The Old Testament's importance does not lie only in its being the source of some New Testament symbols, however. For the expressive force of those symbols itself rests on the dialectic generated between their expressive role in their Old Testament content and the use to which they are put in the New. For example, the symbol "Messiah" is used in the Old Testament to express a hope for a coming military hero who will free his people from political bondage; that gives it the force of expressing the giving side of an anticipated saving-revealing event in which the central figure is a powerful savior. The symbol is used in the New Testament to express an actual saving-revealing event in which the central figure was a powerful liberator all right, but in a paradoxical way. For his "power" was effective only in the brokenness and weakness of the cross. It is precisely the tension between the Old Testament expressive force of the symbol and the force it has in the New Testament that gives it its peculiar expressive significance as part of the biblical picture of Jesus as the Christ. "Mes-

siah" would not have the authoritative import it does have in the
New Testament did it not also have importance in the Old Testament. Thereby New Testament and Old are ordered in a unitary
whole.[34]

Now all this is said of the picture as authoritative because it
expresses original revelation. We saw earlier, however, that a religious symbol is also authoritative because it may occasion contemporary dependent revelations. How is scripture used and construed
when taken as authority on those grounds? And in either case, just
how is the picture brought to bear on theological proposals so as to
authorize them? It is just at this point that a peculiar discrepancy
in Tillich's use of scripture comes to light. It turns out that there
are two quite distinguishable theological tasks for Tillich, one corresponding to scripture's expressive function and the other to its
occasioning function, and scripture is brought to bear on each of
them quite differently.

As we have seen, it is in an essay *outside* the "System" that Tillich announces that the theologian must "conceptualize," "explain,"
and "criticize" religious symbols; and that is just what he has done
in his discussion of "The Reality of Jesus." But in the introduction
to the *Systematic Theology* itself he says that a theologian must
show that Christian symbols contain the "answers" to existential
"questions" men are asking today.[35] Where the first task clearly
appeals to scripture as *expressive* of original revelation, the second
deals with it as *occasioning* dependent revelation now. When Tillich
analyzed the biblical picture in "The Reality of Jesus," he tried to
show how it was an apt expression by focusing attention on the
patterns and overall structure of the picture. That is, he attended to
some intrinsic properties of the picture. When he turns to show how
the picture contains answers for men's questions today, however, he
attempts to show how it functions to occasion revelatory events
now, and in the process seems to ignore entirely the intrinsic formal
features of the picture.

When he tries to explain how the picture functions today, he
turns to his analysis of "being" and to his analysis of revelatory
events. He develops an ontological anthropology, i.e., an account of
the being of man. Using that, he shows how it is possible for a
man to become so radically estranged from God, neighbor, and self.

He sketches the dynamics of man's being whereby in estrangement
he is subjected to the threat of "nonbeing." He argues that at the
same time men have an immediate consciousness that they are ontologically disintegrating and that this consciousness sends them on a
quest for healing. He contends that men express this quest in existential questions such as, "Is there any meaning to my existence?",
"Is there meaning to history?", "Why is there something rather
than nothing?". Then using his ontological anthropology Tillich
tries to explain how healing might take place; not to prove that it
does take place, just that it *could*. It *can* happen if man regains his
immediate apprehension of the ground of being, or God. It *will*
happen only if the power of being, or God, grasps a man, overcoming his alienation and thereby making him whole.

Tillich then turns to his outline of the dynamics of revelatory
events to show that *that* is precisely what happens in them: The
power of being *is* mediated to men through holy objects. At this
point Tillich then returns to the biblical picture of Jesus. He simply
reports that it is the Christian claim that the biblical picture of Jesus
as the Christ does sometimes serve as the occasion for such healing
events today. It can be the "miracle" or giving side in a dependent
revelatory event now. In that way the picture and all its component
sysmbols provide answers to questions men ask out of their awareness of their estrangement. But it is important to note that the
"answer" is not a statement given in response to a request for information. It is rather the power that brings cessation to a personal
quest for ontological healing. The content of the biblical symbols'
"answer" is not stateable information or advice, but a power. It is a
power that transforms the inner reality, the private side of man's life.

Evidently there are two ways in which scripture is brought to
bear on theology. Biblical symbols bear *directly* on theological proposals about original revelation. The symbols provide our sole access to the original event in virtue of the structure by which they
express the dynamics of the giving side of the original event. Consequently, theological proposals about that event are directly controlled by the symbols, whether taken separately or as a whole, much
as a close reading of a poem is directly controlled by the text of the
poem.

However, biblical symbols bear very *indirectly* on theological proposals about dependent revelatory events. Those proposals are directly authorized, first, by analyses of human subjectivity that describe its deepest diseases and the roots of its endemic quests. Religious symbols play no role in that ontological venture. Theological proposals about dependent revelatory events are authorized, secondly, by generalizations about the dynamics of revelatory events. The original Christian revelatory event provides the hermeneutically normative or paradigmatic instance of revelatory events as a class. It is certainly not the only member of the class from which the generalizations are made, but the picture of Jesus is useful in this enterprise. Indeed, only by shaping what is said about revelatory events does the picture thereby indirectly shape what is said about dependent Christian revelatory events.

This creates a problem. How does analysis of the picture as a symbol that *expresses* the occurrence of original revelation fit with discussion of the picture as a symbol that *occasions* dependent revelatory events? It is important that they do fit together. For it is the picture and the picture alone that establishes the continuity between the original event and the dependent ones. It alone guarantees that the later events truly are dependent on the first one, really have the same content and so genuinely depend on Jesus Christ. When he discusses original revelation in "The Reality of Jesus," Tillich appeals to the picture in its expressive function and depends on the patterns and structure of the picture in virtue of which it is reliably "expressive." The patterns of relationship among the picture's component symbols appear to be the theologically important features of the picture. They are the means by which the picture adequately expresses just the way in which the original event took place. But when he discusses dependent Christian revelatory events today Tillich appeals to the picture's occasioning function and depends on analysis of the power it mediates to estranged men. The picture's religiously important content now turns out to be the power which can end men's existential quests. But just how is the fact that the picture can mediate power related to the peculiar structure it has? Tillich does not explain that. Perhaps an explanation could be worked out, but it probably would require a discussion of how the structure of complex symbols causes them to have certain effects on men—a discussion Tillich does not provide.

As it stands, no connection has been shown between what one learns when scripture is brought to bear very indirectly on proposals about saving and revealing events today, and what one learns when scripture is brought to bear very directly on proposals about the "person of Jesus" (not to mention his "work") and original revelation. That lack of connection is serious because it seems to suggest that what the theologian has to say today to and about the world does not depend on what he can say about Jesus and his significance for *his* world. The question is left open, Why insist that saving events today depend in any way on Jesus? Why should the church make the biblical picture of Jesus as the Christ central to saying what it must say today? If there is no connection between what is said (with only indirect appeal to scripture) about making human life whole today and what is said (with direct appeal to scripture) about the person of Jesus, then Christology would seem to have become logically dispensable for contemporary Christian theology.[36]

MYTH AND ESCHATON

Although it may be the only thing he has in common with them, Rudolf Bultmann shares with Thornton and Tillich the view that what is authoritative in the Bible are passages that express the revelatory and saving "Christ event" and occasion contemporary saving and revealing events.

According to Bultmann, the subject matter that theology is to explicate is the "self-understanding" inherent in faith.[37] "Faith" is the name for a particular mode of human subjectivity central to which is a particular way of "understanding" oneself. This sort of "understanding" is a sense of those capabilities that define my range of choices of ways to act. Thus it is a non-theoretical kind of "understanding" more like "knowing how to do x" or "possessing skill y" than it is like "knowing that p." Like knowing a skill and unlike theoretical knowing, it allows no distinction between what is known and what the knowledge is about. If I know how to hit a bullseye, what is my knowledge about except hitting bullseyes? Also like knowing a skill and unlike theoretical knowledge, to exercise it is to perform an overt act that produces changes that have to be explained in terms of my intentional agency and not solely in causal terms. Like knowing a skill and unlike theoretical knowledge, moreover,

it is non-evidential. I do not wait until I finish exercising a skill to
know how to do it; what I have after successfully performing the
skill is evidence for the theoretical knowledge that I can perform it.
Possessing a skill is not generated by collecting evidence.

On the other hand, "self-understanding" is not quite like knowing *a* skill in that it does not consist in knowing how to do some one
thing "with oneself," as it were. It is rather like one important
aspect of knowing a skill, viz., my *sense* of my capabilities that
always goes along with exercise of a skill. If I exercise certain intellectual skills with confidence and verve rather than hesitation, I
show that I "understand" my capabilities even though I may continue to protest that I lack the skills. My grasp of my capabilities
sets the range of choices of ways to act. If you have reason to believe that I have the "native ability" to perform certain skills well,
I may still never learn them if my own sense of myself is that I lack
"what it takes" to learn. If you can change my grasp of my own
capabilities, my own non-theoretical self-understanding, you can
change the range of choices of action open to me. Thus, to change a
man's self-understanding is to transform him.[38] Bultmann contends
that revelation changes men's self-understanding and thereby transforms them. Their new way of being is existence in faith.

Inherent in faith is an understanding, not just of self, but also of
world and God. The theologian's task is to explicate that. But he
has no direct access to it. Fortunately, men of faith bring their transformed self-understanding to public expression in a variety of ways.
The theologian has to base his explication of faith's self-understanding on those "expressions." The paradigmatic expressions of Christian self-understanding are found in the New Testament. Bultmann
appears to take them as normative because they are the earliest ex-
tant expressions of faith. Consequently, the theologian must turn to
scripture to authorize his particular ways of explicating faith's self-
understanding. And scripture contains a variety of kinds of ways in
which Christian self-understanding comes to expression.

Note that the unity of both theology and scripture follows from
the coherence and integrity of the subjectivity of the man of faith.
The variety of things a theologian says hangs together, not because
they all can be deduced from the same first principles, but because
in one way or another they describe the understanding of self,

world, and God that is ingredient in the subjectivity of a man of faith. Correspondingly, the variety of material in scripture holds together only to the extent that it all expresses that same subjectivity.

To see one way this works out in practice, let us take as a case study Bultmann's discussion of faith's "understanding" of man as "reconciled" to God and examine how he appeals to scripture to authorize his proposals.

Bultmann's first move is to assimilate New Testament accounts of reconciliation to accounts of eschatological existence.[39] The point of doing so is to do justice to the historical fact that eschatological claims are the heart of the New Testament message. Claims about "reconciliation" with God are implied in and secondary to the eschatological claims and cannot be separated from them without distorting their meaning. He justifies this by studies of the relationship between the concepts "reconciliation" and "eschatological righteousness," showing that if a New Testament passage is a description of reconciliation, then it is giving a description of one aspect of a more basic and much richer state of affairs called "eschatological existence,"[40] i.e., that existential state that is apt to the "end of history."

For example, in the writings of Paul "reconciliation" turns out to have two sides whose relationship is hard to understand. On one side, it is an "objective, factual situation" and not a subjective process. On the other side, it is a cessation of man's hostility to God, which does sound like a subjective state. In any case, it is a change in some kind of relation brought about by God's "not counting their trespasses" against men.[41] However, this must be understood "in terms of" Paul's account of eschatological existence. This is a mode of existence brought about by God's "acknowledging" men.[42] God's "not counting trespasses," which brings reconciliation, is just one implication of his more basic act of acknowledging men. It is marked by personal wholeness and freedom, which includes cessation of hostility, but is much richer than that alone. It embraces the "world," understood as the world of mankind;[43] this implies the "objectivity" of the situation of reconciliation, but at the same time makes it clear that what is "objective" is an inter-personal situation and not an impersonal cosmological structure.

Above all, eschatological existence is a new historical situation;

hence the "relationship" reversed in reconciliation is to be understood in "historical" and not, say, metaphysical terms. This historical situation is marked by a peculiar tension between its present
reality and future realization.[44] This tension is the basis of the
duality of reconciliation, so that if one could get clear just what this
tension is, then he could see how the two sides of reconciliation
cohere. Thus far Bultmann seems to be engaged in a variant of
"biblical concept" theology. However, so far he has simply been
making a *historical* point about how the concepts "reconciliation"
and "eschatological righteousness" were used in first century Christian discourse.

Bultmann's own proposal is that "eschatological existence" bears
all the marks of what Martin Heidegger calls "authentic existence."
Consequently it may be redescribed today using the terms Heidegger
uses to describe "authenticity." The faithful man's way of being-in-
the-world is determined by the gospel's word of personal address in
which he encounters a love accepting him for what he is. Living as
one who understands himself that way, he is freed of the compul-
sion to assert himself against his neighbor in order to coerce acknowledgment from him. Hence he is free to discern and meet the
unique needs of his neighbor. He sees his whole world in a new
way, as "gift." His old way of being, the old history of his existence
has ended; for it the *eschaton* has come. Compared with his ontic
state apart from this accepting word, his very being is new, and his
life has entered a new era. This new creation is a present reality, and
yet is ever future for it has to be realized anew again and again in
repeated decisions to acknowledge himself acknowledged by God.
He has eschatological existence, existentially understood.

Bultmann appeals to scripture in two ways to authorize this
proposal. More exactly, he appeals to what he takes to be two different kinds of biblical utterance. They bear on his theological proposal in quite different ways.

A primary distinction is to be made within the New Testament
between *kerygmatic statements* and *theological statements*. They
seem to be distinguished more by their respective functions than by
their form or content. A *kerygmatic statement* is an utterance that
may be heard as a word of personal address, a "questioning and
promising word, a condemning and forgiving word" in which a man

is told by God, in effect, "I acknowledge you." It demands a response by the one who hears it. When the kerygma functions effectively, it evokes a peculiar sort of judgment from the hearer, a judgment that constitutes his new self-understanding.[45] The hearer's inwardness, his subjectivity is decisively changed. Thus kerygmatic utterances can be said to present to the hearer the objective possibility of a new mode of existence, if I respond by acknowledging that I håve been acknowledged. My ontic condition,[46] my mode of subjectivity when I live out this acknowledgment, is called "faith." It is characterized by all the marks of freedom and openness that Heidegger says indicate *existentiell* "authenticity." *Theological statements* in scripture, in contradistinction to kerygmatic statements, are expressions of the self-understanding of the man of faith. They express his acknowledgment of his having been acknowledged by God. They express publicly the kind of inwardness he has come to have when he heard the kerygmatic word as personal address.

The distinctive functions played by kerygmatic and theological statements can be brought out by noting their apparent logical force. In different ways, they both seem to have the force of "self-involving performative utterances."[47] A performative utterance does something in saying something. For example, "I forgive you" does not report or describe anything, as would "I forgave you" or "He forgives you"; if truly spoken, it accomplishes your forgiveness by me. There are several types of performatives of which two are especially important here. "Commissives" are performative utterances like "I promise . . ." in which the speaker commits himself to the one he addresses in more than a verbal way. "Behabitives" are performative utterances like "I apologize for . . ." or "I repent for . . ." in which the speaker relates himself to another person in the context of human behavior. Both of these are "self-involving" as well as "performative." That is, in uttering "commissives" and "behabitives" a speaker involves himself with others in more than verbal ways.

Just what kind of involvement this is comes out when we consider how performative utterances ought to be appraised. They are open to two kinds of evaluation. On one hand, performative utterances often include content that can be abstracted from the utterances' performative force. Sometimes the abstractable content may be appraised as to its truth or falsity. If I say, "I pledge my word that County Dodge is asking twice the price I'm asking for this car," I make a performative utterance ("I pledge my word . . .") with abstractable content that makes a truth-claim ("County Dodge is asking twice the price I'm asking . . ."). However, in the case of commissives, the abstractable content must be appraised in terms of fulfillment or unfulfillment of the implied intention. (Commissives imply *intentions* whereas behabitives imply *attitudes*.)

On the other hand, with respect precisely to their performative force, performative utterances invite judgment, not of truth or fulfillment, but (in J. L. Austin's happy word) of their "felicity." One kind of infelicity a performative may suffer is being null and void. This may happen if there is no established conventional procedure to be invoked, or if I make a mistake in the procedure. For example, if I fail to use the Trinitarian formula in baptising somebody, then my baptismal pronouncement is null and void. So too, a performative utterance will be null and void if I lack the proper authority for invoking the relevant procedure, for example, if I pronounce a couple "man and wife" without being either an ordained minister or a justice of the peace.

Clearly, what Bultmann calls "kerygmatic statements" and "theological statements" are distinguishable by the functions they fill in Christian life *in virtue of* their performative force. One never finds a "pure" instance of either kind of "statement." The two are so closely intertwined in the New Testament, according to Bultmann, that it is impossible to separate "kerygmatic" verses from "theological" ones. Sometimes, indeed, one single passage will at one and the same time serve as "kerygmatic statement" and as "theological statement."[48] The difference between the two, then, is not literary or grammatical. Instead, it appears to be a difference between ways in which the same sentence or utterance can *function*, a difference in the *uses* to which the utterance may be put, in the life of the Christian community.

An utterance is "kerygmatic" if it is heard as having the force of "I acknowledge you" or "I accept you," or interchangeably in the New Testament, "I forgive you" and "I love you." An utterance is "theological" if it is understood as an acknowledgment of having been acknowledged, i.e., addressed by a "kerygmatic statement." In effect, then, theological statements are expressions of appraisals of

the felicity of "kerygmatic statements." They express the judgment
that the "speaker" of the "kerygmatic" utterance is One with authority to forgive men and One who can be trusted absolutely to
fulfill the intention expressed in the kerygmatic utterance. As such,
theological statements are themselves self-involving performative
utterances. For if I acknowledge that the kerygmatic utterance does
not fail in respect to the utterer's (i.e., God's) intentions and subsequent actions (i.e., if I acknowledge its felicity), then I imply my
trust in those intentions and actions. I have involved myself in certain relationships and attitudes and policies for future action by my
acknowledgment. To acknowledge God's acknowledgment is to have
faith and faith's self-understanding, and to utter a "theological statement" is to *express* that self-understanding.

Thus "kerygmatic statements" are performative utterances with
at least commissive force, and "theological statements" are performatives with at least commissive and behabitive force. In virtue of
their performative force, "kerygmatic statements" serve to occasion
saving and revealing events, i.e., events in which men's "inauthentic" existence is transformed by giving them a new "understanding"
of self, world, and God. Through their performative force "theological statements" are expressive of the occurrence of that event and
of the new understanding that comprise it. Accordingly, it is in virtue of their performative force that the two sorts of "statement" are
authoritative for contemporary theology. A theologian is to explicate the "understanding" of self, world, and God inherent in Christian faith today. Scripture as "kerygmatic statement" is directly
authoritative, however, not over theological proposals today, but
over the concrete existence of the man of faith today. By its performative force it "authors" new self-understanding in him. His
newly "authentic" self-understanding then directly authorizes theological proposals. Thus scripture as "kerygma" bears on Bultmann's
theological proposals only indirectly as it first and very directly determines the life of the man of faith.

However, there is always the question whether a man today
has heard scripture's "kerygmatic statement" properly. Is the
self-understanding he has in his response to it truly "Christian" self-
understanding? It is to scripture as "theological statement" that one
must turn for *normative* expressions of genuinely Christian self-

understanding. Bultmann brings scriptural "theological statements" to bear on his own theological proposals about "reconciliation" very directly. It is precisely because they are the earliest expressions of Christian faith that they are normative; and they are expressions (and not, say, merely "descriptions") of faith in virtue of their performative force. That makes them authoritative.

It also makes a problem. Generally it is their "abstractable content" that Bultmann actually brings to bear on his theological proposals in order to authorize them. And the "abstractable content" comes in several forms, some of which are well nigh unintelligible to modern men. Consider several examples.

Some theological statements in scripture have abstractable content that Bultmann labels "myth." He is making a logical and not just a literary point. These passages tell stories that appear to make truth claims. For example, they tell of a celestial being who descends to earth and does certain things whereby the entire cosmos is transformed into a "new creation." Bultmann's point is that, while in their original historical contexts (say, in gnostic religious discourse) such literary units may well have been used with the logical force of a description of an event, they have been borrowed by the New Testament writers and put to different uses. They now are used to signal, perhaps unselfconsciously, a particular mode of self-understanding. Their logical force now is that of a verbal *symptom* that manifests to the canny eye trained by Heidegger an underlying ontic state.[49]

Other theological statements in scripture have abstractable content describing God as acting. Bultmann holds that this sort of talk is not myth. It is not a symptom of an ontic state, but rather is to be construed as making a truth-claim. However, it makes its claim using "analogical" rather than "literal" modes of expression. Bultmann apparently believes that the cognitive character of analogical discourse, which seems so dubious to so many "modern men," can be firmly established through philosophical argument.[50]

Still other theological statements in scripture have abstractable content that straightforwardly describes the ontic state of the man of faith. For example, the man of faith is said to be a man whose relations to his possessions, projects, and even his wife is such that he can live "as though not," i.e., he relates to them with such inner distance that it is as though he did not have them. Such content, of course, may be accepted as having the logical force of a truth-claim about certain features of faith's self-understanding. It invites appraisal of its truth. But no single biblical passage is to be accepted uncritically as an adequate description of "eschatological existence" even though it is found in scripture. Any individual text may mis-describe it in some way. Its authority over a theologian's description of faith as a mode of subjectivity is qualified, then, by the fact that it must itself be weighed and, if necessary, its claim corrected by what we already and independently know about authentic existence. The criteria by which it is to be evaluated are provided by Heidegger's philosophical account of authentic existence.

Since it can be shown, Bultmann believes, that in general the New Testament account of the self-understanding of the Christian man coheres with Heidegger's account of authenticity, then Heidegger's more systematic and conceptually tight account may be used to evaluate any particular New Testament description of Christian existence.[51] This implies an expansion and major qualification of our earlier observation about the unity of scripture. Now we must say that for Bultmann the variety of material in scripture holds together only to the extent that it all either expresses the kerygma that calls faith's self-understanding into being, or to the extent that it serves as symptom of that subjectivity, or provides descriptions of it. And Heidegger provides a set of categories by which to assess just to what extent any particular passage does the latter. To the extent that passages of scripture can be found that give inadequate accounts of faith's self-understanding, to that extent scripture lacks both authority and unity.

In summary, when scripture is used as it is in this case, two kinds of biblical expression serve to authorize theological proposals. The two kinds of expression are distinguished by the function each plays in the life of faith. A "kerygmatic statement" is any biblical passage that serves as an expression of God's word of personal address "I acknowledge you." And a "theological statement" is any passage that serves as an expression of the hearer's self-involving acknowledgment that he has been acknowledged, i.e., as an expression of his ontic state when he existentially "understands" himself as one acknowledged. It is precisely in virtue of these functions of occasioning faith's self-understanding and expressing faith's self-understanding that such passages are "authoritative" for contemporary theology. Despite their different functions, when they are taken as authoritative such biblical passages are construed as having the same logical force: they are self-involving performative utterances. Finally, the two kinds of expression bear on theology in quite different ways. Scripture that functions as "kerygma" shapes contemporary theological proposals only very indirectly by first determining quite directly the ontic state of the man of faith whose self-understanding the theology seems to describe. Scripture that functions as "theology" may rule the content of contemporary theological proposals quite directly. Its "abstractable content" contains the paradigm expressions of Christian self-understanding with which contemporary theological descriptions of that understanding must cohere. But the abstractable content must only be used as the standard expression of Christian self-understanding after it has been properly interpreted and evaluated in the light of Heidegger's analysis of authentic existence. Consequently, the more directly scripture may bear on theological proposals, the more qualified is its authority.

"AUTHORITY" AND EVENT

The three ways of construing and using scripture in theology that we have examined in this chapter concur on one point: scripture is authoritative insofar as it expresses the occurrence of a revelatory and saving event in the past and occasions its occurrence for someone in the present.

To be sure, that is "agreement" at a very high level of generality. The three differ most sharply at just this point on which, in other respects, they stand together in contrast to the "cases" we have studied in the two preceding chapters. The point at which they differ is this: Where is the "revelatory and saving event" to be located? As an event in a public world, over against, prior to, and independent of any and all knowing subjects? Or as a private event in individual men's inwardness that transforms their subjectivities? Or somehow both?

Thornton characteristically stresses that "creation" images are more basic than "redemption" images.[52] His point seems to be that the images first of all express the basic character of the most embracing context within which human life is set (viz., that chaos has seeped into it but has been overcome), and only then and therefore are also expressions of the inwardness of the man who lives in a way most apt to that cosmic context (viz., as a redeemed man). Revelation is a disclosure concerning the public and common world and only for that reason also a revelation concerning me. As a generalization about the basic gist of scripture on this topic, that has a *prima facie* plausibility. However, Thornton holds cosmic and personal redemption together by subsuming both under images and concepts of "organic process" and the cosmic and eternal laws governing radical change in such process. As we indicated, those images and categories are open to the objection that they fail to do justice precisely to *personal* existence (and hence to personal redemption), and in particular to man's radical creativity and his capacity to transcend any prior "definitive" account of "laws" allegedly governing all change, including human creativity.

Bultmann assumes that the revelatory and saving event is located in the subjectivity of the man of faith and is in no way a "cosmic" event at all. He takes scripture as occasioning a new self-understanding which is at bottom an insight into what constitutes one's true self-identity. By casting his technical discussions of "redemption" in terms developed by Heidegger to do justice to personal existence, Bultmann can claim to have avoided the sort of objection that may be leveled at Thornton's way of "locating" the revelatory and saving event. However, Bultmann does so at the price of opening himself to the objection coming from several quarters that he thereby systematically distorts an obvious and central feature of most canonical scripture.[53] Whatever else it is, the Bible clearly is talking about revelatory events occurring in a public world of power structures and politics, whereas "kerygmatic statements" and "theological statements" seem to express events that are utterly private.

Tillich tries to avoid privatizing the "revelatory and saving event" by stressing the communal and hence public dimensions of human life and hence of events that transform men's lives. Thereby he seeks to locate the saving event at once in the public world and in the private, without reducing either to being a function or projection of the other. He offers an account of both individual existence and the nature of the "world" that is cast in terms of their respective relations to historical communities. An individual is who he is only as he participates in a community with which he shares the symbols that invest life with coherence, meaning, and vitality. The "world" is the full range of human experience as ordered and thematized by communally shared symbols. If the central symbols of a community are radically changed (e.g., in a revelatory event), that change transforms both the quality of individuals' existence and the nature of their "world."[54] In this way Tillich tries, in effect, to stand with Bultmann against any account of the revelatory events expressed by scripture that might, like Thornton's account, turn it into an impersonal happening or depersonalizing process, and to stand with Thornton against any account of those events that might, like Bultmann's account, end up privatizing what clearly is expressed by scripture as public events with public consequences.

Often these differences are supposed to be so decisive that these kinds of theology are taken as polar opposites. We lump them together in order to stress how much they have in common just at the point at which they also so deeply differ. They all stress the radically "event" character of revelation and share a common decision to construe the Bible as a collection of expressions of the occurrence of that event. Hence what is authoritative about scripture is not its surface content of doctrine, concept, or narrative, but its non-informative *force* as expression. This decision about how to construe scripture, whether its expressive force is said to take the form of literary image, religious symbol, or kerygmatic myth, continues to play a very influential role in Protestant theology.[55]

NOTES

1. London: Dacre Press, 1952, hereafter cited as *Dominion*.
2. *Dominion*, pp. 5, 9, 11, 58.
3. *Dominion*, p. 192.
4. *Dominion*, p. 189.
5. *Dominion*, p. 166.
6. *Dominion*, p. 167.
7. *Dominion*, p. 168.
8. *Dominion*, p. 167.
9. *Dominion*, pp. 170–171.
10. *V. Dominion*, p. 180 for the way Thornton traces this through Jeremiah and Isaiah.

11. *V. Dominion*, pp. 176–179.
12. *Dominion*, p. 183; *v.* pp. 182–184.
13. E.g., Ephesians 4: 8–10; Philippians 2: 5–11.
14. E.g., *v. Dominion*, pp. 148; 176.
15. *Dominion*, p. 165.
16. *Dominion*, p. 15.
17. *Dominion*, p. 17.
18. *Dominion*, p. 16.
19. *Dominion*, p. 2.
20. *Dominion*, p. 113.
21. *Dominion*, p. 189.
22. *Dominion*, p. 149.
23. *Systematic Theology* (Chicago: University of Chicago Press, 1963), Vol. III, p. 201; hereafter cited as *ST*, with appropriate volume number.
24. *ST*, I, pp. 6–8.
25. *ST*, II, pp. 97–165.
26. For the account of "revelation" in the *Systematic Theology*, see ST, I, pp. 101–147; for a more complete discussion of this "functionalist" interpretation of Tillich's doctrine of religious symbols, see my *The Fabric of Paul Tillich's Theology*, Ch. 2.
27. *ST*, II, p. 97.
28. *ST*, II, p. 148; cf. pp. 126, 136.
29. *Religious Symbolism*, ed. F. E. Johnson (New York: Harper & Bros., 1955) hereafter cited as *RS*.
30. *RS*, pp. 111–113.
31. *ST*, II, pp. 153–154.
32. For detailed defense of the thesis that Tillich uses both of these ways to show how symbols are related to the power of being, see *The Fabric of Paul Tillich's Theology*, Chs. 2 and 3.
33. *ST*, II, p. 116.
34. For Tillich's discussion of the symbol "Messiah" see *ST*, II, pp. 88–89, 95–96, 110–111, 138.
35. *ST*, I, pp. 6–8.
36. For a more detailed development of this contention see *The Fabric of Paul Tillich's Theology*, Chs. 5–6.
37. Rudolf Bultmann, *Theology of the New Testament*, trans. by Kendrick Grobel (New York: Scribners, 1955), Vol. II, pp. 237–238, hereafter cited as *TNT*, with appropriate volume number.
38. Bultmann, of course, relies on Martin Heidegger's *Sein und Zeit* for the concept of "understanding." My explication of Bultmann's use of this term follows Richard Schmitt's explication of Heidegger's concept, *Martin Heidegger on Being Human* (New York: Random House, 1969), Ch. 5.
39. Cf. *Kerygma and Myth*, Vol. I, ed. H. W. Bartsch (London: SPCK, 1957), pp. 20, 30; *Jesus Christ and Mythology* (New York: Scribners, 1958).
40. *TNT*, I, p. 285.
41. 2 Cor. 5: 19; oddly, Bultmann does not at this point relate reconciliation to Christ's death, despite 2 Cor. 5:14–15, although much earlier in *TNT* he notes in passing that Paul is almost unique in relating the two.
42. *TNT*, I, p. 272.

43. *TNT*, I, p. 254.
44. *TNT*, I, p. 279.
45. *TNT*, II, pp. 238–241.
46. A statement is "ontological" if it tells us about the being of something and its range of possibilities; it is "ontic" if it tells us about some entity in its actual relations with other entities. A man's possibilities are *"existentiell"* possibilities when they are the concrete practical possibilities of his individual being-there (*Dasein*); the "horizons" of *Dasein's* possibilities, the "range" of its (*existentiell*) possibilities—indeed, the range within which the concrete possibilities of every individual *Dasein* must fall—are called "existential" possibilities. Cf. John Macquarrie, *An Existential Theology* (London: SCM Press, 1955), pp. 30, 34.
47. V. J. L. Austin, *How to Do Things With Words* (Cambridge: Harvard University Press, 1962) for the original discussion of performative utterances, and Donald Evans, *The Logic of Self-Involvement* (London: SCM Press, 1963), pp. 27–44 for a discussion of the "self-involving" force of many performative utterances.
48. *TNT*, II, p. 240.
49. V. *Kerygma and Myth*, I, pp. 35–43, *TNT*, I, p. 258, II, p. 150.
50. *Jesus Christ and Mythology*, Ch. 5.
51. E.g., see Bultmann's criticism of Paul's argument in 1 Cor. 15: If Paul argues that belief in the resurrection of Jesus is warranted by the number of eye-witnesses he can cite, he misdescribes the nature of faith by suggesting it is like belief resting on evidence.
52. *Dominion*, pp. 48, 159, 172.
53. E.g. Karl Barth, "Rudolf Bultmann—An Attempt to Understand Him," *Kerygma and Myth*, II, pp. 91–92; Jürgen Moltmann, *Theology of Hope*, pp. 182–190.
54. *ST*, I, pp. 168–178; III, Part IV, "History and the Kingdom of God," pp. 297–427.
55. The way of construing and using scripture in theology illustrated here by the "case" drawn from Tillich's writings is represented in recent Protestant theology by Gilkey's *Naming the Whirlwind*. If and when Paul Ricoeur's philosophical analyses of personal existence and evil are appropriated by a systematic theologian, it will involve the judgment, very like Tillich's, that religious symbols are what are important in scripture; cf. Ricoeur's *The Symbolism of Evil* (Boston: Beacon Press, 1967). The way of construing scripture in theology illustrated here by the "case" drawn from Bultmann's writings is represented in more recent Protestant theology in the writings of such post-Bultmannians as Ernst Fuchs and Ernst Käsemann. They introduce an important change in Bultmann's stress on the "expressive" and wholly "functional" character of "kerygmatic" utterances. Rather than see them as verbal manifestations of otherwise private and inaccessible transformations of the subjectivities of men of faith, Fuchs, and Käsemann construe biblical writings as the preserved form of originally wholly oral "speech events" that transform the language men speak and thereby transform the men who speak the language. Among other things, this move is an effort to do justice to the "public" and contextual dimension of the saving and revealing event—the dimension, we noted, that Bultmann has been criticized for distorting. Cf. Fuchs, "The

Essence of the 'Language-event' and Christology," *Studies of the Historical Jesus*, trans. Andrew Scobie (London: SCM Press, 1964), esp. pp. 221–225; Käsemann, "The Problem of the Historical Jesus," *Essays on New Testament Themes*, trans. W. J. Montague (London: SCM Press, 1964), esp. p. 33 on the way the NT stresses the *extra nos* of our salvation. In *Language, Hermeneutic, and Word of God* Robert W. Funk has worked out an account of the way language constitutes the "public world," and how changing the language transforms, not just the subjectivity of the language-user, but his world as well (New York: Harper & Row, 1966), esp. Chs. 5–9. The way of construing and using scripture that is illustrated here by the "case" drawn from Thornton's writings has, of course, had much less influence on Protestant theology. It has marked parallels in Austin Farrer's exegetical works, *A Rebirth of Images* (London: Dacre Press, 1949), *A Study in St. Mark* (London: Dacre Press, 1951), *St. Matthew and St. Mark* (London: Dacre Press, 1954), his study of "inspiration," *The Glass of Vision* (London: Dacre Press, 1948) and his essay on "Revelation," *Faith and Logic*, ed. Basil Mitchell (London: George Allen & Unwin, 1957), pp. 84–108. In attenuated form it appears in I. M. Crombie's development of the "parable" theory of what is authoritative in scripture in his essays "The Possibility of Theological Statements" in *Faith and Logic* (pp. 31–84) and "Theology and Falsification" in *New Essays in Philosophical Theology*, ed. Antony Flew and Alasdair MacIntyre (London: SCM Press, 1955), pp. 109–130, and in Donald Evans' *The Logic of Self-Involvement*, Ch. 6 (where the "parable" theory is applied specifically to the notion of creation).

Chapter 5

"Scripture"

The seven case studies provide the basis for some remarks about the concept "scripture" as it is used in theological statements such as, "This scripture is the authority for this theological proposal." In this chapter I want to draw attention to four points in particular; two of them bring implications concerning the grammar of related theological concepts: 1) Part of what it means to call a text or set of texts "scripture" is that its use in certain ways in the common life of the Christian community is essential to establishing and preserving the community's identity. That throws some light on the grammar of the concept "tradition" and its relation to "scripture." 2) Part of what is said in calling a text or set of texts "scripture" is that it is "authority" for the common life of the Christian community. "These texts are authority for the church's common life" is analytic in "These texts are the church's scripture." 3) To call a text or set of texts "scripture" is to ascribe some kind of "wholeness" to it. That throws some light on the grammar of the theological concept "canon." 4) The expression, "Scripture is authoritative for theology" has self-involving force. When a theologian says it, he does not so much offer a descriptive claim about a set of texts and one of its peculiar *properties*; rather, he commits himself to a certain kind of activity in the course of which these texts are going to be *used* in certain ways.

A terminological caution: I shall frequently refer to the case studies by using the name of the theologian from whose writings the case was taken. It must be emphasized again that no single case is

89

necessarily representative of any one theologian's "position" or of his ways of using scripture. I am analyzing some ways theologians have in fact construed and used scripture to authorize particular theological proposals, so my comments are at most only incidentally significant as comment on any particular theologian's general "method." Instead, they are intended to throw light on a variety of particular methods all of which are logical possibilities for a theologian and several of which may in fact be employed by any one theologian.

"CHRISTIAN SCRIPTURE" AND "CHRISTIAN CHURCH"

To take biblical writings simply as "texts" is, notoriously, not necessarily to take them as "Christian scripture." They may be studied as literature or as historical source by methods of inquiry to which their status as "scripture" makes no difference whatever. But it is precisely as "Christian scripture" that they are used by the theologians from whom we drew our case studies to help authorize theological proposals. What does it mean to say of a text or set of texts that it is "Christian scripture"?[1]

Part of what it means to call a text "Christian scripture" is that it *functions* in certain ways or *does* certain things when used in certain ways in the common life of the church; and that draws attention to some aspects of the logical relation between the concepts "Christian scripture" and "Christian church." That, in turn, throws some light on the grammar of the theological use of the concept "tradition."

The case studies themselves showed that biblical texts are taken as "scripture" in virtue of their *doing* something. On further examination it is apparent that what they do is shape persons' identities so decisively as to transform them; and it turns out that the texts do this when used in certain ways in the common life of the church.

Take each point in turn: That biblical texts are taken as "scripture" in virtue of their doing something is brought out by the responses each "case" gave to the question, "In virtue of what is the scripture appealed to 'authoritative'?" In every instance the answer was cast in terms of something the scripture was said to *do*: It refers or "points" the reader to the sequence of God's mighty acts in history which constitute *Heilsgeschichte* (Wright); it *renders* a character (Barth); it *expresses* the occurrence of a cosmic redemptive event and *occasions* a transformation of my vision of the world so that I come to live in ways apt to its true character (Thornton); it *occasions* an event in which my personal and private life is transformed (Bultmann); it *expresses* the occurrence of a saving and revelatory event for an earlier community and *occasions* an event of encounter with the holy here and now (Tillich); it *proposes* or commends concepts men should use to construe their experience, their word, and themselves (Bartsch). At first it seemed that in the case drawn from Warfield scripture was said to be authoritative in virtue of an inherent property, not its function, viz., its inerrancy created by God's inspiration of its authors. However it turned out that its inerrancy is a contingent fact about it believed because scripture claims it for itself; and the claim is accepted in part because of the way scripture functions in the context of Christian piety: It occasions an experience of the holy. On this question Warfield and Tillich are closer to each other than either is to any other theologian we examined: scripture is authoritative in virtue of the fact that what it says confronts men as a numinous and holy object. Thus in every case biblical texts were said to be "authoritative scripture" in virtue of something they *do* when used in certain ways. But what sort of things is it they do, and in what context? That brings up the other two points.

Part of what it means to call a text "Christian scripture" is that *it functions to shape persons' identities so decisively as to transform them*. This is clear from the immediate theological contexts from which the case studies were drawn. It is through the way the text is used that men are "redeemed" by being drawn into salvation-history or by being placed in the presence of the redeeming agent; by personally appropriating beliefs, or concepts, or images in such a way that they are made new men; or by being brought to "authenticity" or to "new being." This is central to *what* the text is said to do when it is called "Christian scripture."

The third point is that part of what it means to call a text "Christian scripture" is that it decisively shapes persons' identities *when it is used in the context of the common life of Christian community*. The applicability of this claim is severely limited. It is made here only of theologies like those from which we drew the case studies; perhaps it does not apply to all kinds of Christian theology. It does hold, however, of those theologies that a) take the theological task to be one of the activities that are constituent of the life of the church, and b) that hold that theological proposals must be authorized by scripture. Admittedly, the evidence that the theologies from which we drew the case studies share these two theses lies outside the materials we examined; it lies in the larger theological context of each of the cases. However, I take it to be uncontroversial that they do share these two themes. For such theologies the concrete contexts in which biblical texts function precisely as "Christian scripture" are a set of activities that are constituent of the church's life: preaching the gospel, celebrating the sacraments, doing the liturgy, teaching the doctrine and lore of the faith, giving pastoral care, offering service to the world's needy, making prophetic judgment on immorality both in the lives of members of the community and in society generally, etc.

Clearly, these remarks in no way exhaust what it means to call a text or set of texts "Christian scripture." In particular, they scarcely touch the theological content of the concept. But they do bring out an important point about the theological concepts "Christian scripture" and "Christian church," which, in turn, allows us to unpack further what it means to call a text "Christian scripture." The point is: Logically, the concept "Christian scripture" and certain concepts of "Christian church" are dialectically related.

Begin with the concept "church." It seems fair to say, albeit at a nearly stratospheric level of generality, that, according to the doctrines of the nature and purpose of the church developed in the sorts of theology we have been studying, the church's reality lies in her engaging in certain activities ordered to a certain end. The *activities* are many and diverse, largely ones we have already suggested: preaching, sacramental acts, liturgy, pastoral care, teaching, and the like. The *end* to which these activities are ordered as a task or mission is characterized in quite different ways in different theologies: conversion of all people to the faith through preaching (*kerygma*), creation of a genuine community of the reconciled (*koinonia*), service to the world (*diakonia*), or some combination of the three. The activities constitutive of the church's life may be thought of as having their end in themselves (e.g., as ways of glorifying God), or in goal-oriented terms (e.g., as having their end in the creation of a more truly humane social order). This is not to say that for all these doctrines of the church, she is *constituted* by these activities done to some end. It is to claim that, for all the variety of characterizations of the end to which they are done, these concepts of "church" do define her in terms that make these activities *constitutive* of her reality. She is defined in terms of the things she exists to *do*.[2]

Furthermore, according to these concepts of "church," her continued *faithfulness* to her task depends on two factors. The first is that her faithfulness to her task depends on God's presence to her. The ends to be achieved through the church's activities are conceived as God's purposes. They are realized only as God makes himself present in and through the activities that are essential to the church's reality. The second factor on which the church's faithfulness to her task depends is her use of certain writings in various ways in her common life to nurture, criticize, and reform herself. That is, it depends in part on her use of those texts precisely as "scripture." This may not be true of every community that calls itself "Christian church." But for communities that do understand themselves this way, use of scripture in their common life is essentially a way of shaping and preserving identity—both corporate identity as an intergral community, and the personal identities of the individuals that make up the community.

These two bases of the church's continued self-identity, moreover, are dialectically related. As Hans von Campenhausen has put it in discussion of the view of the church common in the first two centuries of the Christian era (of which the views of the church we have been discussing are historical and logical extensions), the scriptures are indisputably the church's book, basic to her self-identity. Nevertheless, "Christianity is no longer a 'religion of a book,' in the strict sense" [e.g., in contradistinction to Islam] "since Christians believe in the lordship of the living Christ and in the present reality of the Spirit."[3] Theologically speaking, such communities say that in and through their use of the texts God also uses the texts to transform men's lives.[4] Put non-theologically, we may say that for such communities, part of what it means to call the community "church" is that certain uses of scripture, in which God is said to make himself present, are essential to the preservation and shaping of their self-identity. *These* concepts "Christian church," at least, are understood in terms of the concept "Christian scripture."

Correlatively, part of what it means to call a text or set of texts "Christian scripture" is that they are the texts that ought to be used in the common life of the church in ways such that they can decisively rule the community's forms of life and forms of speech. Theologically, this point may be made in several different and perhaps conflicting ways: when heard by minds illuminated by the presence of the Holy Spirit, the texts may be said to teach revealed truths; by God's grace, use of the words may become the Word of God; or they may become a saving word-event; or the occasion for the Spiritual Presence. Put in a theologically neutral way, the point is that just as some concepts "Christian church" are defined in terms of "Christian scripture," so the concept "Christian scripture" is defined in terms of some concepts "Christian church."

It is very important to note that implicit in this discussion is a distinction between scripture's uses in the common life of the church and its uses in theology. A great deal of our analysis, both in this chapter and in Part III, follows from this distinction, and failure to keep it in mind will tend to obscure the point being made. Thus far we have shown only that part of what it means to call a set of texts "scripture" is that they function in certain ways in the common life of the church. So when a theologian calls a set of texts "scripture" in an expression like "This scripture is authority for Christian theological proposals," he is remarking, not in the first instance on the use of the texts in his own doing of theology, but on the use of the texts in the life of the church.

In short, we have urged simply as a point about the concepts involved, that by definition "scripture" is the church's book. At this point a question is certain to rise about the implications of these observations for the concept "tradition" and its relation to the concept "scripture." Our analysis is supposed to be theologically neutral. But hasn't it ended up siding, in the well-worn dispute over *sola scriptura,* against the "Protestant" position that scripture creates the church and alone is "authority" over her, and *with* the "Catholic" position that since scripture is the church's book, it follows that the church's tradition is authority along with scripture?

I think that some further remarks about the concept "tradition" show that we have not lost our theological neutrality.

Used as a theological concept, "tradition" names a process. It is the process that embraces both the church's use of scripture and the presence of God which, in dialectical inter-relationship, are together essential to the church's self-identity.

More precisely, "tradition" is used as a theological concept to refer to the handing on of the Christian *kerygma*.[5] It has become commonplace among Protestant and Roman Catholic theologians alike to distinguish between two dialectically inter-related senses of "tradition" as a theological concept. It may be used in reference to the *activity* of handing-on the gospel ("active tradition" or *actus tradendi*). In that respect it names the activity in which the Word of God is made present among the faithful. Or it may be used in reference to *that which* is handed-on ("passive tradition" or *traditum tradendum*). In that respect it refers to Jesus Christ the Risen Lord himself, who is present in and through the act of handing-on the gospel.

Concretely speaking, however, tradition both as the handing-on and as what is handed on consists in specific ways of speaking in homiletical, liturgical, and doctrinal modes of discourse and in specific ways of acting in ritually sacramental modes of action. Specific creedal and liturgical formulae and specific ritual acts are characteristically used as the *concrete* modes in and through which the Risen Lord makes himself present among the faithful. These ways of speaking and acting, in turn, either consist in or are based on use of scripture. To call this "Apostolic" tradition, then, is not to locate it historically, but logically. It is to say: This tradition in all its complexity is the concrete mode of use of scripture that is essential to shaping and preserving the church's identity because it provides the mode in which God is present among the faithful.

Thus "tradition" and certain concepts "church" are dialectically inter-related. "Tradition" is used by Catholics and Protestants alike to refer to those activities that are constituent in, if not constitutive of, the church's reality, but not as they are ordered to an overarching end, i.e., not taken *qua* task or mission, but as they comprise the actual, concrete life of the church in the present. Thus part of what it means to call a set of practices "tradition" is that they are to be taken as a *single* activity or event in which scripture is so used as to constitute the mode of the presence of God and thereby to shape and preserve the church's self-identity. And part of what it means to call a group of people "church," according to some uses of the concept, is that their communal and individual personal identities are shaped by a set of practices taken as a *single complex whole* in which scripture is used in a variety of ways and through which God is believed to make himself present.

When these features of the grammar of the concepts "tradition" and "scripture" are kept in mind, the concepts themselves, far from subtly leading us to take sides in theological controversies, make it possible to state fairly what is at issue in such conflicts. For example, it allows us to state in a neutral way what is at issue in disputes about *sola scriptura*.[6]

Our remarks about the concepts "tradition" and "scripture" bring out the fact that they are not on a logical par. "Tradition" is used to name, not something the church uses, but something the church *is*, insofar as her reality lies in a set of events and practices that can be construed as a single activity. "Scripture" is used to name, not something the church is, but something she must *use*, according to some concepts of "church," to preserve her self-identity.

Now, since "scripture" and "tradition" are not logically on a par, it is misleading to contrast them as alternative and competing authorities for the church's forms of action and speech. Indeed, it is commonly acknowledged now by Protestant and Roman Catholic theologians alike that the issue raised by *sola scriptura* is not whether there are two sources for Christian theology ("canonical scripture" and "tradition") or only one ("canonical scripture" alone).[7] Both sides now agree that "scripture" is that set of writings whose *proper* use serves as the occasion by God's grace for his presence, as they both agree that it is permissible to call the complex comprised by the dialectic between proper use of scripture and gracious presence of God by the name "tradition."[8] "The comprehensive problem," as Joseph Ratzinger has put it, "is the *mode* of the presence of the revealed word among the faithful."[9] For the Reformers, God is present among the faithful only in the mode of *viva vox* proclamation. The "proper" use of scripture is its use in preaching and sacramental act. That constitutes the only activity (*sola scriptura*) which is the occasion for the presence of the revealed word. "Tradition" is merely the *context* within which that takes place, and the church itself is in no respect part of the modality in which the revealed word is present. Oscar Cullmann puts the point for the Reformers quite precisely: An apostolic writer continues "himself to fill his function in the church of today: *in* the church, not by the church, but *by his word* . . . in other words, by his *writings*"[10] as they are used in preaching and sacramental act. For the Roman Catholics, God is present only in the mode of uses of canonical scripture ruled by the divinely instituted teaching office of the church which is to be identified with "tradition" unambiguously ("Scripture and Tradition"). Hence, one aspect of the reality of the church, (viz., the *magisterium*) is not just context but *part of* the modality in which the revealed word is present. For the exercise of the church's teaching office is itself a part of the activity that constitutes the modality in which the revealed word is present.[11]

"SCRIPTURE" AND "AUTHORITY"

Our remarks about the concepts "scripture," "church," and "tradition" bring out another point about the use of "scripture" in expressions such as "This scripture is authoritative for the life of the Christian church" and "This scripture is authoritative for Christian theology." The judgment "These texts are authoritative for the life of the Christian church" is *analytic* in the judgment "These texts are Christian scripture." "Authoritative" is part of the meaning of "scripture"; it is not a *contingent* judgment made about "scripture" on other grounds, such as their age, authorship, miraculous inspiration, etc. And the judgment "These texts are authoritative for theology" is in turn *analytic* in the judgment "These texts are authoritative for the life of the church." The texts' authority for theology is logically grounded in and dependent on their authority for the life of the church generally. But since, concretely speaking, the life of the church taken as some sort of organic whole *is* "tradition," that means that the texts' authority for theology is dependent on their being authority for "tradition."

These remarks follow from the *functional* terms we have used to elucidate the concept "scripture": To call certain texts "scripture" is, in part, to say that they ought to be *used* in the common life of the church in normative ways such that they decisively rule its form of life and forms of speech. Thus part of what it means to call certain texts "scripture" is that they are authoritative for the common life of the church. It is to say of them that they *ought* to be used in certain ways to certain ends in that life. But, given how "tradition" is used, that is to say that the texts ought to be used in certain normative ways in "tradition" understood as a set of activities.

Why? On what grounds is that judgment made? Part of the force of our proposal is that this is an analytic rather than contingent judgement. Writings are not declared "scripture" and hence "authority" because as a matter of contingent fact they exhibit certain properties or characteristics (e.g., "inerrancy" or "inspiredness") that meet some pre-established criteria for inclusion in a class called "Christianly authoritative writings." Rather, they are declared "scripture of the church" and hence "authority for church life" because it is part of relevant concepts "church" to do so. "Scripture" and certain concepts of "church" are dialectically related concepts. Part of what it means to call a community of persons "church," according to some concepts "church," is that use of "scriptures" is essential to the preservation and shaping of their self-identity; part of what it means to call certain writings "scripture" is that according to certain concepts of "church" they ought to be used in the common life of the church to nourish and reform it.

Our next step is to show that, for at least some understandings of the nature of "theology," the judgment "These texts are authoritative for theology" is analytic in the judgment "These texts are Christian scripture."

Here, of course, everything hangs on how "theology" is understood. The term is ambiguous. It may name a body of literature, i.e., "theological writings," or an activity through which those writings are produced, i.e., "doing theology." In the second sense "theology" is one of the activities, or an aspect of the activities in which, we saw, the church has her reality. Indeed, it is essential to preserving her self-identity. There is, we saw, the constant danger that the forms of speech and action in which the church has her reality will become faithless to her "task." That is why, according to certain doctrines of the church, she needs to use scripture in conjunction with the presence of God to nurture and reform her. We also saw that the theological concept "tradition" is used to name the entire complex activity in which these two are conjoined, taken as a single, integral activity. Now, to say that the practice of certain kinds of intellectual activity as part of the common life of the church is "doing theology" is to say that they are activities in which the forms of speech and action current in the church are self-consciously criticized as to their aptness or faithfulness, and in which proposals are made for reform of these forms of speech and action so that they will be more faithful.

This is not the only way the theological task may be understood, of course. Nothing prevents anyone from defining it quite without reference to the church, or indeed without reference to specifically Christian existence. But it does fairly represent the variety of activities we examined in the case studies as diverse instances of "theology." For such theologies, "theology" and "church" are dialectically related concepts. To call a set of practices "doing theology" is to say that they are activities in which the church self-consciously criticizes her own faithfulness to her task. And to call a community "church" is in part to say that she is a community that has her reality in a variety of activities done to a certain end, i.e., taken together as a task or mission, among which, *inter alia*, is the activity of self-consciously criticizing her own faithfulness to that end, i.e., "doing theology."

Accordingly, if a set of texts is said to be "authoritative for the common life of the church" it follows analytically that it is also "authoritative for theology," since "doing theology" is one aspect of the activities comprising the church's life. Hence, if a theologian who shares this understanding of "theology" calls a set of texts "scripture" he thereby commits himself to take part in a range of activities which are in some way ruled by certain uses of those texts, and one of those activities is "doing theology."

Moreover, the particular concrete ways in which a theologian construes how the texts function authoritatively in the common life of the church seems to determine the particular way he construes them as he uses them in theology. We noted in Section 1 of this chapter that theologians characteristically ascribe different *sorts* of function to scripture as used in the church: "teaches," "express," "occasions," etc. The case studies also showed that when theologians appeal to scripture to help authorize their theological proposals, they must make a decision about what sort of logical force the texts have. Note now how the decision about how to characterize the function the text fills in the common life of the church determines each theologian's decision about the sort of logical force to ascribe to the text when he uses it in the course of doing theology.

If the texts serve to teach, then when used in theology they are construed as a text-book of doctrine having the force of *asserting* (infallibly) some eternal truths about objective states of affairs (Warfield); or the logical force of *proposing* a set of concepts by which to reform the conceptual schemes we hitherto have used to order experience, either in the form of a lexicon (Bartsch); or in the form of a historical narrative that uses concepts to "interpret" events (Wright). If the texts serve to "express" and "occasion" something, then when used in theology they are construed as having the *expressive-but-non-informative* force of certain kinds of poetry (Thornton); or religious symbolism (Tillich); or as having a *self-involving* force with abstractable content that sometimes is straightforwardly descriptive and sometimes expressive, using mythic language (Bultmann).

For such theologians, the texts' "authoritativeness" for theology could not consistently be said to have grounds independent of their authoritativeness for the common life of the church. On the contrary, their "authoritativeness" for doing theology is logically entirely dependent on their general authoritativeness over the church's life.

"SCRIPTURE" AND "CANON"

To call a text or set of texts "scripture" is not only to say that their use in certain ways in the church's life is essential to the preservation of her identity, and therefore to say that they are "authoritative" over that life, it is also to ascribe some sort of *wholeness* to the text or set of texts. However, *there is an irreducible variety of kinds of wholeness that may be ascribed to the texts.* Thus "scripture" turns out to be, not one concept, but a set of different concepts that bear one another some family resemblances. All uses of "scripture" are dialectically related to uses of the concept "church" and entail ascribing authoritativeness and wholeness to the texts called "scripture"; this much all uses of "scripture" share. But in the actual practice of appealing to scripture in the course of doing theology, there turns out to be an irreducible logical diversity of ways the texts are concretely construed as "whole." If each is called "scripture," then "scripture" is used in a variety of importantly different ways.

This can be brought out by reviewing another result of the case studies. They showed that when a theologian tries to authorize a theological proposal by appeal to scripture he is obliged to decide what it is *in* scripture that is authoritative. On closer examination, moreover, it turned out that what he appeals to are certain *patterns* characteristically exhibited by the aspect of scripture he takes to be authoritative. When a text is construed in terms of such a pattern, it is construed as though that pattern constitutes it a whole whose unity is analogous to that of some other familiar kind of literature.

Recall the variety we discovered: Appeal may be made to the doctrines taught in scripture. But when Warfield does so, he does not appeal merely to individual doctrines, but to doctrines in their logical inter-relations within the systematic structure of biblical doctrine as a whole. The pattern of systematic inter-connections of biblical doctrines constitutes authoritative scripture a whole like that of a work of systematic philosophy or theology. Appeal may be made to concepts proposed by scripture. But when Bartsch does so, he appeals to concepts in their historical relations to other concepts employed at earlier times and in their inter-relations with other concepts used in the same texts. The pattern of relationships among biblical concepts constitutes authoritative scripture a whole like that of a lexicon of technical terms used in some one area of specialization. Appeal may be made to narratives in scripture. But when Wright does so, he appeals to patterns of promise, disappointment, and unexpected fulfillment that unify the narratives into a single, organic history of salvation. The patterns ordering biblical narratives into a unified recital of a single history constitute authoritative scripture a unity like that of a work offering a particular interpretation of, say, a nation's history. And when Barth appeals to narratives in scripture, he appeals to diverse patterns of intention and enactment that are recounted in different kinds of biblical narrative that, when the irreducibly diverse narratives are themselves taken together in complex patterns of juxtaposition, give an identity description of an agent. The patterns by which biblical narratives render a particular agent in history constitute authoritative scripture a whole like that of a novel centering on a single character.

Appeal may made to biblical images, or symbols. But when Thornton does so, he appeals to the pattern of images' inter-relations as they allude to one another and echo each other, for it is the pattern that reflects the specific form of the cosmic redemptive event that the images express. The rich literary structure composed by biblical images in their inter-relationships constitutes authoritative scripture a whole like that of a long, complex, artfully constructed poem. And when Tillich appeals to biblical symbols, he appeals to their inter-relations within the biblical picture of Jesus as the Christ. The pattern of their inter-relationships constitutes authoritative scripture a whole like that of a verbal icon portraying someone in an "expressionist" style. Bultmann appeals to biblical "theological statements," but only insofar as their patterns of inter-relationships adequately express the structure of authentic existence in faith, which "kerygmatic statements" (for all their apparent diversity of content) summon us to appropriate personally. That all authoritative scripture refers to the same possibility for authentic existence constitutes it a whole like that exhibited, in Bultmann's view, by any document that is humanly significant, i.e., any document that presents a possible "how" for a person's existence.[12] In every case, when a theologian appeals to scripture to help authorize a theological proposal, he appeals, not just to some aspect of scripture, but to a *pattern* characteristically exhibited by that aspect of scripture, and in virtue of that pattern, he construes the scripture to which he appeals as some kind of *whole.* Part of what it means to call a text or set of texts "authoritative scripture" is to ascribe to it some kind of wholeness or unity when it is used as authority.

This brings out a second point. The kinds of "wholeness" or "unity" that may be ascribed to a text in calling it "authoritative scripture" are logically irreducibly diverse. Its "wholeness," we have seen, is a function of the kind of pattern to which appeal is made in appealing to the text to authorize a theological proposal. But the patterns are logically utterly diverse. What have "patterns in logical inter-relationships among doctrines or concepts," "patterns among religious symbols used in a particular religious tradition," "patterns recurring in a stretch of world history" in common save the trivial point that they are all patterns? What is common to the modes of unity exhibited by systematic works in philosophy or theology, by lexicons of technical terms used in specialized forms of inquiry, interpretations of a nation's history, novels, poems, portraits in the "expressionist" style, or representations of possible "hows" for human existence, except the empty remark that they are, after all, modes of unity? They are utterly, irreducibly diverse.

That brings out the third point: "scripture" is not so much a single concept as a family of concepts sharing some similarities while remaining irreducibly different concepts. There is no one "standard" concept "scripture." This follows from what we have just said. Part of what it means to call a text "authoritative scripture" is that it is taken as some kind of "whole." But there is a logically irreducible variety of kinds of "whole" it may be taken to be. Each is thereby part of a logically different concept "scripture." That is to say, what it *means* to call a text "authoritative scripture" varies with the sort of wholeness that is thereby ascribed to the text. Put the matter another way: theologians do not appeal to scripture-as-such to help authorize their theological proposals. In the concrete practice of doing theology, they decide on some aspect or, more exactly, some pattern in scripture to which to appeal. That is to say that they decide on some one *kind* of unity to ascribe to the texts, and not some other kind. Not the text as such, but the text-construed-as-a-certain-kind-of-whole is appealed to. What it means, then, to call the text "scripture" varies with the kind of "wholeness" ascribed to it in the concrete decision about which pattern is to be appealed to. In Part III we shall return to the question how that decision is made.

These observations about the "wholeness" ascribed to a set of texts in calling them "scripture" raise questions about another, related theological concept, "canon." Although often they are used interchangeably, we have kept the concepts "scripture" and "canon" distinct because it is not self-evident that theologians who agree that "scripture" is authority for theological proposals would also agree that the "scripture" to which appeal should be made is identical with the historical Christian canon, whether comprised of the literatures of the Old and New Testament alone (the "Protestant" canon), or comprised of those writings in addition to the so-called "Apocrypha" (the "Catholic" canon). We need now to explore what more is said when a set of texts is called, not just "scripture," but "canonical scripture."

It may be helpful to begin by introducing a distinction between a theologian's "working canon" and the "Christian canon." By "Christian canon" I mean the historical canon, "Protestant" or "Catholic." In contrast, a theologian's "working canon" is simply that set of texts to which he does in fact appeal to help authorize his theological proposals. We have stressed that a theologian's "working canon" may or may not be identical with the "historical canon." In any case, we have argued, in calling his working canon "scripture" he necessarily ascribes some sort of "wholeness" to it. "Working canon" is thus logically a necessary part of the meaning of "scripture."

It must be stressed that a "working canon" is not necessarily what Ernst Käsemann has called a "canon within the canon." Strictly speaking, the wholeness of a "canon within a canon" is a function of its doctrinal content. For Käsemann it is a function of its uniformly teaching the doctrine of justification by faith.[13] The wholeness of a "working canon," however, may be a function of any of several different kinds of patterns within the text, including patterns among concepts or doctrines, to be sure, but not confined to them.

But while "working canon" is part of the meaning of "scripture," "Christian canon" is not. A theologian makes no conceptual mistake if he takes certain biblical texts as "scripture" to which he appeals to help authorize his theological proposals and to which he ascribes some kind of "wholeness," but does not appeal to all of the texts in the historical "Christian canon" nor ascribe any kind of wholeness to it.

This brings us to a second point. We can now specify what more is said of a set of texts by calling them "Christian canon" than by calling them simply "Christian scripture." Although "canon" is not necessarily part of the concept "scripture," "scripture" is necessarily a part of the meaning of "canon." When a community of Christians calls a set of writings the "Christian canon," she affirms that it is her "scripture." It is to say that this set of writings ought to be used in certain ways in the church's common life. But more than that: It is to say that *just these* writings are *sufficient* for the ends to which they ought to be used in the church. This is the important point where "canon" means more than "scripture." Thus, for a community to call itself "church" is to say, *inter alia*, that it is a community whose continuing self-identity depends on the use, not just (vaguely) of some writings, but precisely use of just these writings. Hence, when any community calling itself "church" does acknowledge these writings to be her "canon" she is, in James Sanders' image, taking them as a "mirror for the identity of the believing community which in any era turns to it to ask what it is and what it is to do, even today."[14]

It follows, thirdly, that to call a set of writings "Christian canon" is an analytic judgment: To say, "These writings are the Christian canon" is analytic in "This community is a Christian church." The historical process through which the canon was formed was a process of selecting certain writings out of a larger literary pool.[15] When the church was forced to *justify* its selection of certain books and rejection of others in the face of attacks like Marcion's, she represented it as a contingent decision: They alone were selected because they alone did, as a matter of objective and contingent fact, meet certain historical criteria, chiefly that they had been written by prophets and apostles or apostles' secretaries.[16] However, Hans von Campenhausen has shown that the "truly crucial factor" in selecting writings for the canon was not the contingent facts about their authorsip but simply "the usage and judgment of the one true church, spread throughout the world."[17] That is, in declaring just these writings "canon" the church was giving part of a self-description of her identity: we are a community such that certain uses of scripture are *necessary* for nurturing and shaping our self-identity, and the use of "just these," i.e., "canonical," writings is *sufficient* for that purpose. The judgment, "These writings are 'canon'," is analytic in the judgment "This community is 'church'," *if* one adopts the appropriate concept "church."

Karl Rahner has put this point succinctly by trading on a distinction between two levels of the church's collective self-consciousness. At the level of "primal self-consciousness" the church's "primal

memory of the days of her birth, when she first heard the revelation
of God in Christ" is fully and adequately "concretized" in the Bible.
Having the Bible play this role is part of "the integral and full con-
stitution of the Church, according to the plan of God." At a second
level of consciousness the church has a " 'concomitant' consciousness" *that* "this is her Scripture, canonical and inspired."[18] One does
not need to share Rahner's phenomenology of consciousness, collective or individual, to accept the implicit suggestion about the logic
of the concept "canon:" The church's acknowledgment that just
these writings are sufficient as her "canon" is part of her self-
description.

A fourth point, as with "scripture," so with "canon": to call a
set of writings "canon" is to ascribe some kind of "wholeness" to it.
The "wholeness" is a function of the *singularity* of the end to
which the uses of these writings is said to be sufficient, viz., that
the use of these writings be sufficient as the occasion for the presence of God among the faithful. To call them "canon" is to say
that the writings taken together, no matter what their diversity from
one another, function *ensemble* when used in the common life of
the church and serve as the sufficient occasion for that presence of
God that preserves the church's identity as a single, integral, living
reality. No matter how great its inner diversity, this set of writings
is to be taken as mirroring in a wholeness of its own the unity of the
church's own identity.

It should be noted that ascribing "wholeness" to the canon is
not identical with ascribing "unity" to the canon. The canon's
"unity" would consist of a coherence or even consistency among its
contents. It could only be demonstrated by exegetical study. The
canon's "unity," if it has any, might be invoked to account for its
effectiveness at accomplishing the end to which it is used. But it is
not logically necessary that the canon actually exhibit such "unity" in
order for it to be construed as some kind of "whole." Its being an
ensemble can be accounted for on other grounds, namely, that when
used in certain ways in the common life of the church it does all taken
together serve to establish, nurture, and preserve the church's self-
identity.

It is, in any case, a "whole" of irreducibly different "parts." The
"parts" are distinguished from one another on exegetical grounds

by their respective contents and literary and historical characteristics. Von Campenhausen has shown that in the early history of the church the canon was taken as having a bipartite "wholeness" comprised of the Old and New Testaments.[19] Its "wholeness" was construed in different ways depending on how the relation between the two parts was construed. Moreover, each of these parts sometimes was, on exegetical grounds, taken as comprised of sub-parts: "Law" and "Prophets" in the Old Testament, "Gospels" and "Epistles" in the New Testament. Here too, the canon's "wholeness" could be construed in quite different ways depending on how the relations between the sub-parts of each "part" were construed and on how that then influenced the ways in which the relation between the main "parts" was construed. Hence, while calling a set of writings "canon" means construing it as an ensemble, it does not entail any particular orchestration, any one mode of "wholeness." On the contrary, if a theologian calls a set of writings "canon," he takes on a responsibility to suggest what its singular "wholeness" is *like*. It requires a metaphorical judgment declaring what it is like, an act of the imagination.

Concretely, then, there is logically irreducible diversity of *concepts* "canon." To call a set of writings "canon," we said, is to take it as a "whole" comprised of "parts," an ensemble that may be orchestrated in any of several ways. The differences among the various ways in which it may be orchestrated as a "whole" are *differences in ways in which uses of the parts are inter-related in actual practice*. The "parts" are differentiated through exegetical studies. But the way they are taken as a "whole" will vary with the ways in which the *use* of each "part" is inter-related with the uses of all the other parts. Thus in the actual practice of doing theology, every theologian who takes, not just (vaguely) "scripture," but (more particularly) "canon" as his authority must decide just how his use of one "part" of the canon is to be inter-related with his "use" of other parts of the canon.

Consider some of the possibilities: A theologian's use of Old Testament material may be subordinated to and controlled by his use of New Testament materials (as in, e.g., Bultmann); or (as seems to have happened in early forms of Christianity that took Jesus as a revealer of a new Torah) his use of New Testament materials may be subordinated to his use of Old Testament materials; or (as in, e.g., Barth) he may try to keep his use of materials from each major "part" of the canon in some kind of dialectical tension with his use of material from the other "part." There are important variants on each of these possibilities, however. What "New Testament" means in each case varies with the way in which use of each of its sub-parts is related to use of its other sub-parts; so also with "Old Testament." Thus the New Testament "Gospel" materials may be used in ways subordinated to and controlled by uses of "Epistle" material, or *vice versa*; or an effort might be made to keep use of each sub-part in some sort of equipoise. "New Testament" means something significantly different in each case. So too in use of the Old Testament, "law" materials may be used in ways subordinated to and controlled by "prophecy" materials, or *vice versa*; or an effort may be made to keep uses of each of these sub-parts in some kind of equipoise. "Old Testament" means something significantly different in each use. Thus, in the actual concrete practice of using scripture to help authorize theological proposals, each of the different ways of relating use of Old with New Testament materials will itself vary depending on how uses of the sub-parts of each Testament are inter-related. Each constitutes a different way of orchestrating the ensemble; each is a different concrete kind of "whole" for the "canon." To call each "canon" is to say something significantly different in each case.[20]

"AUTHORITY OF SCRIPTURE": DESCRIPTION OR INVOCATION?

We noted above that if a theologian, who shares the view of the nature of theology reflected in the case studies, (despite their diversity on other scores) calls a set of texts "scripture," he thereby commits himself to take part in a range of activities which are in some way ruled by certain uses of those texts, and one of those activities is "doing theology." This suggests something about the logic of expressions like "Scripture is authority for Christian proposals!" It might seem that such an expression uses "authority" as a logical predicate naming a property of the referent of the logical subject "scripture." Taken that way, it would be an informative remark if it were clear what "scripture" means and what sort of property "authority" is and, further, if it were possible to check whether scripture does in fact have the property claimed for it. However, to take the expression this way would be to misunderstand its logical force. It ought not to be taken as a claim about a property of scripture. It ought rather to be taken as having self-involving performative force. It is a performative utterance in that by it the speaker effectively acknowledges a rule governing the practice of theology: In the making of theological proposals, scripture is to be used in such a way that it helps somehow to authorize the proposals.

This follows from three points we have made about the grammar of the use of the concept "scripture." First, the judgment "Scripture is authority" turned out to be analytic in the judgment "These texts are Christian scripture." So "Scripture is authority" is not, strictly speaking, an informative remark. It ascribes no property to the texts whose presence in them could be checked out independently of the judgment itself. Secondly, to say "Scripture is authority" turned out not to be drawing attention to a property implicitly ascribed to texts in calling them "scripture," but rather draws attention to functions they fill. To say "Scripture is authority" means in part "These texts must be used in certain ways in the common life of the church." Thirdly, given certain understandings of "theology," to say "Scripture is authority" is in part to say "These texts must be used in certain normative ways in the course of doing theology." That is, it is to adopt a rule governing how one does theology. Such a rule is part of the definition of the nature of theology common to theologies that take scripture as authority for the life of the church. Scripture's "right" to be put to use as authority is logically analytic in the very concept "theology." The utterance, "This scripture is authority for this theological proposal" is self-involving in that by it a speaker commits himself to follow this rule when he does theology. Accordingly, such expressions do not ascribe a property to scripture; instead, they locate scripture in a certain way in the context of the activity of doing theology.

Allow a parable: A group of boys gather on an empty lot. One has a soft rubber ball about the size of a grapefruit and he says, "Come on, play ball." They begin to divide up into teams. An observer knowing nothing else about the sorts of games they customarily play, and hearing nothing else of what they say to one another, could not know at that point just what game they are going to play. They might be getting ready to play baseball, but it might be either hardball, softball, or a variant of stickball; or they might be getting set to play basketball, or football, or even soccer. The observer also has grounds for the more interesting belief that whatever game they play, the *point* of the game will involve doing something specifiable with the ball (hitting it as far as possible with a bat; or throwing it as quickly as possible to one of the basemen; or throwing it through a hoop; or moving it down to the end of the field and into a net between two upright posts by kicking alone), and the things done with and/or to the ball will be done according to some commonly agreed on set of rules. Moreover, in this case their decision about which game to play will involve "construing" the ball in one way or another: as being like a baseball, a basketball, a football, a soccer ball. It will also involve their "construing" other things too, e.g., the empty lot as a baseball diamond, a basketball court, a football or soccer field. The "construals" will depend on which sort of activity they take to have been invoked by the cry "Come on, play ball!" The decision about which game to play will determine among other things what the point is of the specific things done with and to the ball, by what rules it is done, and so what "scoring" will consist in. The decision to play ball—or we might say: play-ball-as-such!—however, rules out certain other games they might (logically might) have taken up instead. Whatever sort of game they do play, it must be one in which the point of the game involves doing something with and to the ball. Hence they cannot set out to play jump rope, chess, or bridge when they commit themselves to play ball.

So too when, in his actual practice of theology, a theologian says "Scripture is authority for this theological proposal," he thereby commits himself to participate in one or another of a family of activities called "doing Christian theology." At one level of generality, what all members of this family have in common is that the *point* of doing them is to make "theological proposals." At that level of generality they also share a *rule*: In developing theological proposals, scripture shall be used in such a way that it helps authorize the proposals. Hence, at this level of generality, to say "Scripture is

authority for theology" is to exclude certain other activities that
might appear to be similar in other respects but use in the authorizing roles passages from the New York Times, the Koran, or aborig-
inal Patagonian legends instead of passages from the Bible.

More concretely, however, the members of this family of activities differ from one another radically precisely because in each the
point of doing the activity, and in some respects the *rules* according
to which it is done, are different. The task of theology is variously
understood. For that reason it really is no more illuminating to say
that the point of doing theology is to make "theological proposals"
than it is to say that the point of playing ball games is to "score
points." What a "theological proposal" is, what the phrase means,
depends in large part (though probably not entirely) on how the
task of theology is specifically understood. When a particular theologian says "Scripture is the authority for this theological proposal,"
he is not making a descriptive claim about scripture, nor is he committing himself to an entire family of activities as such. Rather, he
is committing himself to a particular member of the family which
is specified by a particular understanding of theology's task. And,
just as in our parable the boys' decision about which ball game to
play determined just how they construe the ball and what they do
with it, so a theologian's decision about what the task or point is of
"doing theology." determines how he will construe scripture and
by what rules he will use it so as to authorize his own theological
proposals.

In short, a theologian who marshals his proposals under the emblem "Let theology accord with scripture" does not thereby announce that he has made a methodological decision, but only that
he has taken on an awesome array of methodological problems. He
announces that he is going to undertake the practice of theology
understood in a certain way, viz., as governed, *inter alia*, by the rule
that in the course of defending theological proposals scripture shall
be used in ways that help authorize the proposals. He thereby commits himself to making several decisions regarding logically diverse
matters: what aspect or, more exactly, what pattern it is in scripture
that is to be taken as authoritative; what of its uses in the common
life of the church make it authoritative; consequently, what sort of
logical force to ascribe to the scripture to which he does appeal; how

to bring the scripture to which he does appeal to bear on his theological proposals so as to authorize them. But in saying "Let theology accord with scripture" or "Scripture is authority for Christian theology" he has not yet committed himself on just what he will decide on these matters.

In particular, he will not yet have decided just how he will *use* scripture in the course of doing theology so that it bears on his proposals. That is a major decision because it determines how in actual practice scripture does "authorize" someone's theology. It bears further close analysis, to which we turn in Part II.

NOTES

1. The importance of distinguishing between the Bible as a text and the Bible as "scripture" is brought out forcefully by Wilfred Cantwell Smith in "The Study of Religion and the Study of the Bible," *Journal of the American Academy of Religion,* 39 (Je 1971), pp. 131–140. V. also F. F. Bruce and E. G. Rupp, eds., *Holy Book and Holy Tradition* (Manchester: Manchester University Press, 1968) for a study of this question in regard to several different religious traditions.
2. Notice that this is not to say that for any conceivable doctrine of the church, the reality of the church is *constituted* by these activities done to some end, only that they are *constituent* in its reality. One advantage of putting the matter this way is that it provides terms in which to state opposing views of the church fairly. If the church is understood in existentially "actualist" or quasi-empirical "functionalist" terms, then her reality simply is identical with the doing of these activities. In that case (by definition) there can be no "sinful church": either the constitutive activities are actually done, or there is no "church" at all. If the reality of the church is grounded in God's eternal election of men for salvation or in the presence in the church of a structure, say an office, established by God and continued in unbroken succession (from the time of its establishment) until today, then the reality of the church is comprised by these activities but does not simply consist in them. Even if none of these activities is properly done, the community is still truly "church," since its reality is constituted by something else; but it is "sinful church."

This characterization of views of the church in terms of what she does seems fair to contemporary Roman Catholic, Eastern Orthodox, and "mainstream" Protestant accounts alike. Cf. Hans Küng, *The Church* (New York: Sheed and Ward, 1967), esp. Parts 'A' and 'C'; Georges Florovsky, *Bible, Church and Tradition* (Belmont: Norland, 1972), esp. Chs. III ("The Catholicity of the Church") and IV ("The Church: Her Nature and Task"), and "The Ethos of the Orthodox Church" in *The Ecumenical Review,* Vol. 12 (Jan. '60), pp. 183–198; Langdon Gilkey, *How the Church Can Minister to the World Without Losing Itself* (New York: Harper & Row, 1967); Gustavo Gutierrez, *A Theology of Liberation* (New York: Orbis, 1973), esp. Ch. 12 ("The Church: A Sacrament of History"); Lesslie Newbigin, *The Household of God*

(New York: Friendship Press, 1954); *The Church for Others* (Geneva: World Council of Churches, 1968).

3. *The Formation of the Christian Bible* (Philadelphia: Fortress Press, 1972) tr. J. A. Baker, p. 1; cf. pp. 62–63. Cf. the Reformers' stress that biblical writings are only truly "Word of God" when use by the church is dialectically related to the presence of the Holy Spirit and the Spirit's use of the writings to his own ends. Oscar Cullmann has argued that the same theme is present in St. Paul. Certain formulaic expressions had been received by Paul (*paradosis*) and he acknowledges, in effect, that their use is essential to the church's continuing self-identity. But they are authoritative and fulfill that function only as the Lord (*kyrios*) makes himself present in and through their use; *v.* "The Tradition," *The Early Church* (Philadelphia: Westminster, 1956), pp. 69–71.

4. Again, we must stress the qualification we put on this claim. These remarks hold only for *some* concepts of "church." We have not tried to make the case that the concept "church" as such logically necessitates "use of certain writings in the church's common life" as part of her definition. Since we have not tried to specify *which* are the writings whose use is essential to the preservation of the "church's" self-identity, it might be logically impossible to make such a case! If there are communities that call themselves "Christian Church" and do not understand the use of scriptures as essential to the preservation of their self-identity, then our remarks simply do not apply to them.

5. In relation to the content of this paragraph see: Albert Outler, "Traditions in Transit" in *The Old and The New in the Church* (Minneapolis: Augsburg, 1961), ed. Paul Minear, and *The Tradition and the Unity We Seek* (New York: Oxford, 1959); and K. Skydsgaard, "Scripture and Tradition," *Scottish Journal of Theology,* Vol. 9, pp. 337-358. See Skydsgaard, "Scripture and Tradition" in *Challenge and Response* (Minneapolis: Augsburg, 1966), ed. W. Quanbeck, pp. 25–59 for a good survey of Roman Catholic views and Protestant responses; J. P. Mackey, *The Modern Theology of Tradition* (New York: Herder and Herder, 1963) for a survey of Roman Catholic views.

6. That these remarks about the grammar of the use of the concept "scripture" and "tradition" enable rather than hinder fair statement of what is at issue in well-worn theological disputes can be shown by other examples. They allow us to state fairly some issues on which influential concepts of "church" differ. It is misleading to say that the major issues dividing Roman Catholic, Eastern Orthodox, and characteristically Reformation doctrines of the church turn on whether "tradition" is affirmed as part of the meaning of "church." They all affirm that. The issues lie elsewhere. To call the activities in which the church has her reality "tradition" is to construe them as a single, integrally complex whole. But what kind of whole; what is it *like*? Differences in judgment about *that* are the root issue.

For example: Some theologians liken it to an *organic process.* That allows stress on its continuity through time and, perhaps, its capacity for "evolving" one way or another. Others liken it to an existentially important *event.* That allows stress on its person-transforming power. (Cf. Skydsgaard, *Scottish Journal of Theology,* Vol. 9, p. 356.) The differences are not whether "tradition" is part of the meaning of "church," but how best to characterize the *whole* that is "tradition." Again: Does characterizing "tradition" as "process" or as "event" imply that there is a being that undergoes the process or does

the event? Many Roman Catholic theologians assume that "activity" (whether
as "process" or "event") is intelligible only on the supposition of a substantial "agent" whose being is independent of its performing just this activity.
There has to be an "organ" or "organism" for there to be "activity." [Cf.
Mackay, *passim.*] Others seem to hold that it is intelligible to say that the
church's being is simply constituted by this activity. The issue is not whether
"tradition" is part of the meaning of "church," but how best to construe the
single complex activity that constitutes "tradition."

Another example: We saw that "tradition" is used as a technical theological
concept to refer to the same concrete, empirically describable forms of speech
and action which are referred to by "tradition" used in phenomenological
contexts, i.e., in history or sociology. Should it be assumed that the two concepts "tradition" not only are used to *refer* to the same phenomena, but also
that "tradition" in the theological sense wholly and unambiguously includes
"tradition" in the phenomenological sense? The issue here is not whether
"tradition" is part of the meaning of "church," but whether it is intelligible
to say of a particular community that it is truly "church" but also "faithless"
or "sinful." A characteristic Protestant response is to declare the two uses of
"tradition" ambiguously related at best. That way it is possible to judge
theologically that the church's forms of speech and forms of action phenom-
enologically identified as "tradition" are in fact largely heretical and sinful,
and still affirm intelligibly that, by God's grace, those activities are "tradition"
in the theological sense and the community is nevertheless genuinely "church,"
albeit "sinful church." The church itself is *simul justus et peccator.* A second
possibility, sometimes adopted in Roman Catholic discussions of the church
and tradition (Cf. Mackey, *passim.*) accepts the first proposal with the reser-
vation that certain particular organs within the church's common life (say, the
teaching office in the person of the Pope when speaking *ex cathedra*) and certain particular forms of speech and ritual action (say, the eucharist duly celebrated by a priest and understood as valid *ex opere operato*) are unambiguously identical with "tradition" in the theological sense. These "traditions," in
the phenomenological sense of the term, cannot be sinful and so are unambiguously part of the meaning of "tradition" in the theological sense. A third
possibility would be to affirm that the totality of the empirically describable
life of the church (phenomenological "tradition") is unambiguously part of
the meaning of "tradition" as a theological concept. In that case the church
cannot intelligibly be said to be sinful. Some discussions of the matter by
Eastern Orthodox spokesmen seem to express or imply this view; cf. Panagi-
otis P. Bratsiotis, "The Fundamental Principles and Main Characteristics of
the Orthodox Church," *The Ecumenical Review,* Vol. 12 (Jan. 1960), pp.
154–163; Georges Florovsky, *Bible, Church and Tradition* (Belmont: Norland,
1972), esp. Chs. III ("The Catholicity of the Church"), IV ("The Church:
Her Nature and Task"), and V ("The Function of Tradition in the Ancient
Church"); C. Konstantinidis, "The Significance of the Eastern and Western
Traditions Within Christendom," *The Ecumenical Review,* Vol. 12 (Jan. 1970),
pp. 145–153. Non-orthodox commentators are struck by the way in which
Eastern Orthodoxy's understanding of "tradition" (as a theological concept,
in our terms) construes it concretely as an eternally unbroken act of liturgical
doxology which constitutes the context of all mankind's life. Hence scripture

used in it is not so much an "authority" as a "whole world" (Louis Bouyer, p. 51) and dogma is not so much the church's legal charter as its aptest mode of doxological expression; cf. Louis Bouyer, "Holy Scripture and Tradition as seen by the Fathers," *Eastern Churches Quarterly*, Vol. VII (1947), pp. 2–16; Edmund Schlink, "The Significance of the Eastern and Western Traditions for the Christian Church," *The Ecumenical Review,* Vol. 12 (Jan. 1960), pp. 133–142.

The point each of these examples underscores is this: When a theologian understands "tradition" to be part of the meaning of "church," as most Roman Catholic, Eastern Orthodox, and "mainstream" Protestant theologians do, he undertakes to construe the activities in which the church has her reality as a single though complex "whole" and is obliged to offer some characterization of that "whole," some proposal about what it is like. And that is an act of the imagination. It is at the point of making that metaphorical proposal that concepts of the "church" most basically begin to diverge. [*V.* also footnote #20, below.]

7. *V.*, in Roman Catholic discussions, Yves-Marie Congar, *Tradition and the Traditions* (London: Burns & Oates, 1966), E. T. of *La tradition et les traditions*; Joseph Geiselmann, S. J. *The Meaning of Tradition* (New York: Herder & Herder, 1966), tr. W. J. O'Hara, and "On the Interpretation of the Tridentine Decree on Tradition" in Rahner and Ratzinger, *Revelation and Tradition* (New York: Herder & Herder, 1966) pp. 50–69; George Lindbeck, *The Future of Roman Catholic Theology* (Philadelphia: Fortress Press, 1970), Ch. 5; George Tavard, *Holy Writ or Holy Church?* (London: Burns and Oates, 1959); and in Protestant discussions Oscar Cullmann, "The Tradition" in *The Early Church* (Philadelphia: Westminster, 1956) ed. A. J. B. Higgins, p. 59–105; Gerhard Ebeling, " 'Sola Scriptura' and Tradition" in *The Word of God and Tradition* (Philadelphia: Fortress Press, 1968), tr. S. H. Hooke, pp. 102–148; K. E. Skydsgaard, "Scripture and Tradition" in *Challenge and Response*, ed. W. Quanbeck; and essays by Jaroslav Pelikan, Albert Outler, and K. E. Skydsgaard in *The Old and the New in the Church* (Minneapolis: Augsburg; 1961), ed. Paul Minear.

8. Even spokesmen for theologically conservative "low church" Protestant traditions are prepared to admit that scripture is always used in the context of some kind of "tradition"; cf. F. F. Bruce, *Tradition: Old and New* (Grand Rapids: Zondervan, 1970), esp. the Introduction and Chs. 8–10.

9. *Revelation and Tradition*, p. 34; my italics.

10. "The Tradition," p. 80. For Roman Catholic critique of Cullmann's claim that this was also the view of the earliest church, see Josef R. Geiselmann, *The Meaning of Tradition*, pp. 24–27, and George Tavard, "Scripture, Tradition and History," *Downside Review*, Vol. 72, pp. 234 ff.

11. This point seems unambiguously clear in those Roman Catholic theologians like Pesch and Dieckmann who equate "tradition" with the *magisterium* taken as an "organ" in the church. More than that, it is the common assumption among Roman Catholic theologians who otherwise disagree about the concept "tradition." "Active tradition" in dialectical inter-relation with scripture-in-use is the mode in which the revealed word is present among the faithful. The disagreements can be construed as turning on the question which or how many parts or "organs" of the Body of Christ are identical with "tradition":

magisterium alone, *magisterium* and Fathers and major theologians, the faithful, the entire complex of activities constituting the life of the church? That is, all agree that part or parts of the church are themselves part of the activity that constitutes the modality in which the revealed word is present, but some disagree about just which part or parts; *v.* the useful survey of the literature by J. P. Mackey in *The Modern Theology of Tradition.*
12. V. "The Problem of Hermeneutics," *Essays,* tr. J. C. G. Greig, (New York: Macmillan, 1955), pp. 234–262.
13. Cf. Ernst Käsemann, *Essays on New Testament Themes* (London: SCM Press, 1966), Chs. II and IV, and Diem, *Dogmatics,* pp. 229–234.
14. *Torah and Canon* (Philadelphia: Fortress Press, 1972) p. xv–xvi; cf. p. 117.
15. *Cf. von Campenhausen, passim,* and in regard to the Christian canon of the Old Testament, Albert C. Sundberg, Jr., *The Old Testament of the Early Church* (Cambridge: Harvard University Press, 1964) for the view that the early church received a fixed set of "Law" and "Prophets," but a fluid collection of "Writings" from which she made her own selection independently of and prior to Judaism's selecting her own canon of the same materials.
16. The earliest known statement on the matter, the Muratorian canon, c. 200 AD, cites the following principles of selection for the canon: (a) the authors of the canonical books are apostles; (b) the authors are eyewitnesses to the resurrection; (c) the writings must be addressed to the whole church; (d) the message must be a unified one. Kurt Aland has pointed out that, as the Muratorian canon itself acknowledges, each of these is violated by some writing admitted into the canon: re (a) and (b), Luke and Mark are not technically apostles, and Luke is not an eyewitness; furthermore, some writings held by many to have apostolic authorship are rejected (e.g., the "Apocalypse of Peter"); re (c) Paul writes to individual churches and even to individual persons, and not to the whole church; re (d), the *principia* (= "beginnings" or "basic assumptions"?) of the Gospels are different (*v.* Kurt Aland, *The Problem of the New Testament Canon* [London: A. R. Mobray, 1962], p. 9). In a provocative attack on the very concept "canon," Christopher Evans points out that in any case the image of "apostle" "is almost, if not entirely, fantasy, and the literature which promoted it in the form of liturgy, church order, canons as well as gospels, Acts, and epistles, is the literature of the imagination." Historical research has shown that the received image of "apostle" is so blurred that "the adjective 'apostolic' comes to be used in an increasingly Pickwickian sense." Sometimes an "apostle" is thought to have authority because he is one of the twelve Christ sent to extend his own mission into all the world. But "such evidence as we have suggests that, with the exception of Peter, they remained in Jerusalem exercising their function of being the Twelve." Sometimes an "apostle" is thought to have authority because he holds an office to which he has been appointed by the Lord to serve as the original and sure basis of the church and its faith. "The image is of the church's origination from an unfailing source in a divine history, and of its pedigree—an image not of what it is for, as in the missionary understanding, but of what it is from. And this begets its own legend, that of the so-called 'apostolic age'," of a unified and pure faith "from which all later ages must trace their descent." Evans objects that this sense of "apostle" can be read back into the New Testament usage of the term only by dubious linguistic and historical arguments about

the basis of the concept "apostle" in the Jewish concept *shaliach* (a legal arrangement by which one who was sent on a task had a power of attorney, expressed in the dictum "he who is sent by a man is as the man who sends him") (*v.* Christopher Evans, *Is "Holy Scripture" Christian?* [London: SCM Press, 1971], pp. 26–29). The merits of the linguistic arguments aside, however, a larger problem is raised by the picture of an "apostolic age" in which the church is united in a normative orthodoxy and from which she subsequently falls into division, with some parts maintaining continuity with the orthodox past and others drifting into heresy. This picture is well-nigh universally assumed backdrop to discussions of the meaning of "canon." But it is probably historically incorrect. Walter Bauer contends that there is good evidence that in many localities (e.g. in Edessa, Egypt, parts of Asia Minor) the historically original form of Christianity was a sort later judged heretical. Hence "heretical" forms of Christianity cannot be pictured as a decline from a historically prior orthodoxy. Rather they must all be seen as variants in a highly pluralistic and fluid situation that eventually lost ground before other variants that were ultimately taken as normative Christianity (*v.* Walter Bauer, *Orthodoxy and Heresy in Earliest Christianity* [Philadelphia: Fortress Press, 1971], E. T. of *Rechtgläubigkeit und Ketzerei in Altesten Christentum* [Tübingen: Mohr-Siebeck, 1934]). Our point is that uncertainty about the historical accuracy of traditional justifications for selection of "just these" writings as the church's "canon" are logically irrelevant to use of "canon" as a theological concept. The historical uncertainties undercut the judgment that "just these" writings are "canon" only if it is a *contingent* judgment. Our contention is that, where "canon" is used as a theological concept, it is rather an *analytic* judgment.

17. von Campenhausen, p. 261; cf. pp. 253–262.

18. *Inspiration in the Bible* (New York: Herder & Herder, 1964), tr. C. H. Henkey, S. J., pp. 36–37.

19. On the development of a view of the canon as "bi-partite," *v.* von Campenhausen; the phrase is his, e.g., p. x.

20. Just as our remarks about the concepts "scripture" and "tradition" enabled rather than hindered fair statement of what is at issue in disputes about *sola scriptura* and about the concept "church," so these remarks about the grammar of the use of the concept "canon" enable us to state more fairly what is at issue in certain theological disputes [cf. above, pp. 100–108 and footnote 6]. Consider, for example, a recent dispute about how the unity of the church is related to the unity of the canon. In 1951 Ernst Käsemann delivered a lecture advancing the thesis that the New Testament canon does not, as such, constitute the foundation of the unity of the church. On the contrary, as such (that is, in its accessibility to the historian) it provides the basis for the multiplicity of the confessions [*V. Essays on New Testament Themes* (London: SCM, 1964), tr. W. J. Montague, p. 103; cf. p. 95.] The dis-unity of the canon is then the basis of the dis-unity of the church. However, he argues, the basis of the church is not the canon but the Word of God, and "the canon is not the Word of God *tout simple*." The Word of God is God's gift and "the gift is a mode of the Giver's presence, not a substitute for him" [p. 105]. The canon becomes Word of God, i.e., the mode of God's presence, only as it is so used that its very use is an event the hearer experiences as his being justified by

grace. Here the "authority" of canonical scripture is understood in *functional* terms, i.e., in terms of the function it fills in the church's common life. Hence the question, " 'What is the Gospel?' cannot be settled by the historian according to the results of his investigations but only by the believer who is led by the Spirit and listens obediently to the Scripture." (Käsemann calls this "discerning the spirits," i.e., testing the canonical writings to find the Word of God.) Correlatively, "the unity of the Church is never immediately accessible; it exists only for faith" [p. 106].

Hans Küng offered a Roman Catholic response. He implicitly agreed with Käsemann's functionalist construal of the canon's "authority" and he accepts the dis-unity of the New Testament as exegetically well established. But he wants to argue that the New Testament's dis-unity "is indeed a necessary *presupposition* and *occasion* for confessional multiplicity, but not strictly its root or cause." The cause of the multiplicity of confessions is "not seriously accepting the Canon as one thing, for all its lack of unity, not striving, through all the difficulties confronting each other in it, to reach a *comprehensive* understanding of it" [" 'Early Catholicism' in the New Testament," in *The Church in Action* (New York: Sheed & Ward, 1963), tr. Cecily Hastings, p. 172. *V.* also Hermann Diem, *Dogmatics* (Edinburgh: Oliver & Boyd, 1959), esp. Ch. 9, "The Unity of Scripture," for another critique of Käsemann's views.] Protestants, he suggests, characteristically see the church's unity as a function of the canon's wholeness and so are driven to find some kind of unity in the canon even if the price is an arbitrary selection of some parts of it as "authoritative" and an exclusion of other parts. Käsemann does this by using "justification by faith" as his "material principle of selection" (p. 173) of the parts that do fall together as a "unity" and are "authoritative," and his systematic rejection of parts of the New Testament that reflect a fundamentally "catholic" view of the church and of grace [pp. 181–183]. By contrast, Roman Catholics characteristically see the canon's "wholeness" as a function of the church's "unity." Küng's implicit logical point seems to be that ascription of "wholeness" to the canon is analytic in acknowledgment of "unity" to the church, and not *vice versa.*

How should we state what is at issue here? It would be misleading to say that the issue is whether ascription of "wholeness" to the canon is analytic in acknowledgment of "unity" in the church (Roman Catholic view) or, on the contrary, "unity" in the church is grounded in "wholeness" in the New Testament canon (Protestant view), for Käsemann rejects the latter also and grounds the church's unity in the identity of all events of "justification." So, too, Küng states the issue misleadingly when he suggests that the issue is the attitude brought *to* the New Testament: Roman Catholics characteristically being "open" to all of the New Testament in all its diversity (especially, open to the "early catholic" elements in it), and Protestants being arbitrarily selective of the parts to which they will be open (especially excluding its "catholicizing" tendencies). It is a tendentious way to state the issue because it fails to note the variety of senses of "whole" in which the New Testament may be said to be some one thing. Käsemann's and Küng's proposals are more fairly seen as different proposals about *how* to take the New Testament precisely as some kind of "whole." The two proposals share a common logic in one other respect: both take the ascription of "wholeness" to scripture, i.e., the judgment that it is "canon," to be analytic in the judgment that the "church" is somehow one. The "wholeness" of the canon is somehow dependent on the "unity" of the church. As our remarks about the concepts "tradition" and "canon" lead us to expect, what divides these two proposals is an act of the imagination, not of conceptual or doctrinal analysis. They diverge at the point where they must characterize *concretely* just what the church's "unity" is *like*. Since the specific kind of "wholeness" ascribed to the canon follows from the specific kind of "unity" ascribed to the church, their proposals about what the canon's "wholeness" is *like* also differ. Käsemann proposes that the church's "unity" is the unity of the existentially decisive event of "justification" which is always self-identical despite the temporal multiplicity of its occurrences. And the New Testament is a "whole" insofar as it is so used as to occasion that event. This alone is the mode of God's presence. Küng proposes that the church's "unity" is that of the singular activity that comprises the life of an integral organism. The New Testament canon is a "whole" in that in all its diversity it may be taken together as describing the paradoxical dialectics that characterize that life. This includes the fact that the church itself serves not only as context for, but as *part of* the mode in which God is present. In short, what is basically at issue in this dispute is how best to characterize metaphorically the singular mode of God's presence.

PART II:

USING THE TEXT

Chapter 6

"Authority" and

Arguments

"Proving a doctrine from Scripture": Jowett's phrase draws attention to the relational character of the authority scripture is supposed
to have for theology. To talk about the "authority of scripture for
theology" is, at very least, to talk about a *relation* that must obtain
between scripture and theological proposals. To say that theology
must be authorized or "proved" by scripture is to say that scripture
must be *brought to bear on* theological proposals in such a way as
to authorize them.

Can the relation be characterized with any greater specificity?
Discussions of the relation between theology and authoritative scripture sometimes trade on the metaphor of "translation." They suggest that there is a straight-line relation between scripture and
theological proposal, as though they were the two ends of a chain
and the only point at issue among doctrines of biblical authority
were the number of links in the chain. This is a fair description of
these theological positions in which the theological proposals are
seen as restatements of biblical concepts or doctrines. In Part I we
examined a couple of illustrations of theological proposals on which
scripture is brought to bear just this directly. But we also saw illustrations of positions in which scripture is brought to bear on theological proposals very indirectly. Theological proposals may be seen
as descriptions of modes of subjectivity, or of the dramatic structure
of history-as-a-whole, or of the ontological structure of the cosmos.
In such cases what bears directly on the proposals are, obviously,

a mode of subjectivity, or the structure of history, or the structure of the cosmos. Scripture may bear on the subjectivity, or on our participation in history, or on our insight into the cosmos, and *thereby* bear on theological proposals. In these cases too, theological proposals may justly be said to be made "on the basis of" scripture. But the relation "on the basis of" is far more indirect and complex than the relation between Homer's *Iliad*, say, and Latimore's English translation of it.

A PROBLEM OF STRATEGY

This poses us a strategic problem. We need to find a way to state the general question we wish to pursue in such a way that the very terms we use do not end up being unfair to some of the cases we wish to analyze. Instead of employing the standard picture of the relation between scripture and theology as "translation," which may be misleading about some theologians' ways of actually using scripture as "authority," it will be more illuminating to consider a theologian's appeal to scripture as part of an *argument*. After all, when a theologian appeals to scripture to authorize his theological proposal, his appeal is part of an effort to make a case on behalf of his proposal.

Obviously, not every reference to scripture in a theological document is an appeal designed to strengthen a case. Sometimes biblical allusions or quotations may be introduced simply to provide an illustration for a point or to acknowledge the source of a useful phrase. Furthermore, the notion of "argument" is open to wider and narrower understandings. Robert Funk points out that several New Testament scholars have suggested that the parables of Jesus have their authority precisely in that they are "argumentative."[1] He points out that this is different from their being illustrative, and goes to some pains to make the case that they are not illustrations of particular religious or ethical ideas.[2] It becomes clear, however, that Funk wants to use "argumenative" in a very broad way. It need not mean that Jesus used his parable in the "context of debate and controversy."[3] Rather, to say that the parables are "argumentative" is to say that they are "provocative,"[4] that they elicit insight and are a "revelation"[5] to their hearers, that they demand a judgment from their hearers. Indeed, the basic point Funk wants to make is that parables are authoritative in that they found for their hearers a "world"[6] which was also Jesus' "world," where "world" means not an aggregate of discrete objects, but a "preconceptual totality of significations" within which, as a kind of "penumbral field," things are "located" as tools in a workshop—tools whose employment is dictated by the horizons of someone's *existentiell* projects.[8] This is to say that parables are "authority" in that they serve to "author" person's lives by founding their worlds.

This is not yet authority for, precisely, *theology*. Funk argues that theology arises in the New Testament when writers such as Paul begin to reflect on the fate of Christian proclamation, i.e., on how and why it is being mis-heard.[9] In an analysis of 1 Corinthians, he argues that Paul's theological proposals are not christological doctrines advanced to dispute erroneous christological doctrines, but are efforts to help the subject matter or intended "object" (i.e., the Crucified Christ) of Christian preaching come into view for its miscomprehending Corinthian hearers.[10] That to which Paul can appeal is not the parables of Jesus, nor latter day Christian proclamation (for both are misfiring with the Corinthians) but the reality that was rendered by both: the kingdom of God. Thus, despite the fact that he uses the metaphor himself,[11] it is misleading to characterize the relation Funk describes between theology and parable within the New Testament as "translation." On the other hand, the authority of parable for theology cannot be described in terms of the role of parable in "argument," *in Funk's broad use of that concept.* For him parables are authoritative in terms of "argument" only when one is speaking of their authority for an individual's *Existenz* and precisely not for theological proposals. If we analyze scripture's authority for theology in terms of the use of scripture in arguments making a case for theological proposals, we will be using "argument" in a far more narrow way. That is not to deny that scripture may be "authority" in just the sense Funk outlines: but it is authority *for* something else, viz., *for* the shape of one's personal life, not *for* one's Christian theological proposals. There is no reason to suppose that "authority" may be used in only one of those ways and not in the other; but there is also no reason to suppose that it means the *same* thing to speak of scripture's "authority" *for* my life and to speak of its "authority" *for* my theological proposals.

AN ANATOMY OF ARGUMENTS

Our suggestion is that scripture may properly be said to be "authority" for a theological proposal when appeal is made to it in the course of making a *case* for the proposal. Perhaps the theologian hopes to persuade his reader that his proposal is true. Perhaps he hopes to persuade him that the proposal is, at any rate, one a Christian ought to agree with. We need not settle here the question whether a proposal's being accepted as aptly "Christian" entails its being accepted as "true." Nor need we discuss whether a theologian has a responsibility to try to persuade his reader that his proposals are not only "Christian" but also "true"—or whether, if so, an appeal to scripture would be relevant to the latter task.

The sole point of importance here is that in making an appeal to scripture in order to justify or *authorize* a theological claim, a theologian is in fact framing an informal *argument*. As such, it is *formally* analogous to another man's appeal to certain diplomatic documents to help make a case for his historical claim that Emperor Hirohito was in fact partly responsible for Japanese policies that resulted in Japan's attack on the United States in 1941. It is formally analogous to another man's appeal to certain statutes to help make a case for his legal claim to the right to vote. It is formally analogous to another man's appeal to his listeners' responses to the performance of a play to help make a case for his dramaturgical claim that the director misunderstood the play. It is formally analogous to another man's appeal to the results of controlled experiments to help make a case for his pharmaceutical proposal that taking large doses of vitamin C prevents contracting the common cold.

Arguments like these are formally alike in that, no matter how great the other differences among them, they all exhibit the same *pattern* of argument. Stephen Toulmin[12] has shown how this pattern can be laid out in a "candid" form that exhibits the different "functions of the different propositions invoked in the course of the argument and the relevance of different sorts of criticisms which can be directed against it."[13] Toulmin's analysis of the form exhibited by informal arguments provides us a useful way to chart how theologians so bring scripture to bear on their theological proposals as to authorize them, i.e., to make a case for them.

The proposal for which a case is made may be considered as a

conclusion to the argument. When the proposal is challenged by a
question like, "What have you got to go on?", an attempt is made
to make a case for the conclusion (C) by appealing to some data
(D). Toulmin points out that the conclusion (C) and data (D) in
each of two arguments need not belong to the same logical type of
statement. If they do belong to the same logical type, the two arguments are said to belong to the same "field of arguments."[14] Fields
of argument are not to be confused with what are called "fields of
study" in the academic world, e.g., the "field of geology" or the
"field of law." "Fields of argument" are specified by the logical
type of the propositions constituting the data and conclusions of
arguments in the field. By contrast, "fields of study" are far more
vaguely specified by the "subject matter." And arguments concerning the "subject matter" in a given "field of study" may in fact belong to several quite different "fields of argument."

So far the move from data (D) to claim (C) seems straightline.
To use one of Toulmin's stock examples: The claim (C), "Harry is
a British subject," may be justified by an appeal to the data (D),
"Harry was born in Bermuda." The move may be diagrammed:

D(Harry was born ——————————————— So C(Harry is a
  in Bermuda)   British
                                                 subject)

However, C may be challenged in a second way. The question
may not be, "What have you got to go on?", but, "How did you get
there (to C) from here (D)?" This calls for an appeal, not to additional data, but to a rule or inference-license or warrant (W) that
authorizes the move from D to C. Toulmin points out that whereas
data (D) are expressed in explicit and categorical statements of
fact, warrants (W) are "general, hypothetical statements."[15] They
will often be appealed to only implicitly as a case is made for a particular conclusion (C). Appeal to a warrant is logically prior to
appeal to data in support of a claim, for warrants constitute the principles of selection of the data relevant to the conclusion: "We should
not even know what sort of data were of the slightest relevance of
a conclusion, if we had not at least a provisional idea of the warrants acceptable in the situation confronting us."[16] Warrants vary
in the degree of force they confer on a conclusion. Some authorize

us to accept a claim unqualifiedly. We may qualify such a conclusion with "necessarily." Other warrants authorize us to move from data to conclusion only tentatively, or only subject to certain conditions, exceptions, or qualifications. We modify the conclusions in such cases with adverbs such as "probably" and "presumably." Such modifiers of the conclusion may be called "qualifiers."

This reminds us that the move from D to C is not necessarily a straight-line move. It may have to be mediated by a warrant (W) and the qualifiers (Q) appropriate to it.

D(Harry was born ————————— So, Q(presumably), C(Harry is a
  in Bermuda) | British
                         | subject)
                         |
                    Since W
            (A man born in Bermuda
             will generally be a
             British subject)

This, in turn, may be challenged in either or both of two more ways. It might be objected that the warrant (W) simply does not apply to the case under discussion. Or, secondly, the truth of W might be challenged. In order to deal with the first question, we must set conditions of rebuttal (R). They indicate the circumstances in which the authority of W would have to be set aside. In order to deal with the second question, it is necessary to produce backing (B) for the warrant.

Backing are assurances standing behind the warrant, without which the warrant would have neither authority nor currency. The only arguments for which no backing is necessary are those whose warrant is trivial or analytic. For example, the warrant for the argument, "Harry's hair is red, and so it is not black," is the analytic judgment, "What is red is not black." Of course, the bearing of a proffered backing on the questioned warrant may itself be challenged. In that case the original argument must be set aside while a second argument is mounted, in which the proffered backing becomes the data, and the challenged warrant becomes the conclusion and a new warrant is exhibited to license the move from the one to the other. Obviously, some warrant must at some point be accepted by all parties to a dispute, or no arguments of any sort on the topic at hand could be developed by any one of them.

Toulmin points out[18] that backing (B) and confirmation or rebuttal of the applicability of the warrant (R) may be expressed in categorical statements of fact. In that case neither their logical nor their grammatical characteristics would distinguish them from expressions of data (D) in the same argument. The propositions that express each of them in a given argument can be distinguished from one another only by noting carefully their *roles* in the total argument, i.e., whether they are appealed to in order to justify the conclusion (in which case they serve as D), or to show that the warrant is true (in which case they serve as B), or to show that the conditions for rebuttal are excluded (in which case they are R).

All of this brings sharply into focus how little like a direct, straight-line move it is to get a claim "authorized."

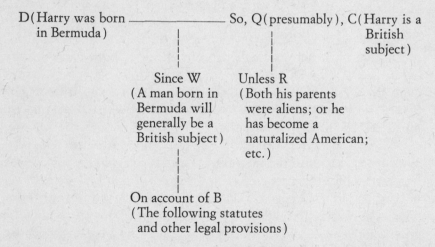

D(Harry was born —————————— So, Q(presumably), C(Harry is a
    in Bermuda)   British
                                                                   subject)

                            Since W   Unless R
                          (A man born in   (Both his parents
                           Bermuda will   were aliens; or he
                           generally be a   has become a
                           British subject)   naturalized American;
                                                etc.)

                            On account of B
                          (The following statutes
                           and other legal provisions)

That is to say that in the course of an argument in support of a claim, the claim (C) is *authorized in several different senses of the term.* "Data," "Warrant" (with its appropriate "Qualifier"), "Condition of rebuttal," and "Backing" each designates a different *role* that some expression or expressions play in an argument. Each is brought into play when the claim (C) is *challenged* in some way or other, in order to "authorize" C in face of the challenge. D are produced to authorize the claim in the face of the challenge, "What do you have to go on?" W is produced to authorize the claim in the face of the challenge, "How did you get to C from D?" Evidence that conditions of rebuttal (R) have been excluded are produced to authorize the claim in the face of the challenge that the warrant is inapplicable to this move from these data to this conclusion. B is produced to authorize the conclusion in the face of challenge to the truth of W. When an argument is fully and explicitly laid out candidly, all of these different kinds of "authorizing" are pointed up.

Toulmin's way of laying out the pattern of arguments that men actually use in their ordinary efforts to persuade one another is roughly analogous to the pattern of procedures in Anglo-American jurisprudence, whereas traditional logic formalizes arguments on analogy with mathematics. His proposal has the advantage, in Toulmin's view, of stressing that the logical form of a valid argument is a *procedural* matter, whereas the more usual way of setting out the structure of an argument stresses that the logical form of a valid argument is something quasi-geometrical.[19] Our interest in it is confined to the *pattern* it exhibits in every argument, for that pattern provides us a chart on which to plot the various places in theological arguments where an appeal to scripture might be entered. It has the advantage of exhibiting with equal fairness the structure of moves from scripture to theological proposal that are direct and those that are very indirect. Toulmin's analysis of the layout of arguments throws no light, of course, on where theologians get the proposals they want to make. It exhibits the structure of the arguments to justify our claims, not a guide to the sources of our claims. So too, while Toulmin believes that laying out arguments on the jurisprudential analogy improves on the syllogistic form traditionally used in logic and thereby facilitates assessment of the validity of arguments,[20] we may safely leave aside any consideration of the merits of that contention. That is a problem for logicians to settle. We only look to his proposal for help in exhibiting the anatomy of theological arguments; we are not concerned to diagnose their logical diseases.

THEOLOGICAL MACRO-ARGUMENTS

Toulmin's analysis of the standard pattern of informal arguments draws attention, first, to the variety of "fields of argument" that may turn up in a "system" of theological proposals. By "system" here I mean a theological "position"; a comprehensive exposition of the whole body of Christian divinity that not only makes many proposals about different theological *loci* (God, Jesus Christ, man, church, etc.) but self-consciously develops those proposals with an eye to their logical inter-connections. Toulmin points out that any two arguments belong to different "fields of argument" if the backing or conclusions in each of the two are of different logical types.[21] Now the arguments entered in support of proposals a theologian may make concerning a particular theological *locus* may belong to different "fields of argument," as may the arguments he advances in support of proposals concerning different *loci*.

We can illustrate this by examples drawn from Tillich's theology and, more briefly, from Barth. Each of these illustrations is a complex and extended argument which in fact subsumes many shorter arguments. To use Toulmin's image, they are like organisms that have a "gross, anatomical structure and a finer as-it-were physiological one."[22] Toulmin thinks his way of formalizing arguments on a

I.

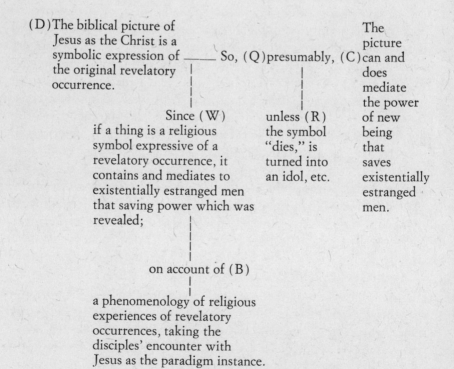

(D) The biblical picture of Jesus as the Christ is a symbolic expression of the original revelatory occurrence. ——— So, (Q) presumably, (C) The picture can and does mediate the power of new being that saves existentially estranged men.

Since (W) if a thing is a religious symbol expressive of a revelatory occurrence, it contains and mediates to existentially estranged men that saving power which was revealed;

unless (R) the symbol "dies," is turned into an idol, etc.

on account of (B)

a phenomenology of religious experiences of revelatory occurrences, taking the disciples' encounter with Jesus as the paradigm instance.

jurisprudential model is an especially sharp implement for doing detailed physiological study of "micro-arguments," but we are going to use it here to do a gross anatomy of some "macro-arguments."

Paul Tillich has said that the "direct object of theology is not God; the direct object of theology is . . . religious symbols"[23] and theology is to explicate the meaning of those symbols. A major argument in Part III of Tillich's system ("Existence and the Christ") may be abstracted and put in candid form like this:[24]

In this argument D is an exegetical claim about the New Testament (viz., that it presents a picture of Jesus that arose under certain circumstances) taken under a certain description in which technical terms like "religious symbol" and "revelatory occurrence" are key. Clearly, this exegetical claim could itself be challenged. The argument made in support of it would have as *its* supportive data specific passages of scripture, whereas the datum in this argument (Argument I) is not scripture itself but a generalization about a large and internally diverse section of the historical Christian canon (i.e., the Gospels). W is a hypothetical generalization about how religious symbols function in both religious discourse (they "express" a speaker's involvement in a revelatory event) and in subsequent religious life (they "mediate" to others a power revealed in the original revelatory occurrence). B for this W is provided by an extensive phenomenology of religious experience and revelatory occurrences that Tillich gives in Part I of the system ("Reason and the Quest for Revelation"). The conditions for rebuttal (R) are provided by the same phenomenology. This shows how misleading it is to characterize C as a *translation* of D or of the passages of scripture from which D is generalized. If it were a translation, the W would be of a totally different sort. It would then have to be, "If *x* is a religious symbol, then we can substitute for it a technical term defined by its use in Tillich's ontological system." And the backing would be a theory of language showing how Tillich's ontological system allows for more precise and exact statement of the same things that religious symbols express more vaguely. But Tillich does not concentrate on the relation between religious symbols and his technical ontological language. Instead his move from D to C is based on remarks about the role of peculiarly religious language ("religious symbols") in ordinary religious contexts.

Contrast to this a second major argument in Part III of Tillich's system. It can be abstracted and laid out in candid form like this:

II.

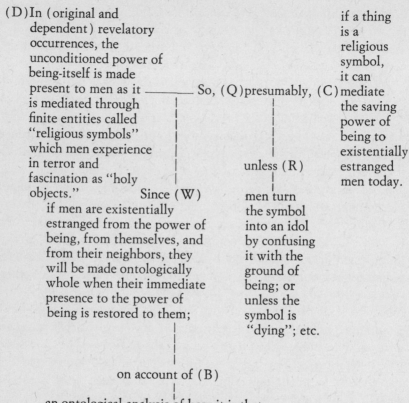

(D) In (original and dependent) revelatory occurrences, the unconditioned power of being-itself is made present to men as it —— So, (Q) presumably, (C) is mediated through finite entities called "religious symbols" which men experience in terror and fascination as "holy objects."

if a thing is a religious symbol, it can mediate the saving power of being to existentially estranged men today.

unless (R) men turn the symbol into an idol by confusing it with the ground of being; or unless the symbol is "dying"; etc.

Since (W) if men are existentially estranged from the power of being, from themselves, and from their neighbors, they will be made ontologically whole when their immediate presence to the power of being is restored to them;

on account of (B)

an ontological analysis of how it is that men can become "existentially estranged," and what the necessary ontological conditions are for restoring a man in that state to ontological wholeness.

In *this* argument, obviously, C is the warrant used in Argument I. It is a generalization about how religious symbols function in both religious discourse and religious life. It is a statement of a quite different logical type from C in Argument I, which was a Christian theological claim about the contemporary religious importance of the picture of Jesus as the Christ. D used in Argument II is obviously the statement that functioned as B in Argument I. Thus Argument II is an argument to justify the move in Argument I from B to W. W in Argument II is a hypothetical generalization about the conditions under which existentially estranged men may be made ontologically whole. B for *this* W is provided by the ontological analysis Tillich develops in Parts II ("Being and God") and IV ("Life and Spirit") of the system, an analysis that for all its claims to absolute generality concentrates on *man's* "being." Clearly, this sort of B consists in statements of a quite different logical type from the statements making up B in Argument I. The B and C, respectively, in Arguments I and II are of different logical types. Thus, although both arguments belong to the same theological "system," and indeed are part of its discussion of one theological locus, viz., Christology, they belong to different "fields of argument."

Contrast to the second argument the following one. I offer it as a fair representation of a family of arguments found frequently in Karl Barth's discussion of the perfections of God in *Church Dogmatics* II/1, although it is abstracted and set in candid form here and is not a direct quotation of any particular passage in the pages of the *Dogmatics*:

III.

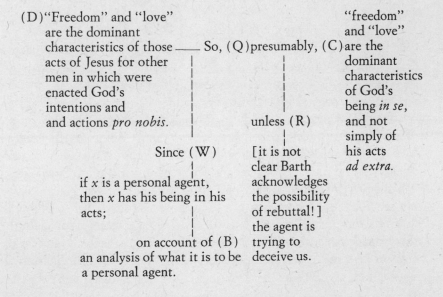

(D) "Freedom" and "love" are the dominant characteristics of those acts of Jesus for other men in which were enacted God's intentions and and actions *pro nobis*.

— So, (Q) presumably, (C) are the dominant characteristics of God's being *in se*, and not simply of his acts *ad extra*.

unless (R)

[it is not clear Barth acknowledges the possibility of rebuttal!] the agent is trying to deceive us.

"freedom" and "love"

Since (W)

if *x* is a personal agent, then *x* has his being in his acts;

on account of (B) an analysis of what it is to be a personal agent.

Here C is a theological claim about the being of God as he is in himself and quite apart from his relation to creation. It is a logically different type of statement from C in Argument II, but very likely the same logical type as C in Argument I. D are two claims about the actions of Jesus of Nazareth: the first a historical claim that Jesus' actions toward other men were marked by "freedom" and "love"; the second a theological claim that the actions of Jesus were not only enactments of the intentions of the man Jesus, but also were enactments of God's intentions. W is a hypothetical generalization about the relation of "being" and "acts" in personal agency. B for this warrant is a rudimentary ontology of personal agency that Barth sketches in Paragraphs 28 and 29 of *Church Dogmatics* II/1.[25] The statements constituting this backing are of the same logical type as the backing in Argument II; both are arguments whose warrants rest on ontological analyses. However, B in Argument III belongs to a very different type of statement than B in Argument I. Thus this (hopefully) representatively Barthian argument belongs to a different "field" of argument than either of the arguments from Tillich: its C belongs to the same logical type of statement as C in Argument I, but to a different type than C in Argument II, while its B belongs to logically different type of statement than B in Argument I and to the same logical type as B in Argument II.

FROM ANATOMY TO DIAGNOSIS

Once these features of the gross anatomy of theological macro-arguments are noted, several important guides to the diagnosis of theological arguments come into view.

First, it becomes clear that so far as the arguments it employs are concerned, theology is "field encompassing." That is, in the course of making cases for their claims in regard to different theological *loci* theologians make arguments that belong to many different "fields of argument." This means that there is no one distinctively "theological method," if that means a single characteristically "theological" field of arguments. So too, there is no special theological "way" to argue or "think," if that is taken to imply a peculiarly theological structure to argument. Accordingly, analysis and criticism of theological "systems" are not likely to be illuminating if undertaken on the tacit assumption that they may be measured by an ideal or standard mode of "theological thinking," "theological method," or "theological way of arguing." Arguments in theology have the same pattern as arguments actually used in connection with any other subject matter, but belong in several different fields of argument.

Second, setting theological macro-arguments into candid form shows that several logically different kinds of statement may all serve to help authorize a given conclusion, although in different senses of "authorize." A conclusion is authorized in one way by the data on which it is based, but the data may be provided by statements belonging to any of several different logical types. The same conclusion is authorized in the same argument in a second way by a warrant which, with its backing, may belong to a quite different logical type of statement than the data appealed to in the same argument. Thus, a conclusion that is authorized by data which consist of direct biblical quotations may also be authorized by backing consisting in a section of an ontology. It is at least logically possible that a theological proposal might be authorized by data provided by an ontological analysis and also authorized by warrants backed by direct quotations from scripture.

It would be a meaningless question to ask which of the two was more genuinely authorized by appeal to scripture; "meaningless" in that every answer would, in the nature of the case, be arbitrary. Accordingly, it is pointless to *contrast* "authorizing a theological proposal by appeal to scripture" to "authorizing it by appeal to an ontology (or to a phenomenology or to historical research)," as though, if it were genuinely authorized in one way, it would not also be authorized in one of the other ways in the same argument.

Third, this exercise in comparative anatomy suggests the inappropriateness of a familiar way of going about critical analysis of theological systems or "positions." It is not uncommon to find critical analysis opening with the question, "Where does this position *begin?*" The supposition seems to be that if a theology "begins" at the wrong place it will inevitably and systematically distort the Christian message it seeks to elucidate. So Tillich's theology is criticized for "beginning" with an ontology, Bultmann's for "beginning" with Heidegger's analysis of *Dasein*, Barth's for "beginning" discussion of every *locus* with Christology, Schleiermacher for "beginning" with religious experience, etc. For example, this procedure is especially notable in Gustaf Wingren's *Theology in Conflict*, an acute and penetrating analysis of Barth, Bultmann, and Nygren. He contends that each of their theological positions inadvertantly distorts the Christian gospel because each begins with a view of man that centers on man as knower and his difficulty in knowing God,[26] a view of man that is "different from the conception which the biblical writings themselves represent."[27] In short, there seems to be something like a standard test question to put to theological systems as the key to diagnosing their weaknesses and strengths. It is some variant on: "Does this theology begin with revelation or religious experience?" (Or: with scripture or ontological speculation? Or: with Jesus Christ or with man's natural understanding of himself? etc.), with a prior judgment usually smuggled in about where Christian theology *ought* to "begin."

This is an inappropriate way to start critical analyses of theological positions because it trades on a very misleading picture of how such positions are organized. It supposes that a theological position is held together by, or indeed consists in, one long overarching argument. It suggests that the discussions of all other theological *loci* are fairly tightly controlled by what is said on the *locus* with which the system "begins," either because they are analytically contained in it or because they may be inferred from it on the basis of a few unacknowledged inference licenses. It is as though the component parts of a theological system all flowered out of one stalk rooted at one point (such that there is one possible correct beginning point and innumerable possible wrong ones and the critic knows which is which ahead of time), (think of Schleiermacher's feeling of absolute dependence!), or as though they hooked together in one long train, curving and doubling back on itself no doubt (think of Barth's *Dogmatics*!), in one long line whose beginning is an engine that moves in one direction.

But surely theological positions *taken as wholes* ("Bultmann's theology," "Barth's Dogmatics," "Tillich's System," etc.) are not arguments, no matter how many arguments they may include, and they are rarely if ever as tightly organized as these familiar pictures suggest. Perhaps it would be less misleading to picture the component parts of a single theological position as arranged and held together rather like the component parts of one of Alexander Calder's sculptures. That is, a theological position is a set of several different families of arguments, but it is not itself *taken as a whole* ordered as an argument; rather theological positions taken as wholes might be looked at in a quasi-aesthetic way as a solicitation of mind and imagination to look at Christianity in a certain way. The component parts of such a proposal are the several families of arguments, each family dealing with a different theological *locus* or problem (Christ, man, God, church, etc.). Within a "position," families of arguments may be related to one another in a variety of ways. In some cases several families of arguments may hang from some one family of arguments. The connections among them may be loose in various degrees, so that some systems taken as wholes may be structures rather like one of Calder's mobiles and others rather more like one of his stabiles.

The "position" taken as a whole would then be more aptly discussed in quasi-aesthetic terms as the expression of a particular vision of the basic character or "essence" of Christian faith and not in logical terms as though it were one large argument. An aesthetic entity, after all, unlike an argument, doesn't logically "begin" at any one point except in the trivial sense in which a play "begins" with its first word, and a sonata begins with its first note, and a painting, looking from left to right, begins with the edge of its canvas (or does it?). The point of suggesting that theological systems be taken on analogy with a sculpture by Calder rather than on analogy with a train or a plant is not to deny that different sorts of questions and different sorts of intellectual inquiry do tend to dominate different theological "systems," nor to deny that this difference helps give each system its peculiar characteristics. As we saw in Part I, Tillich's interest in ontological questions has a lot to do with the differences between his theology and Barth's, and Thornton's interests in literary imagery in scripture has a lot to do with the differences between his theology and Bultmann's. The point is, rather, that it will be more illuminating if, instead of asking where it "begins," we analyze a theological "position" by asking (a) what *roles* are played in the structure of the whole position by its discussion of each of several theological *loci*, and (b) by asking what *roles* are played in the arguments found in each of those discussions by various kinds of intellectual inquiry such as historical research (including biblical scholarship), phenomenology of religious experience, metaphysical schemes, etc., asking what they do, i.e., what they are *used* for within the "system" as a whole.

NOTES

1. *Language, Hermeneutic, and Word of God* (New York: Harper and Row, 1966), p. 143. Funk cites C. H. Dodd, Amos Wilder, and A. T. Cadoux, *v.* pp. 133 ff.
2. Funk, pp. 146–152, 236.
3. Funk, p. 144.
4. Funk, p. 161.
5. Funk, p. 145.
6. Funk, p. 233; cf. p. 244.
7. Funk, p. 237.
8. Funk, pp. 234–235.
9. Funk, p. 238.
10. Funk, pp. 276, 280–281, 284.
11. Funk, p. 132.
12. *The Uses of Argument* (Cambridge: Cambridge University Press, 1964), pp. 97–102.
13. Toulmin, p. 9.
14. Toulmin, p. 14.
15. Toulmin, p. 98.
16. Toulmin, p. 106.
17. Toulmin, p. 98.
18. Toulmin, pp. 103, 106.
19. Toulmin, p. 95; *v.* pp. 15–17, 41–43.
20. Toulmin, pp. 107–145.
21. Toulmin, p. 14.
22. Toulmin, p. 94.
23. Paul Tillich, "Theology and Symbolism," *Religious Symbols,* ed. F. E. Johnson (New York: Harper, 1955), p. 108.
24. The following analyses of Tillich are defended in considerable detail in my *The Fabric of Paul Tillich's Theology* (New Haven: Yale University Press, 1967), esp. chs. 2 and 3.
25. Barth often develops his point about the "being" of a person by explicit reference to God as "person." But the analysis has more general applicability since God is the one of whom "person" is said properly and the rest of us are called "person" analogously. Cf. *CD*, II/1, p. 272.
26. Wingren, esp. pp. 74, 79–82; cf. Hermann Diem, *Dogmatics* (Edinburgh: Oliver and Boyd, 1959), tr. Harold Knight, Chs. 2 and 3 on Barth, Bultmann, and Käsemann.
27. Wingren, p. xiii.

Chapter 7

"Authority"

Our study in the gross anatomy of theologians' arguments exhibits
a variety of logically diverse ways in which scripture can be used to
help authorize a theological proposal, and provides the basis for
some remarks about the grammar of the concept "authority" as used
in expressions like "Scripture is authority for theological proposals."
Like the concept "scripture," the concept "authority" turns out to
be a family of related but importantly different concepts, and there
is no one normative or standard concept "authority." The first two
sections of this chapter will show how our analysis of the variety of
decisions a theologian must make about how to *use* scripture brings
with it analyses of different things it means to call a text "authority"
in the actual practice of theology. Picking up a theme developed in
Chapter 5's discussion of various meanings of "scripture," the third
section will suggest how the diversity of senses in which scripture is
"authority" in theology has its roots in a diversity of senses in which
it is authority in the common life of the church. A fourth section of
this chapter will bring out some of the family resemblances that
these concepts "authority" share despite their differences.

DIRECT AND INDIRECT "AUTHORITY"

Perhaps the first important point brought out by our inspection of
informal arguments by which theological proposals are authorized is
that scripture generally is brought to bear on the proposal indirectly
rather than directly, though it could be brought to bear on the proposal either way. Each is a different way in which scripture might

139

serve to "authorize" a proposal. Hence, a theologian's decision to bring scripture to bear on his proposal indirectly, say, rather than directly, brings with it a different sense in which scripture is "authority" for that proposal.

The difference between "indirect and "direct" modes of "authority" can be brought out by noting how difficult it is to bring scripture to bear on a proposal directly. Even if direct quotations from scripture serve as data in a theological argument, they bear on the argument's conclusion only by the mediation of a warrant that requires the support of a backing. Clearly, if direct quotations from scripture serve as backing in an argument, they help authorize the argument's concluding theological proposal only indirectly, i.e., only as they directly support the argument's warrant which, in turn, authorizes the move from data to conclusion. Again, it may be that passages of scripture help authorize a conclusion by providing the conditions for rebuttal or by providing evidence that the conditions for rebuttal have been excluded. In that case too scripture would bear on the conclusion of the argument only indirectly, since it would serve only to show that the warrant which directly authorizes the conclusion does in fact apply.

However, one way in which an argument for a theological proposal might be so ordered that scripture does directly authorize the proposal would be for the warrant in the argument to be itself a direct quotation from scripture. Not a paraphrase or a generalization made on the basis of numerous passages of scripture, but a direct quotation in the proper form: a hypothetical generalization. In such a case scripture would directly authorize a conclusion, i.e., authorize it without the mediation of any other authority, in response to the challenge to the conclusion, How did you get to that conclusion from this data? (where the data themselves need not be drawn from the Bible). Obviously, however, the number of such arguments would necessarily be small, given the paucity of biblical passages in the proper form.

Another way in which an argument for a theological proposal might be ordered so that scripture does directly authorize the proposal would be for the data to be quotations from scripture and the warrant be either analytically true (i.e., a tautology) or in some other way taken as self-evident. There is an example of such an argument in B. B. Warfield's essay in support of the doctrine of the plenary verbal inspiration of scripture.[1] If the argument is abstracted and set in candid form it looks like this:

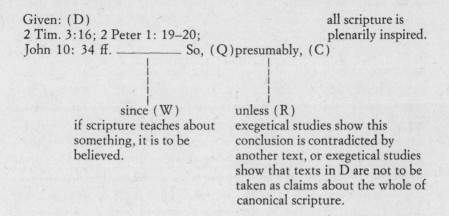

Given: (D)   all scripture is
2 Tim. 3:16; 2 Peter 1: 19–20;   plenarily inspired.
John 10: 34 ff. ——————— So, (Q)presumably, (C)

            since (W)   unless (R)
        if scripture teaches about   exegetical studies show this
        something, it is to be   conclusion is contradicted by
        believed.   another text, or exegetical studies
                                         show that texts in D are not to be
                                         taken as claims about the whole of
                                         canonical scripture.

The warrant in this argument is, on Warfield's terms, self-evident, given a certain definition of "scripture." We saw in an extended analysis of this theological argument in Part I that in order to commend this definition Warfield resorts, not to another argument, but to a direct appeal to the reader's own religious experiences of the Bible as a holy object. That appeal is, I think, not so much backing for the warrant as a heuristic device to disarm the readers' inclinations not to accept that definition of "scripture."

If and when the warrant of a theological argument is analytically true or self-evident, then the move from data (D) consisting of quotations from scripture to a theological proposal as conclusion (C) is direct in the strict sense of the term. It is not mediated by a warrant whose truth itself needs to be argued. In such cases scripture would authorize theological proposals by serving as the response to the challenge, "What have you got to go on?" Arguments of this sort too are necessarily rare, for there are very few warrants that would generally be acknowledged to be self-evident. There are, then, these two ways in which scripture might serve to authorize a theological proposal directly and without the mediation of any other sort of authority. But they are not really two instances of a (probably quite small) class, for here too "authority" means something quite different in each case. In the one case scripture bears on a theological

proposal directly in the way in which data are authority for a conclusion, i.e., as response to the challenge, "What have you got to
go on," while in the other scripture bears directly on a theological
proposal in the way in which a warrant is authority for a conclusion,
i.e., as response to the challenge, "How did you get from that data
to this conclusion?"

Setting theological arguments out in candid form draws attention
to a second and quite different sort of reason why it is difficult and
generally uncommon for scripture to authorize theological proposals
directly. When scripture is the basis for the data of a theological
argument it is more likely to be just that; the *basis* and not the
explicit *content* of the data. That is, data in such cases are more
likely to consist of claims about scripture than of quotations from
scripture. We saw in the case studies in Part I that the data theologians introduce to help authorize their theological proposals are
related to scripture in an astonishing variety of ways. The data may
consist of remarks about biblical concepts based on exegesis of biblical texts done in accordance with generally recognized historical-
critical methods (as illustrated by Hans-Werner Bartsch's study of
the biblical concept of peace, or by G. Ernest Wright's study of the
biblical understandings of history and God). The data may consist
of remarks about symbols or images in scripture and their relationships with one another based as much on literary and aesthetic
methodologies as on critical methods, and in any case showing little
concern with historical methods (as illustrated by Tillich's comments
on the biblical picture of Jesus as the Christ and by Thornton's study
of creation imagery). The data may consist of remarks about the
mode of subjectivity or *existentiell* self-understanding expressed by
biblical texts and based on historical, and especially form-critical,
study of the texts combined with some theories about the way
myths "express" modes of subjectivity (as illustrated by Bultmann's
discussion of "reconciliation"). Or the data may consist of remarks
about characteristic features of a living agent who is "rendered" or
given an "identity description" by biblical narratives, based on a
combination of critical study of the texts and some (mostly implicit)
notions about how narrative renders agents (as illustrated by Barth's
uses of scripture in Christology). In short, as our analysis in Part I
showed, even when scripture does provide the data for a theological

argument, it is generally not biblical texts themselves that serve as data, but the texts *construed* in terms of a certain set of patterns found, to be sure, in the texts.

Now, when scripture is brought to bear on a theological proposal quite directly, it is said to be "authority" for that proposal in the same sense of "authority" as that employed when we say that an English translation of the Gospel of Mark, say, is "authorized" by its Greek original. But when scripture is brought to bear on a theological proposal indirectly, it is said to be "authority" for the proposal in some other sense of "authority."

As I shall try to show in greater detail in Part III, this has important material implications for the way in which we describe the relation between scripture and theology. The variety of ways in which scripture can be brought to bear on a theological proposal, and the even greater variety of ways in which scripture can serve as basis simply for data in a theological argument, show that in the context of modern theology the concept "biblical authority" does not entail any one "method" for getting from scripture to theological proposal. Nevertheless it has become commonplace to characterize the move from scripture to theology as "translating" and to speak of theological proposals as "translations" of scripture. Our discussion in this section shows that the metaphor "translation" is seriously misleading. It suggests that one method *is* normative. It suggests that all theological arguments, including those in which scripture bears on theological proposals only indirectly, use scripture in the way in which it is used in arguments where it bears on theological proposals directly. Furthermore, it misleadingly suggests that there is a standard sense of "authority." It suggests that scripture serves as authority in all theological arguments in exactly the same sense of "authority" as is appropriate in characterizing the use of scripture when it authorizes proposals directly. "Translation" is simply inappropriate as a metaphor for the way many, if not most, theological proposals are actually "authorized" by scripture.

ROLE IN ARGUMENT AND "AUTHORITY"

In addition to having to decide whether to bring scripture to bear on his proposals directly or indirectly, a theologian has to make a second set of decisions about the roles in which he will use scripture in his theological arguments. Each of them, too, brings with it a slightly different sense of "authority." Now, in Chapter 6 we studied the anatomy of theological macro-arguments, i.e., extended and complex arguments and families of arguments dealing with particular *loci* in the full body of Christian Divinity and constituting, we suggested, major component parts of theological "positions" or "systems." If we shift focus now to the physiology of theological micro-arguments, i.e., arguments in support of very limited theological proposals, we can sort out the decisions a theologian must make about which roles to assign to scripture in his arguments, and with them a variety of concepts "authority."

It is evident by a glance at the layout of arguments set in what Toulmin calls candid form that there are several different points in the structure of an argument for a theological proposal where scripture might be introduced. If we may take the theological proposal itself as the conclusion (C) of the argument, then it is obvious that a passage or passages of scripture might be entered as data (D), or as warrant (W), or as backing for the warrant (B), or even as conditions for rebuttal (R). Each would be a somewhat different role scripture might play in the argument, a different way in which scripture could authorize the argument's concluding theological proposal.

Accordingly, a theologian's decision about which *uses* to make of scripture to authorize his proposal brings with it a different *meaning* to "authorize" and "authority." The meanings are logically irreducibly diverse. Scripture used, say, as data (D) would authorize the conclusion in a quite different sense of "authorize" than it would if used, say, as warrant (W). The logical differences among senses of "authority" can be brought out by noting how each sort of "authority" is a response to a quite different kind of challenge, "What have you got to go on in making that proposal?"; in that case it functions as data (D). It might be brought in as response to the challenge, "How do you get to that conclusion (C) from these data (D)?"; in that case it serves as warrant (W). Its role might be to show that the warrant (W) is in fact applicable to the topic in hand by showing that conditions of rebuttal have been excluded (R). Or it might serve to show that the warrant is true; in that case it is backing (B). Each of these is a logically different way in which scripture may be said to "authorize" a theological proposal.

Two points follow from this concerning the idea of biblical authority for theology. First, there is little point in asking flatly of any given theological proposal, "Is scripture the authority for that?" or "Is it based on scripture?" Before the question would yield an answer that told one anything about the grounds for holding the proposal in question, one would have to specify in which sense(s) of "authority" one wanted to know the answer. So too, once one sees this diversity of senses of "authority," one sees that disputes between theologians over whether a given proposal is indeed based on what was said by the apostles and prophets will be fruitless unless they specify in which ways they think the proposal ought to be authorized by scripture, i.e., unless they agree on which role or roles ought to be played by scripture in an argument mounted to authorize the proposal.

Second, it is pointless to discuss the biblical authority for theological proposals as though one were confronted with an either/or choice: either authorize the proposals by appeal to scripture, or authorize them some other way (say, by appeal to experience or to an ontology). The very structure of informal theological arguments shows, when it is set out in candid form, that a given conclusion, i.e., a given theological proposal, will necessarily be "authorized" in several different ways all at once. Presumably, it is a logical possibility that scripture would provide all the different sorts of authorization a proposal could get, D, W, B, R and Q. But the *idea* of biblical authority for theology does not necessarily logically legislate that procedure. Indeed, our study of theological macro-arguments in Chapter 6 produced evidence that theological proposals by otherwise very dissimiliar theologians like Paul Tillich and Karl Barth may be alike in being authorized simultaneously by appeal to passages of scripture and appeal to philosophical theses.

For Barth, we saw, a theological proposal about the being of God (C) ("'Freedom' and 'love' are the dominant characteristics of God's being *in se*, and not simply characteristics of his acts *ad extra*") can be authorized at one and the same time by appeal to scripture, functioning as D (summarized as: "'Freedom' and 'love' are the dominant characteristics of those acts of Jesus for other men in which were enacted God's intentions and actions *pro nobis*") and by an appeal to elements of an ontology of personal agency, functioning as W and B (the W: "If x is a personal agent, then x has his being in his acts").

In Tillich, we saw that a theological proposal (C) ("The biblical picture of Jesus as the Christ can and does mediate the power of new being that saves existentially estranged men") can be authorized both by an appeal to the Synoptic Gospels functioning as D ("The biblical picture of Jesus as the Christ is a symbolic expression of the original revelatory occurrence") and by appeal to a generalization about religious symbols, functioning as W ("If a thing is a religious symbol expressive of a revelatory occurrence, it contains and mediates to existentially estranged men that saving power which was revealed") whose backing (B) is a phenomenology of religious experiences and revelatory occurrences.

Now, there are many good reasons for contrasting Barth's and Tillich's theologies, and in particular by reference to their opposed views concerning the possibility of commending Christian beliefs by means of philosophical, or more exactly, phenomenological and ontological, arguments. But it evidently is both pointless and misleading to contrast them as though Barth's theological proposals were authorized *only* by appeal to scripture whereas Tillich is prepared to appeal instead to "philosophy," or more exactly, to his ontology. Ironically, appeal to elements of an ontology comes into play in connection with Tillich's christological proposal much more indirectly than an appeal to elements of an ontology comes into play in connection with Barth's doctrine of God. For Tillich, we saw, appeal to ontology comes in only in a *secondary* argument in which he responds to a challenge to show that the warrant used to help authorize the christological proposal in the primary argument is itself correct.

These observations do not demonstrate that it would be impossible for a theologian so to argue for a theological proposal that *every* role in the argument was filled by some sort of appeal to scripture. Only such authorization for theology could really count as an instance of authorization of a theological proposal *sola scriptura.* Nor, of course, do they show that every theological proposal logically must be authorized by appeal to an ontology as well as an appeal to scripture. But they do serve to point out how misleading it is to conduct debate about the adequacy of various theological positions and theologians' methods as though only one kind of thing could serve as the authority for a theological proposal: either scripture, or if not that, then something else. And they help point out the multiplicity of possible kinds of authority that any one proposal might have all in the same argument: not just appeal to scripture and to an ontology, but also to the results of historical research, to analyses of various aspects of contemporary culture, and to the traditional practices and ways of speaking of the church.

USE IN CHURCH AND "AUTHORITY"

In Chapter 5, at the close of Part I, I tried to show that for theoligans of the sort we have studied the judgment "Scripture is authority for theology" is analytic in the judgment "Scripture is authority for the life of the church." Now note that just as "authority" may be used in any of several senses in expressions like "Scripture is authority for theology" and there is no one standard concept "authority for theology," so too there is no one standard concept "authority for church." In expressions like "Scripture is authority in the life of the church," "authority" is used in several different, though related ways. Furthermore, as the following discussion will tend to show, each different sense in which scripture is "authority" over the church's life seems to bring with it a different sense in which scripture is "authority" for theological proposals.

We noted that to call a set of texts "scripture" is to say that it ought to be used in certain ways in the church's common life so as to nurture and preserve her communal self-identity. However, we also noted that different theologians tend to identify quite different things the texts *do* to fill the role of "scripture": asserting, proposing, rendering, expressing, occasioning, etc. The point to be made here is that each type of function ascribed to authoritative scripture brings with it a different concept of "authority." To say "Scripture is the authority for this theological proposal" simply *means* something different by "authority" when the scripture in question is taken with the force of "asserting" than when it is taken with the force of "non-informatively expressing." The differences in sense of "authority" may be brought out by noting differences in the sort of response and assessment each solicits and the different sorts of phenomena for which each is said to be "authoritative."

For example: To say that scripture is "authority" in terms of its asserting doctrinal truths is to say that it invites *belief* on the part of the hearer and that it is open to various kinds of *logical assessment*. It is appropriate to explore what may properly be inferred from the truths it asserts, how far the assertions are individually self-consistent and mutually coherent, etc. On the other hand, to say that scripture is authoritative in the mode of non-informatively expressing the occurrence of a revelatory and saving event may be to say that it invites a decision by the hearer wherein he surrenders his hitherto inauthentic self-understanding for an authentic one (Bultmann). Involved in this is an assessment of the *"felicity"* of the scripture taken as a "performative utterance" declaring God's love for the hearer.[2]

The phenomena for which each is "authority" are as diverse as the sorts of response each solicits; and different judgments about just what phenomenon it is over which scripture is "authority" in the church's life bring with them correspondingly different judgments about the sense in which scripture is "authority" for theology. To say that scripture is "authority" over the church's life in that it has the force of asserting doctrine is to say that it is directly authoritative for theological proposals one might make now. The relations between scripture and theological proposals are then logical relations like "implying" and "entailing" and "contradicting." Such relations are so direct that the picture of theological proposals as "translations" of scripture seems very appropriate. On the other hand, if scripture is authoritative in non-informatively expressing the occurrence of revelatory and saving events, then its function as "authority" is not to provide premises for other theological proposals; rather, its function is to transform men's lives. Scripture is directly authoritative for or productive of new modes of subjectivity. Theological proposals, in turn, are to be descriptive accounts of that transformed personal being (life-in-faith), of why it needed to be transformed (sin), and of the conditions that make the transformation possible (grace). Here scripture as authority bears on a theologian's proposals only indirectly. The proposals are primarily authorized by appeal to general features of the new mode of subjectivity men have in faith. Since it is scripture that decisively shapes that new subjectivity, however, the appeal is indirectly to scripture too. When scripture bears on theological proposals indirectly, the picture of theological proposals as translations of scripture seems singularly inappropriate. "Asserting" and "non-informatively expressing" are irreducibly diverse functions that scripture may fill as "authority." Each brings with it a quite different order of phenomena for which scripture is authority and, accordingly, quite different ways in which scripture serves to authorize theological proposals.

To take another example: To say that the authoritative aspect of scripture is narrative may mean that scripture has the force of proposing concepts to be used to "interpret" history, or it may mean that in scripture narrative functions to render an agent. If scripture is authoritative in that, through its narrative interpretations of events in ancient Palestine, it proposes to us concepts we are to learn to use to interpret ourselves in our own histories (Wright), then it invites its hearers and readers to learn to appropriate the concepts personally and therewith learn the rules for their use, what other concepts are thereby excluded, what situations call for their use and what do not, and so on. On the other hand, if narrative in scripture is authoritative in that it serves to render an agent present to the hearer or reader (Barth), then it calls for a range of responses appropriate to the unique personal individuality of just this agent, viz., worship of the Lord.

The phenomena in the life of the church for which each of these is "authority" are as diverse as the sorts of response each solicits; and different judgments about just what phenomenon it is over which scripture is "authority" in the church's life bring with them correspondingly different judgments about the sense in which scripture is "authority" for theology. Where scripture is authoritative in that it proposes concepts, there theology's task is to analyze the "logic" of the concepts proposed. In that case, scripture bears on theological proposals very directly, for the latter are best seen as remarks about the conceptual "content" of scripture. It seems quite fitting to see such theological proposals as "translations" of scripture's "content." But where scripture is authoritative in that it renders a character, then its function is not to provide the concepts that theology discusses, but to make the Risen Lord vividly present, at least in imaginative memory and anticipation of his "real" presence. Theological proposals, in turn, are remarks about this agent or (as accounts about the history in which this agent appears, the concepts appropriate to discussing and worshiping him, and descriptions of the mode of subjectivity created by existential encounter with him) are based on such remarks. Here scripture bears on a theologian's proposals only indirectly. The proposals are directly authorized by the character of this agent and thus, strictly speaking, theological proposals are directly authorized by appeal to general features of this agent and therein, since it is scripture that renders this agent through the patterns of its narrative, by an indirect appeal to scripture. In such cases it is very misleading to see theological proposals as "translations" of scripture's "content." The "content" is a person, not a set of concepts, not even ones about this person. "Proposing concepts" and "rendering an agent" are irreducibly diverse functions that scripture may fill as "authority" each of which brings with it a quite different order of phenomena for which it is authority and, accordingly, quite different ways in which scripture serves to authorize theological proposals.

In summary: To call a set of texts "scripture" is, in part, to say that they ought so to be used in the common life of the church as to nurture and preserve her self-identity. However, the way the texts are to fill this role can be described in terms of several quite distinct functions. Differences in the type of function ascribed to the text bring with them differences in the sense in which the text is "authority" in the church's life. To chart the differences, we have shown how ascription of different functions to texts taken as "scripture" brings with it different judgments about the type of *response* the text-as-scripture solicits when used in the church's common life, about the type of *assessment* the text invites when used that way, and about the type of *phenomenon* in persons' lives over which it is authoritative. It simply *means* something different to say of a set of texts that it is "authority" in the church's common life *in that* it solicits one type of response, invites one type of assessment, pertains to one type of phenomenon, and to say that it is "authority" *in that* it solicits another type of response, invites another type of assessment, pertains to another type of phenomenon. Furthermore, insofar as differences in senses in which scripture is "authority" over the church's life are a function of differences in judgment about the type of phenomenon over which it is authority, those differences bring with them differences in the way scripture bears on theological proposals. Given our analysis in Section 1 of this chapter, that means that different senses in which scripture is "authority" over the life of the church bring with it different senses in which it is "authority" for theology. Therefore, it would be very misleading to discuss the notion of biblical authority, or to discuss whether a theologian's proposals truly are governed by biblical authority, in a way that simply assumed that there is some commonly accepted standard or normative concept of "authority" as that is used either in expressions like "Scripture is authority for the life of the church" or in expressions like "Scripture is authority for theology."

FEATURES COMMON TO CONCEPTS OF "AUTHORITY"

What it means to call scripture "authority" for theology varies with a theologian's decision whether to bring scripture to bear on his theological proposals directly or indirectly and with his decision about the roles in which he ought to use scripture in arguments supporting his proposals. His decision on the first score seems to be a function of a logically prior decision about how best to characterize the phenomenon over which scripture is most centrally "authority" when used in the common life of the church. However, there are some features *common* to otherwise logically diverse concepts "authority." We can bring them out by returning to the parable we introduced at the close of discussion of the concept "scripture" in Chapter 5.

We suggested that a theologian's remark "Scripture is authority for theology," said in reference to biblical texts taken as scripture, is like a boy's exclamation "Come on, let's play ball," said in reference to a ball not evidently designed for use in any one ball-game in particular. It no more makes a claim about the texts than the boy's exclamation does about his ball; rather, it self-involvingly invokes an activity. In saying "Scripture is authority for theology," the theologian commits himself to participate in one or another of a family of activities called "doing Christian theology." Moreover, he thereby acknowledges and commits himself to observing a *rule* governing the practice of theology (on certain understandings of "theology"): In defending theological proposals, scripture shall be used in such a way that helps authorize the proposals.

This draws attention to three features common to all concepts "authority" as used in expressions like "Scripture is authority for theology." First, they have all turned out to involve, at least implicitly, a *functionalist* understanding of "authority." To call a set of texts "authority," whether over the common life of the church or in doing theology, always means that the texts ought to be *used* in certain ways. To be sure, theologians' doctrines *about* the Bible as authoritative scripture rarely cast their exploration of the nature and basis of its "authority" in functionalist terms. But we have studied, not their doctrines about scripture's authority, but rather how scripture served as authority in their actual practice of theology. And it turns out that what it means to say of scripture in concrete cases of theologizing that it is "authority" for theology is best explicated in functional terms.

Second, despite the variety of ways in which scripture may actually be used in theological arguments to help authorize theological proposals, to call scripture "authority" for theology in any sense of "authority" is to acknowledge the *normative* status of scripture in relation to theology. This, of course, is central to traditional Christian talk about the authority of the Bible. "Authority" is not conferred on scripture by our decision to treat it as authority. "Authority" is acknowledged by scripture's readers or hearers. It "deserves" that response, and they "ought" to give it, whether they do so or not.

This "objective normativity" of scriptural authority is not undercut by taking its "authority" in terms of scripture's functions rather than its properties. When someone says, "Scripture is authority for this theological proposal," he locates the making and defending of the proposal within the family of activities called "Christian theology." Further, he acknowledges that one rule governing all members of that family is: In defending theological proposals, scripture shall be used in such a way that it authorizes the proposals. That is, to commit oneself to that activity entails acknowledging that scripture *ought* to fill such a role in the doing of it. Hence, to say, "This scripture is authority for this theological proposal," entails an acknowledgment of scripture's normativity and cannot be taken as a conferring of "authority" on it.

To be sure, "normativity" is relative to a specific activity, viz., doing theology. It is not some sort of "normativity-absolute," whatever that might mean. This comes as no surprise, however. We have already seen that "authority" is a relational concept. To say *x* is "authority" is always to say, at least implicitly, "*x* is authority *for y*." What we have been trying to do is map out with care just what sort of relation that is when it is scripture that is said to be "authority" for theology.

Third, expressions like "This scripture is authority for this theology" have their place in discussions of the "Christianness" of theological proposals; they may or may not have a place in discussion of their "truth." This too follows from understanding "authority" in terms of the functions scripture fills in the family of activities called "making theological proposals."

A distinction needs to be drawn between the question of the authorization for a particular theological proposal on the one hand, and the justification for engaging in the activity of making theological proposals at all, on the other hand. In one way or another, theological proposals are proposals about the ways of speaking, acting, feeling, believing, etc., that are called for by Christian faith. The question about the authorization of any one such proposal, therefore, is a question about the aptness of the proposal to Christianity—a question about its "Christianness." As we have seen, one of the rules shared by all the members of the family of activities called "Christian theology" is that scripture is to be used in such way that it serves to authorize the proposals made. It follows analytically that questions about the "Christianness" of any proposal are answered by an appeal to scripture. Scripture is "authority" precisely in relation to the specifically *Christian* character of the proposals.

To ask for the justification for engaging in the activity of making Christian theological proposals in the first place is to ask another order of question. It is to ask for the justification for Christian beliefs, action, affections, and the like, in short, to ask whether Christianity is "true." Some theologians decline to answer this order of question. Those who do not decline may rely on an appeal to scripture for part or all of their defense of the "truth" of Christianity, or they may not appeal to scripture at all. The point is that if they do, they are appealing to scripture in the course of a logically quite distinct kind of activity from the making of theological proposals. It is not a member of the same family of activities. If appeal is made to scripture as part of an argument in defense of the truth of Christianity, scripture will be "authority" for the conclusion that Christianity is true. But it may be "authority" in quite a different sense than the ones we have been discussing. To suppose that what is said about "authority" in connection with the "Christianness" of Christian theological proposals applies equally well to what might be said about "authority" in connection with arguments for the "truth" of the same proposals, would be to overlook the differences between the use of scripture in the framing and defending of Chris- tion theological proposals as "Christian," on one hand, and the possible use of scripture in justifying acceptance of those proposals and the form of life going with them, on the other hand.

To say "Scripture is authority for theology" is to commit oneself to engaging in the doing of theology under a rule that requires one to *use* scripture in certain ways. That involves, at least implicity, a functionalist understanding of "authority," an acknowledgment of scripture's normative status *vis a vis* theological proposals, indeed its normativity specifically in regard to the "Christianness" of the proposals. "Let theology accord with scripture" invokes some in- stance of a type of ruled activity, as "Let's play ball" invokes some instance of the type "ball game." However, again like "Let's play ball," it does not specify which instance of the type is being in- voked; it is not part of the meaning of the expression to specify either the particular *point* of the activity or most of its *rules.* "Scrip- ture is authority for theology" does not logically entail any par- ticular decision either about which of the types of *construal* of text-as-scripture (that we sorted out in Chapter 5) to adopt, or about which of the *uses* in theological argument (that we sorted out in Chapter 6) to assign to scripture. In Part III I shall develop a suggestion about how those decisions are made.

NOTES

1. B. B. Warfield, *The Inspiration and Authority of the Bible* (Philadelphia: The Presbyterian and Reformed Publishing Co., 1948), esp. Chs. 2, 3, and 6; *v.* Chapter 2 above.
2. The classic discussion of "performative utterances" is J. L. Austin's *How To Do Things With Words* (New York: Oxford University Press, 1965) and his essay "Performative Utterances" in *Philosophical Papers* (Oxford: Clarendon, 1961). The most extensive development of the notion in regard to theological discourse is Donald Evans' *The Logic of Self-Involvement* (London: Student Christian Movement Press, 1963), pp. 27–44.

PART III:

THEOLOGY AND SCRIPTURE

Chapter 8

Theologians' Decisions About Scripture

Our analysis so far leaves some questions to which we need now to turn. In Part I we saw that when a theologian appeals to scripture in the course of doing theology he is obliged to make at least three decisions about how to *construe* the texts: To which patterns in the text should he appeal? And in virtue of what function filled by the text in the church's common life? And what logical force should be ascribed to the text? In Part II we saw that our theologian is also obliged to make decisions about how to *use* the texts he construes: Shall they be brought to bear on the theological proposals they help authorize directly or indirectly? And, in which of several possible roles in arguments supporting his proposal should the texts be used? Carefully avoided in both Parts was the underlying question, Why appeal to biblical texts at all in doing theology?

It might seem reasonable to assume that a theologian's decisions about how to construe and use scripture, and perhaps even his decision about whether to appeal to it at all, might be determined by the results of a close study of the biblical texts themselves. The recent claims noted at the start of Chapter 1 that the Bible can no longer serve as authority for Christian theology assume this to be true. They argue in part that it is precisely the results of scientific historical and critical studies of biblical texts and the development of the canon that make it impossible to use the texts as authority in theology. More generally, a common characterization of theology as a "translation" of scripture's "message" makes the same assumption. It suggests that a theological "position" is built up piece by

158

piece as the several parts of the Bible are each studied by sophisticated critical methods and are then "translated" into theological proposals cast in contemporary idiom, until the "position" as a whole is completed.

Our thesis in Part III is that this assumption seriously misrepresents the way theology is related to scripture in many of the theologies that stand under the emblem "Let theology accord with scripture." The results of close study of the biblical texts, as I shall try to show in Chapter 9, are relevant to making the decisions noted above; but, as I shall try to show in this chapter, they are not decisive. More basic to the making of these decisions than the results of biblical scholarship is a decision a theologian must make about the *point* of engaging in the activity of doing theology, a decision about what is the subject matter of theology. And that is determined, not by the results of historical-critical biblical study, but by the way in which he tries to catch up what Christianity is basically all about in a single, synoptic, imaginative judgment.

CRITERIA FOR THEOLOGY AND IMAGINATION

In Chapter 5, I suggested that, for all their diversity, theologies that adopt the emblem "Let theology accord with scripture" agree that "church" and "theology" are dialectically related concepts. To call a community "church" is in part to say that she is a community that has her reality in a variety of activities done to a certain end, among which is the activity of self-consciously criticizing her own faithfulness to that end, i.e., "doing theology." And to call a set of practices "doing theology" is to say that they are activities in which the church self-consciously criticizes her own faithfulness to her task. For such theologies, "theology" is at once a *practical* and a *critical* activity or it is nothing.[1] Of course, nothing prevents one from defining the task of theology in some other way, without reference either to church or to scripture. This characterization of the nature of theology applies only to theologies like those from which our case studies were drawn, in which theology is an activity governed in part by the rule that scripture must be so used in the course of doing theology as to help authorize its proposals.

As a critical activity, theology is inescapably a "reformist" activity. It is not exhausted by descriptive analysis of the forms of action and speech currently practiced in the church's common life. Rather it mainly consists in proposing how they ought to be reformed if the church is to remain faithful to her task and to retain her self-identity.

By what criteria is the criticism made? This question forces us to attend to the role of imagination in doing theology. Our suggestion is that, to speak exactly, theological criticism is guided by a *discrimen*, not by a "norm" or a "criterion." Robert C. Johnson has drawn the important and regularly overlooked distinctions: A *norm* is "assumed to be absolute or, by its very nature, to exclude the acceptance of other theological norms." Extreme statements of *sola scriptura* sometimes take the canon this way, as though it were the single authority over the church. Like the authority of a judge, authority in the sense of *criterion* "is not absolute, but derived and mediate. A judge functions in the presence of other judges, in the context of a particular society and its culture, and under a body of law." *Discrimen*, however, designates "a configuration of criteria that are in some way organically related to one another as reciprocal coefficients."[2]

At one level of generality the *discrimen* is the same for all theologians of the general sort from which we drew our case studies: The conjunction of certain uses of scripture and the presence of God. We have already shown this in Chapter 5.[3] As one attends more closely to the specific characteristics of different kinds of Christian theology one begins to see significant differences. For example, for Roman Catholic theologians the church is usually taken as part of the *discrimen*, whereas for Protestant theologians it is characteristically taken as merely the context of the *discrimen*.[4]

However, when one attends to the specific characteristics of individual theological positions one sees that each differs from all the others in its judgment about how to characterize the *discrimen*. We have already seen that in the course of doing theology a judgment must be made about how to characterize the *mode* in which God is present among the faithful. That is always a complex matter, and the challenge is to hit upon a single characterization of it in all its complexity. That is a judgment about what the *discrimen* is *like*. It calls for an imaginative act.

The seven case studies illustrate three families of ways to construe the *mode* in which God is present. One way is to construe it in the *ideational* mode. That happens when God is taken to be present in and through the teaching and learning of the doctrine asserted by scripture (Warfield), or the concepts proposed by scripture (Bartsch; Wright). It suggests: God's presence is something like understanding the basic truth about oneself and one's world. Or: It is like having personally appropriated a set of concepts with such seriousness that they decisively shape one's emotions, passions, and feelings. A second way is to construe it in the mode of *concrete actuality*. That happens when God is taken to be present in and through an agent rendered present by scripture (Barth) or in and through a cosmic process of re-creation (Thornton). It suggests: God's presence is something like having the terms on which one lives set by the sheer fact that another agent is present who can be described only in the following very peculiar and paradoxical "Chalcedonian" identity description. Or: It is like having the terms on which one must live, if one would live well, set by the cosmic fact that a process of transformation is going on in all realms of being. A third way is to construe it in the mode of *ideal possibility*. That happens when God is taken to be present in and through existential events that are occasioned by scripture's kerygmatic statements which announce the possibility of authentic existence (Bultmann), or occasioned by the biblical picture of Jesus as the Christ which mediates the power that makes new being possible (Tillich). It suggests: God's presence is something like having present the possibility of that mode of subjectivity that the following phenomenological or ontological analyses show to be authentically, and so ideally, "human." Each of these is an imaginative construal of the mode of God's presence *pro nobis* that tries to catch up all its complexity and utter singularity in a single metaphorical judgment. As a characterization of the mode of God's presence, each is therefore a distinctive construal of the *discrimen* guiding theology's critical judgments. Furthermore, each of these imaginative judgments determines the specific features that characterize one particular theological position. The ordering principle peculiar to each position is its peculiar way of imaginatively construing the *discrimen.*

If, for example, a theologian construes the mode of God's presence in the *ideational* mode, as Warfield does, then he takes the central theological task to be the analysis of doctrines or concepts with an eye to proposing reforms in current forms of church belief and speech. The center of gravity in the ensuing "theological position" will fall on believing and on what is to be believed, and traditional theological topics will be treated in the order of their logical dependence. Hence, for instance, the doctrine of revelation, and especially the doctrine of the inspiration of the Bible, will be treated first, to secure the logical ground for what is said on all other topics. Other theological *loci* will be treated in the order in which they may be derived directly from scripture or from scripture and other doctrines together, or solely from other doctrines.

So too, if a theologian construes God's presence in the mode of a *concrete actuality*, e.g., the presence of the Risen Christ, as Barth does, then he takes the central theological task to be a reformist criticism of current churchly form of speech and action in the light of an elaborated identity description of this agent and of the implications of his presence for men's lives. The center of gravity in the ensuing "theological position" will fall on an identity description of the person and work of Jesus Christ. Traditional theological topics concerning the Christian life, like justification and sanctification, as well as such topics as the being and knowledge of God, will then be discussed in terms of, and in subordination to, the account of the identity of this agent.

By contrast, if a theologian construes God's presence in the mode of an *ideal possibility*, i.e., as the possibility for transformation of "inauthentic existence" into "authentic existence," as Bultmann does, then he takes the central theological task to be a reformist criticism of current forms of churchly speech and action in the light of an account of what "authentic existence" is like and how it is possible. The center of gravity in the ensuing "theological position" will fall on an account of the nature and possibility of "justification." Other traditional theological topics like the being and knowledge of God, the incarnation and atonement, will then be discussed in terms of, and in subordination to, an account of the dynamics of the transformation of man's subjectivity.

Each of these is a different way of ordering the proposals that, taken together in some particular arrangement, constitute a particular "theological position." Indeed, as the published controversies between Barth and Bultmann suggest, what is most basically at issue between the two kinds of "theological position" they each represent may not be so much what either side actually *says* on any given theological topic, but rather the *order* in which they are taken up.[5] What is at stake is not which one has done the more adequate conceptual analysis of key Christian ideas, but which has the more adequate or apt imaginative grasp of the basic *discrimen* governing all Christian theology, viz., the mode of God's presence *pro nobis*.

The point can be generalized. The unprecedented theological pluralism marking the neo-orthodox era is sometimes taken as a sign of a breakdown in consensus about the nature and task of theology. However, the suggestion is misleading. The point cannot be that in that era theologians *ceased* to agree about the content of their proposals; there have *always* been deep disagreements among Christian theologians about that! Nor is the point that theologians no longer agreed about the topics on which they are expected to comment. Judging by the sheer magnitude of their publications, it seems fair to say that theologians during the past half century acknowledged an obligation to comment on the traditional array of theological *loci*. Rather, it is because their proposals on a roughly common range of topics are ordered in such radically different ways into such different kinds of "positions" that theologians' writings often conveyed the sense that they were engaged in subtly but importantly different tasks. They are the result of irreducible differences among imaginative construals of the mode of the presence of God; and they are evidence that this act of the imagination is decisive for the particular characteristics that give a theological position its particular specificity and most deeply separates it from other "theological positions."

In short: at the root of a theological position there is an imaginative act in which a theologian tries to catch up in a single metaphorical judgment the full complexity of God's presence in, through, and over-against the activities comprising the church's common life and which, in turn, both provides the *discrimen* against which the theology criticizes the church's current forms of speech and life, and determines the peculiar "shape" of the "position."[6] With this point in hand, we can answer the questions with which we began the chapter.

WHY TAKE BIBLICAL TEXTS AS AUTHORITY?

Our discussion thus far has simply assumed the fact that certain theologians take biblical texts as "authority" for their theological proposals. But why should anyone do that? The first step in an answer to that is to recall a point made in Chapter 5. I suggested there that, given certain concepts of church, the judgment that biblical texts are authority for theology is analytic in the judgment that they are authority over the common life of the church. Hence the answer to our question is, "Because one takes them to be 'authority' in the common life of the Christian community." But that only pushes us back a step to the question: "Why would anyone take these writings to be 'authority' for the common life of the church?" That is the question we need to address, both as a question about these writings taken as "scripture" and, more narrowly, the writings taken as "canon."

The answer to which our entire analysis of "authority" for theology points is this: Taking these writings as "scripture," and even as "canon," is an integral part of certain ways of becoming a Christian. The reasons for adopting just these writings as "authority" are as complex, unsystematic, and idiosyncratic as are the reasons individual persons have for becoming Christians. The point turns on the fact that one can only become a Christian in some concrete fashion. For many, it involves joining with others in a Christian community. Most Christians perhaps would hold that becoming a member of a church is analytic in the idea "becoming a Christian." However, one does not join the church-in-general. The concreteness of the way one does in fact become a Christian is in part constituted by the concreteness and particularity of the mode of "church" one joins as part of becoming a Christian. That means that becoming a Christian always involves adopting, at least implicitly, some concept of "church." In many cases, though not necessarily in all, the concept "church" that is adopted includes as part of its meaning the concept "scripture." And the concept "scripture" brings with it a concept of "authority," for to call a set of writings "scripture" is to say that they ought to be used in certain normative and rulish ways in the common life of the church.

An analogous response must be made to the question, "Why would anyone take the 'canon' as "authority' for the common life of the Christian community?" One of the implications for our analysis is that the decision to adopt these writings as "canon" is not, as Willi Marxsen suggests, a separate decision over and above a decision to become a Christian. Marxsen acknowledges that "the canon was part of the fabric of church history."[7] He rightly points out that "the canon does not exist independently of the ancient church. At best, it is the modern church that has independent existence—vis-a-vis a fourth century decision."[8] But he is misleading when he suggests that the modern church's "independence" is its freedom to decide whether to agree "that the decision on the canon made so long ago was correct . . . ,"[9] as though it were one thing to decide to identify with the "church" and quite another to decide to identify with the decision about the canon. Marxsen suggests this on the supposition, on which von Campenhausen throws serious doubt, that the original decision about the canon was based on the contingent grounds that the writings deemed canonical were in fact written by apostles.[10] We have tried to show, to the contrary, that the canonicity decision is best taken as analytic in another decision about how to take the concept "church." The modern church's very real independence is not vis-a-vis one of the ancient church's decisions, viz., about the canon. It is an independence vis-a-vis the ancient church's self-understanding, an independence over-against her understanding of what it is in concreto to be Christian. To adopt the "canon" as "authority" for the common life of the church is to adopt, for whatever reasons, the particular way of being "Christian" that much of the ancient church also adopted.

No more systematic or logically compelling reasons can be given for taking scripture as authority than for becoming a Christian. Nor, of course, need they be any less compelling either! Probably it is misleading to discuss this decision exclusively in terms of "reasons." Like most personal acts, it may be described both in terms of reasons that might be offered in justification of the act, and in terms of psychological and social causes that might be offered in partial explanation of it. The satisfactoriness of any such account would be limited to the sorts of questions that were actually being answered. In the nature of the case no exhaustive or general and all-purpose account can be given. An account might be given in terms of the particularities of a person's own history, the circumstances in which he grew up, his religious training in childhood, or the lack of it, his continued emotional dependence on his parents or his rebellion against them, etc. Or an account might be given in terms of the particularities of his own wrestling with "big questions," his effort to find "meaning in life," to "make sense of it all," and the sort of illumination and capacity to take experience and take it "whole" that comes when he understands his personal identity in terms of the communal self-identity that the Christian community has in the presence of God. Perhaps the most that can be said in a *general* way about why people adopt just these writings as scripture, and even as canon, is that when they are used in the common life of the Christian community they drive us, as Barth put it in an early essay, "out beyond ourselves and invite us, without regard to our worthiness or unworthiness, to reach for the highest answer in which all is said that can be said, although we can hardly understand and only stammeringly express it. And the answer is: A new world, the world of God."[11]

Theologians, however, do offer much more elaborate and systematic "reasons" for taking biblical texts as "authority." As our discussion in Section 1 would suggest, these "reasons" are never "theological-position-neutral." They always derive their force from a logically prior imaginative judgment about how best to construe the mode of God's presence. That is, they always presuppose a prior decision about what it is to be a Christian. Hence, their force is entirely relative to whether one shares that understanding of what Christianity is all about.

For example, theologians in the neo-orthodox period frequently said that the reason for taking biblical texts as authority for theology is that they preserve the content of "revelation" and that their human words may again become the Word of God. More recently, Marxsen has argued that the true canon is Jesus himself, who "actualizes God" in an event having a "language character."[12] Scripture is "authority" insofar as it witnesses to this event and serves as norm for contemporary preaching in which the presence of God is once again made actual in a language game.

But each of these is a "reason" cast in terms of some one particular imaginative construal of the church's "central reality." The presence of God is construed in terms of a given "phenomenon" called "the-words-becoming-the-Word" or in terms of a "language event" that Jesus inaugurated and in which one becomes authentic. Each "reason" for taking these writings as authority is cogent if one has already judged that the heart of Christianity is best construed in the appropriate way. Each reflects a prior theological commitment, in which "church" is taken a certain way and these writings are *already* taken as "scripture." Each thus has the logical status of a general hypothesis about biblical writings, whether taken ensemble as canon, or only in parts.[13]

CONSTRUING AND USING SCRIPTURE

What underlies a theologian's decision to construe the scripture to which he appeals in a certain way rather than another and his decision to use the scripture he construes in certain roles and not others in theological argument? Here too our suggestion is that these decisions are decisively shaped by a theologian's prior judgment about how best to construe the mode in which God's presence among the faithful correlates with the use of scripture in the common life of the church.

In Section 1 above, I suggested that the criterion by which the church's current forms of speech and action are criticised and re-forms proposed in "doing theology" is a *discrimen* in which the church's use of scripture in her common life is conjoined with God's presence among the faithful. However, this is too general. No theologian simply "uses" this *discrimen*. Rather, that which guides his critical reflections and reformist proposals about the forms of the church's speech and action is a *particular construal* of the *discrimen* in an imaginative judgment that tries to catch up in a single meta-phor the utter singularity and full complexity of the mode in which God is present among the faithful. My proposal is that it is just that imaginative characterization of the *discrimen* that largely shapes his decisions about how to construe and use particular passages of scripture.

For example, when the *discrimen*, i.e., the mode of God's pres-ence, is construed as a reality in the ideational mode, it follows that scripture will be taken with the force of "teaching" the doctrines or "commending" the concepts that comprise it. Hence, what is author-itative about scripture will be said to be the system of doctrine it teaches or the coherent set of concepts it commends; or, more exactly the patterns among the doctrines (Warfield) and the patterns among the concepts (Bartsch; Wright). When the *discrimen* of theology is construed in the mode of an objective actuality, e.g., as the presence of the Risen Christ, then it follows that scripture will be taken with the force of "rendering" this agent by giving his identity description. Hence, what is authoritative about scripture will be said to be the patterns in and among the narratives that give an identity description of this agent by recounting his characteristic patterns of intentional action. And when the mode of God's presence is construed as that of an ideal possibility, e.g., the possibility of a transition from inauthentic to authentic existence, it follows that scripture will be construed as expressing this possibility and evoking its actualization. Hence, what is authoritative about texts will be said to be the patterns obtaining among the, e.g., mythic, forms by which it is usually expressed in scripture. In each case the decision about how to construe texts taken as authoritative scripture is determined by a logically prior decision about how best to characterize in a single judgment the singularity and complexity of the mode of God's presence.

So too with decisions about how to use authoritative scripture in the course of doing theology. We saw in Part II that a theologian is obliged to decide in which of several possible roles to use scripture in arguments mounted to support his theological proposals. The suggestion is that that decision is largely shaped by the way a theologian's imaginative construal of the mode of God's presence dictates where the center of gravity falls in his total "theological position."

Suppose, for example, that God's presence is construed in an ideational mode. As we saw, that tends to throw the center of gravity in the theological position onto a system of doctrines or a set of concepts, and scripture is taken with the force of "asserting" or "commending" these doctrines or concepts. In that case, scripture clearly must provide the data that "authorize" the theological proposals. The warrant for moves from scripture to theological proposal must lie in doctrines about scripture and how it is to be interpreted. This would be an instance in which "translation" is an apt metaphor for the relation of theological proposal to scripture.

On the other hand, suppose God's presence is construed as a concretely actual agent, the Risen Christ (Barth). That tends to throw the center of gravity in the theological position onto giving an identity description of this agent. Not that this constitutes the only subject matter for theological proposals: rather, the subject matter of every theological proposal is discussed in terms of its relation to this identity description. In that case scripture, taken as giving an identity description of this agent, will be used as the basis for data authorizing theological proposals specifically about his identity; the warrants for the move from this data to theological proposals will be backed by some theory about the nature of personal identity and how it is best described. The data for theological proposals about other *loci*, however, say those about the nature and destiny of man, may be drawn from philosophical phenomenology, the physical or social sciences, or from common experience, with scripture providing the backing for the warrants for moves from such data to the theological proposals. Both sorts of arguments could justly be called "christocentric," but in importantly different ways. Both use biblical writings construed as identity descriptions of Jesus Christ to authorize theological proposals, but in different senses of "authority," the one in the mode of "data" and the other in the mode of "backing."[14]

Again, suppose that the *discrimen* that rules theological proposals is construed in the mode of an ideal possibility, as the possibility of coming to have the mode of "authentic" subjectivity exhibited by the man of "faith" (Bultmann). That tends to throw the center of gravity in the theological position onto descriptions of "faith" as a possible mode of subjectivity. The data for theological proposals about that possibility may be provided by a philosophical phenomenology of authentic and inauthentic modes of existence. Scripture will then serve to provide backing for the warrants for moves from such data to the theological proposals.

In each of these cases, theologians' decisions about which role in an argument supporting a theological proposal ought to be filled by scripture is largely determined by a decision about how best to characterize the subject matter theological proposals are chiefly to elucidate. But that is to say that they are determined by the particular way each theologian tries to catch up the full complexity and singularity of the mode in which God is present in a single imaginative judgment. Theologians' decisions about how to use scripture, like their decisions about how to *construe* the scripture they use, are determined by decisions that are literally pre-text, i.e., logically prior to any attention to any particular text taken as authority for any particular theological proposal.

CONTROLS ON IMAGINATION IN THEOLOGY

If decisions about whether to appeal to scripture at all in the course of doing theology and about how to construe it and use it if it is appealed to are largely shaped by imaginative characterizations of the mode of God's presence among the faithful, doesn't it follow that theologians will in fact treat scripture as *gallus in campanili*, "the weathercock in the church tower" which is turned hither and thither by every theologian's imaginative brainstorm?

Not necessarily. In the first place, it must be borne in mind that the argument in this chapter is one-sided and is balanced by the argument in Chapter 9. The thesis here is that while the results of biblical scholarship may be relevant to making these decisions (we'll take that up in Chapter 9), they cannot be *decisive* because these decisions are also shaped by an act of the imagination that a theologian must necessarily make prior to doing theology at all. Just how biblical texts-as-scripture "control" the imaginative act is something we shall explore later. In the second place, our argument hitherto itself draws attention to another range of limits to a theologian's freedom of imagination. Scripture's "authority" for theology, we have held, is grounded in its "authority" over the common life of the church. It is this that makes a theologian's imaginative characterization of the mode of God's presence *prior* to his doing theology and making the decisions called for in that activity. For his imaginative act has its ground in features of the common life of the church as he knows it by participating in it. It is shaped by and arises out of a larger set of activities of which "doing theology" is but one, and out of which it too arises. The point to be made here is that there are certain features of the common life of the church to which the imaginative act is accountable. I want to mention briefly three quite familiar features of the church's life that in this way impose some limits to the range of ways in which theologians may construe and use scripture.

First, the common life of the church is, *inter alia*, a community of discourse in which it is possible to have significant disagreements and mount arguments in support of one's proposals when they are challenged. There are conditions that human utterances must meet if they are to count as intelligible discourse. These conditions impose limits on the ways theologians imaginatively characterize the mode of God's presence. For one thing, it must be capable of consistent formulation. Otherwise it can only be set aside as unintelligible. Beyond that, it must be patient of elaboration into proposals on a variety of theological topics. Moreover, it must be patient of reasoned elaboration. That is, it must be possible to exhibit the logic of the relations obtaining among the theological proposals by which it is elaborated and it must be possible, if they are challenged, to make a case for them. That is the point we made in Part II: It must be possible to formulate self-consistently, not only the proposal itself, but the data on which it is grounded, the warrant licensing the move from the data to the conclusion, and the backing on which the warrant is grounded. For example, if God's presence is said to be like the presence of an agent who acts in history (Wright; Barth), then it must be possible to develop a reasoned elaboration of the concept "act of God in history." If that cannot be done, as has been charged in this case,[15] then the theological position shaped and ordered by this construal of the mode of God's presence is open to the objection that it is utterly arbitrary and capricious.

None of this entails that the imaginative judgment itself must have been arrived at through a reasoned argument. On the contrary, the point is that the judgment is an imaginative act. Neither do a theatrical director's basic judgments about the nature of the characters and the fundamental conflicts and movement of a play come out of a syllogism. What is being asserted is that once the imaginative judgment is made, it is open to reasoned assessment: It must be possible to give good reasons for adopting it. And central among those reasons is the fact that it proves open to reasoned elaboration and to reasoned justification of the elaborations.

The fact that participants in the common life of the church also participate in a wider shared "culture" imposes a second type of limit to the range of ways theologians might imaginatively characterize the mode of God's presence. There are culturally conditioned limits to what either the theologian or his readers can find seriously imaginable. By "seriously imaginable" I mean imaginable as a way of shaping my personal identity and the identity of any community that is personally important to me. Some forms of life can be imagined in a wholly fantastic way, i.e., as possibilities unrelated to what one takes to be the real world, but not as real possibilities for the imaginer. In some cases this is because what is imagined cannot be coherently elaborated. All variants on the Midas image, for example, fantasying a form of life endowed with some sort of omnipotence, whether to create riches or lovers, turn out on further elaboration to be self-contradictory scenarios, as the legend of King Midas itself testifies. In other cases a form of life, while abstractly imaginable, cannot be imagined as a real possibility for *us* because it is so utterly alien to the social world we do in fact inescapably inhabit as members of our culture.

This sets outside limits on ways in which the presence of God and, correlatively, the form of life that is appropriate in his presence, can be construed. However, as the culture changes, what is seriously imaginable may change and with it the force of certain construals of the mode of God's presence may change. For example, we suggested in Chapter 2 that Warfield's way of construing scripture is grounded at least in part in taking the Bible as a holy object in and through which the Christian experiences numinous power. But if that way of construing scripture seems alien to many American Christians it may be because it is simply no longer seriously imaginable for them. Perhaps as a result of that massive cultural change called "secularization"[16] it has come about, as Edward Farley has pointed out in *Requiem for a Lost Piety*, that:

> Pictures of the father reading the Bible daily with the family, Bible reading and study as a regular exercise of the Christian life, "learning the Bible at Mother's knee"—all sound quaint to the modern ear. What do we have instead? . . . [T]he transformation of the piety of the Book into Bible *study* in the Church. We study in groups the history of Hebrew religion, the missionary journeys of Paul, and Johannine theology. This means that our basic relation to the Bible is an intellectual one.[17]

With this cultural change goes the compelling force of Warfield's "hypothesis." The passage of time has not so much disproved him as make him seem terribly culture-conditioned. And to insist that a Christian community now adopt his hypothesis might seem a demand that it archaize itself into a culture now gone, much as though it were being required to adopt pre-Copernican man's attitudes toward the heavens.

Another example is provided by the rise of modern methods of historical inquiry. It can be plausibly argued that, for better or worse, the methods of historical inquiry set limits to what is seriously imaginable for many people who learn to use them or learn to honor them highly. For example, they generate a deeply relativistic attitude that is very nearly unable to imagine an event that is not decisively shaped by antecedent events and conditions, or to imagine a view of the world that is not decisively shaped by, and hence relevant only to, its original socio-cultural setting.[18] Now it may be that the theologian's task is to explicate his theological proposals in terms that conform to such an imagination. Or, it may be that part of his task is so to explicate his proposals that they capture men's imaginations with enough power to alter the very limits of the imaginable. Either way, however, a theologian would be foolhardy to ignore the way historians' methods and working assumptions have shaped and so limited what many people are able seriously to imagine. Those limits impose important checks on a theologian's imagination when he construes the mode in which God is present.

These sorts of limitations are evidence of the culturally conditioned character of Christian theology. That is a danger. In being conditioned by the limits culture sets on what is seriously imaginable, theological proposals may turn out to be merely restatements of what is already imagined in the culture quite apart from Christianity's central reality. Nevertheless, the culturally conditioned character of theological proposals is also evidence of the importance of its grounding in an act of the imagination. Only by an imaginative act can theological proposals capable of capturing the imaginations of real men living in a particular culture be concrete enough to be really "practical" for particular men and significantly "critical" of particular Christian communities. Only because it is grounded in a decisive imaginative act is a set of theological proposals really incarnate in men's real lives.

A third limit on a theologian's freedom to construe the mode of God's presence may be stated more briefly. What is being construed is a complex reality in which the presence of God is conjoined with the church's uses of scripture to nurture and reform both her common identity and the personal identities of her members. In Chapter 5, we saw that "tradition" may be used as a technical theological name for this entire complex. There is a great variety of concrete instances of "tradition" in the theological sense, exhibiting important empirical diversity in many details ("traditions" in a phenomenological, rather than theological, sense of the term). However, they exhibit a characteristic structure. Since it is precisely the entire complex of some concrete phenomenological "tradition" that a theologian tries to capture in his single, metaphorical judgment, his imaginative judgment must be responsible to that common structure. The determinate givenness of the structure imposes certain checks on the range of possible imaginative construals.

This common structure can be described through a phenomenological study of religious traditions as such. In his discussion of "revelation" Paul Tillich gives a sketch of a phenomenology of tradition's structure that can be usefully adapted to our purposes.[19] "Tradition" is a temporal sequence of "situations." It has what may be called both a "horizontal" and a "vertical" structure. Each "situation" exhibits a bi-polar structure: On one hand, a community of people who understand their communal and personal identities to be shaped by the fact that they live "before God"; on the other hand, the presence of God in and through a set of common forms of speech (homiletical, creedal, doxological, and simply "pious"), common liturgical actions, and uses of biblical writings, all related in some way to the life, death, and resurrection of Jesus of Nazareth. Concretely speaking, each such "situation" is dependent for its existence and for its concrete forms of speech, liturgy, and use of scripture on some particular, temporally antecedent "situation" and *its* forms of speech, liturgical action, and uses of scripture. That is, concretely speaking, "tradition" in the technical theological sense always takes place in and through some particular "traditions" in the phenomenological sense of the term. Ultimately, they historically depend to some degree on an original "situation" in which the community was constituted by Jesus' disciples, on one side, and on the other the presence to them of God in and through the appearances of one whom they identified as Jesus of Nazareth who had been crucified. What all the "situations" share, for all their diversity, is this double structure: Horizontally, each one has two poles, a community with its characteristic forms of speech and action in dialectical relationship with a presence (or "power" or "event") that is experienced as "coming to" them and "over against" them; and vertically, each "situation" in "tradition" (in the technical theological sense of the term) is somehow grounded in Jesus Christ's life, death, and resurrection.

Every imaginative judgment that attempts to capture that complex in a single characterization must be apt to that double structure. Thus the very structure of "tradition" rules out any construal of the mode of God's presence that collapses the "over against": that stresses the present "situation" at the expense of its basis in Jesus Christ, or Jesus Christ at the expense of the present "situation."

Conditions necessary for discourse to be intelligible, open to reasoned elaboration, and capable of argued defense; culturally conditioned limits to what is seriously imaginable; the structure of "tradition:" these are three types of limit imposed on the range of ways a theologian might imaginatively characterize the *discrimen* by which he criticizes and proposes reforms of current churchly forms of speech and action. They are imposed by the very fact that the imaginative judgment is made in the context of a culturally situated community of discourse whose common life is ruled by God's presence in dialectical relation to certain uses of scripture, i.e., through "tradition."

WHY SHOULDN'T SCRIPTURE BE "AUTHORITY"?

We noted at the beginning of Chapter 1 that some recent discussions of the matter hold that scripture can no longer be taken as "authority" for at least two different kinds of reasons. Some seem to hold that the very idea of "authority" has been rejected as part of a major change in the values most widely shared in Western cultures, with the result that Christianity can no longer be understood in terms of "authority" in those cultures.[20] Others suggest that once biblical scholarship has demonstrated the lack of theological unity within the Bible, it can no longer be adopted as "canon."[21]

One thing our analysis shows, however, is that these conclusions are neither logically cogent nor psychologically inevitable. We showed that "authority" is used in a large variety of senses. Even if a major change has occurred in the culture, the sense of "authority" it affects is not necessarily any of the senses in which biblical writings need be called "authority." So too, we tried to show that the judgment that a set of writings is "canon" with canon's "authority" is not a contingent judgment resting on the alleged theological unity of the writings' content. Acknowledgment that they are not a theological unity need not undercut acknowledgment of these writings as "canon."

Perhaps a loss of a sense of the reality of "scriptural authority," and especially of "canonical authority," comes with a loss of ability or willingness to appropriate and use any concept "church" that includes the concept "scriptural authority." Theological positions in the neo-orthodox period that stressed a high doctrine of biblical authority took that to entail a high doctrine of the church. The doctrine of the church as the veritable Body of Christ on earth was taken very seriously, helping to account, among other things, for the theological passion of the time about recovery of the organic unity of the church through the ecumenical movement. The dominant way of talking about the congregation pictured it as true *koinonia*, a fellowship of men and women genuinely reconciled to one another. It is suggestive that the period of crisis about biblical authority, at least in the United States, has also been a period of severe social and political dislocations in which many churchmen became disillusioned with the church and her apparent inability to be a true community of reconciled persons in a society rent by deep racial and ideological alienation. "Authority" and "canon" as technical theological terms are specific enough that changes in cultural attitudes to other sorts of "authority" and scholarly demonstration of biblical disunity do not require their abandonment. However, it does follow from our own analysis of the concept "church," that if one gives up a concept of "church" of which the concept "scripture," and especially the concept "canon," is a part, then one is also logically obliged to give up the concept of the "authority" of scripture.

However that may be, the point being made here is this: neither cultural changes nor the results of historical inquiry into biblical texts and canon *logically* imply the "impossibility" of a theologian's taking biblical texts, and even the historical Christian canon, as "authority" for theology while remaining in intelligible and significant conversation with the contemporary mind. And the reason is this: "The Bible is the church's book" makes what is apparently an accurate *historical* claim; but "Biblical texts are the church's scripture" makes an important *conceptual decision* (i.e., self-involvingly to adopt a certain concept "church"), and "Scripture is authority over the church's life" makes a *conceptual claim* that is analytic in the foregoing conceptual decision.

Hence, for example, a theologian's decision about which kind of logical force to ascribe to scripture is perhaps best understood as a *policy* decision. It is a logically different kind of judgment from historical and literary judgments about the same texts. To use a particular passage of scripture as having a certain force is not necessarily to make any historical or literary claims about those passages, nor does it necessarily rest on research on such topics. In any case, what is decisive is a prior judgment about the "essence of Christianity" and the point of doing theology at all.

To be sure, theologians may feel constrained to give reasons for the policy decisions they make on this point. For some theologians, the results of historical and literary study of the texts may weigh heavily in the process of deciding what logical force is to be ascribed to the texts in question. Such research may show how the texts functioned in their original historical settings for their original readers, or how they functioned for subsequent readers in later historical and cultural settings, or it may exhibit the literary structure and history of the texts themselves. Such information is not necessarily irrelevant to a theologian's decision about what force to ascribe to the texts. However, the decision how or whether the results of such research are relevant to this decision must *itself* be grounded in a prior theological judgment about how best to characterize the basic nature of Christianity, what it is "all about." Accordingly, some theologians who make different theological judgments at this point will not take the results of historical or literary study of the Bible as relevant to the decision about what logical force to ascribe to authoritative scripture. In their theological writings there may be marked contrasts between the force they ascribe to a particular biblical passage and the force its inherent literary properties might suggest it has. To see that every theologian's decision about the sort of logical force to ascribe to scripture is a policy decision is to recognize that such contrasts do not necessarily count against these theologians' good judgment. As a policy decision it is simply logically diverse from any historical or literary judgment theologians might make about the texts, and in making it they are not necessarily (though they may in fact be) taking a stand on any controversies about historical or literary questions.

NOTES

1. No theologian has stressed this point more tellingly in his reflections about the nature of theology than Julian N. Hartt, *A Christian Critique of American Culture* (New York: Harper & Row, 1967), esp. Ch. VI.
2. Robert C. Johnson, *Authority in Protestant Theology* (Philadelphia: Westminster, 1959), p. 15.
3. *V.* above, Ch. 5, p. 94.
4. *V.* above, Ch. 5, p. 96, and footnote 6.
5. Cf. Rudolf Bultmann, "The Problem of Hermeneutics," *Essays* (New York: Macmillan, 1955), tr. J. C. G. Greig, pp. 234–261; esp. 259–261; Karl Barth, "Rudolf Bultmann—An Attempt to Understand Him." *Kerygma and Myth*, II (London: SPCK, 1962), tr. Reginald H. Fuller, pp. 83–133, esp. 91–92.
6. James Barr has noted this also, *The Bible in the Modern World*, p. 163, as has Michael Novak, "Culture and Imagination," *Journal of Ecumenical Studies*, Vol. 10 (Winter, 1973), pp. 128–140.
   It should be clear that I am using "imagination" and "imaginative" in a non-technical way to designate a judgment in which one suggests that some complex reality may be grasped holistically when one sees that it is like some simpler, more familiar reality. It is the mode of judgment by which one offers metaphors and analogies. A full-blown account of "theological thinking" would require a technical discussion of the notion of imagination; but I think this essay does not require it. Probably the richest investigation of "imagination" in connection with "revelation" and "doing theology" is Ray Hart's *Unfinished Man and the Imagination* (New York: Herder and Herder, 1968).
7. *The New Testament as the Church's Book* (Philadelphia: Fortress Press, 1972), p. 18.
8. Marxsen, p. 20.
9. Marxsen, p. 18.
10. Marxsen, pp. 27, 63.
11. "The Strange New World Within the Bible," *The Word of God and the Word of Man* (London: Hodder & Stoughton, 1928), p. 34.
12. Marxsen, pp. 61, 92.

13. Recent literature yields two more examples of this point. James Barr suggests that the reason for taking the canon as authority is that it expresses the "structure" of Christian faith. It describes who Jesus is (New Testament) and who God is (Old Testament). *The Church in the Modern World*, pp. 114–5; 158. In a recent study J. Christiaan Beker has suggested that the reason for taking biblical writings as authority is that they express the humanly important "experience" that the biblical writers had, an experience he hopes we can redescribe with the help of conceptual tools provided by Merleau-Ponty. [Daniel Batson, J. Christiaan Beker, W. Malcolm Clark, *Commitment Without Ideology* (Philadelphia: Pilgrim Press, 1973).]

Each of these cases too gives a "reason" for taking scripture as "authority" that is cast in terms of some one particular construal of the church's central reality, as constituted by a "faith" having a perduring "structure" or by a characteristic "experience."

14. Karl Barth seems in fact to shift the sense in which his theology is "Christocentric" in just this fashion. Compare the structure of the overall argument in *CD* IV with the overall argument in *CD* III/2. In the latter, e.g., in discussion of what he calls man's essential "co-humanity" *as man-and-woman*, does he really rely on the NT identity description of Jesus for the data marshalled to "authorize" his theological proposal (as he does in *CD* IV), or does he not use common-sensical observations about common experience as the "data" and rely on NT identity-descriptions of Jesus (as "man for others") for the backing for the warrant that licenses the move from this data to theological proposals about "co-humanity" constituting man's "nature"?

15. Langdon Gilkey has developed this question most effectively in his essay "Cosmology, Ontology, and the Travail of Biblical Language," [*Journal of Religion*, 41 (1961), pp. 194–205.] It is disappointing that G. Ernest Wright has ignored the important question raised in this essay in his more recent *The Old Testament and Theology* (New York: Harper & Row, 1969), especially since Wright stresses there the importance of the Old Testament for the Christian understanding of God. He raises questions that are far more serious for the way scripture is construed in Wright's essay than for the way it is construed in the passages we examined from Barth. Gilkey contends that without further philosophical elaboration, an assertion by a contemporary theologian that "God acts/acted in history" is unintelligible. Scripture and pre-modern orthodox theology might speak that way, Gilkey believes, because it was possible in the prevailing views of the cosmos to speak of God acting in exactly the same sense of "acting" as one spoke or "your father" acting. In the context of their cosmology "acting" could be used univocally. We are unable to. Modern men assume a casual continuum in space-time experience, Gilkey contends, and we do not expect amazing divine events on the surface of experience. Accordingly, while stressing that God is revealed in objective events in history, writers like Wright insist that this "act is not self-evidently *God's* act." It can be known as such only when properly "interpreted" by the eyes of faith. When we say "God acts" and "your father acts" we must use "act" analogically. Now, unless we know how the analogy is to be used and what it points to, it is unintelligible, and "act" is being used equivocally. The difficulty is that to say that "God acted at the Red Sea" is an *interpretation* and not a straight-forward report of a publicly available event implies

that we know what "God" means and how to identify its referent, but it does not tell either one.

Gilkey contends that biblical sources cannot help with these questions. Instead, "only an ontology of events specifying what God's relation to ordinary events is like, and thus what his relation to special events might be, could fill the now empty analogy of mighty acts, void since the denial of the miraculous." (p. 200). At least two prominent philosophical theologians, Schubert Ogden [Schubert Ogden, *The Reality of God*, (New York: Harper & Row, 1966), pp. 164–188.] and Gordon Kaufman, [Gordon D. Kaufman, *God: The Problem* (Cambridge: Harvard University Press, 1972), pp. 119–148.] have taken up Gilkey's challenge. They try to give an ontology "specifying what God's relation to ordinary events is like" from two very different philosophical perspectives. Although this is not the place to discuss their respective merits, it is fair to note that neither view has been available long enough to be subjected to the extensive discussion that must go on before either is likely to command widespread acceptance. Gilkey himself seems to have decided that the direction he pointed in his essay leads to a dead end, and in his recent work he has taken up a quite different approach that avoids making claims about God's acting, even in an analogical use of "act" (Langdon Gilkey, *Naming the Whirlwind*, Pt. II.) In short, continuing philosophical discussion has not yet persuaded any large number of students of the matter that the concept "God's action in history" is intelligible. Until that happens, construing scripture as narrative recital of the acts of God seems less and less likely to strike men as an illuminating or powerfully authoritative way to take it.

The case study we drew from Tillich illustrates a second way in which a construal of the mode of God's presence may be criticized because it violates limits imposed by the conditions of intelligible discourse. In *The Fabric of Paul Tillich's Theology* I have tried to show that the problem is not, as with the case drawn here from Wright, that the proposed construal is not open to reasoned elaboration, but rather that while it is open to reasoned elaboration, the proposals into which it is elaborated seem incoherent with one another. We saw in the case drawn from Tillich that the authoritative aspect of scripture, i.e., the central religious symbol, the biblical picture of Jesus as the Christ, fills two inter-connected functions as used in the church: it is the paradigmatic *expression* of a (past) occurrence of God's presence, and it serves (now) to *occasion* new occurrences. The problem is that, having shown how the formal features of the biblical picture of Jesus as the Christ make it most aptly expressive of that which it is supposed to express, he fails to show how those formal features have any bearing on the picture's serving now to occasion new revelatory events in which God is present among the faithful. And yet, for the coherence of his own theological system, Tillich needs to show such a connection since it is this picture alone that ties the original revelatory event of which it is expressive and contemporary revelatory events which it occasions together in one whole. If there is no connection between what makes the picture apt to the original revelatory event and what makes it effective in revelatory events today, then its aptness to the past event becomes religiously and theologically unimportant in the present. But, in the context of Tillich's system, that would be to say that Christology becomes unimportant—a conclusion Tillich would obviously have resisted strongly.

16. Gordon Kaufman may overstate the claim somewhat, but his description fits a very great many people: "The Bible lies at the foundation of Western culture and in a deep sense, however unbeknownst, has informed the life of every participant in that culture . . . But all this is over with and gone. Though we may recognize and be grateful for its contributions to our culture, the Bible no longer has unique authority for Western man. It has become a great but archaic monument in our midst. It is a reminder of where we once were—but no longer are . . . For the more pious, all this is highly embarrassing: For they would like to regard the Bible as still maintaining—for them at least— the authority which it had for their fathers. But it does not: They cannot and do not actually order their lives by Biblical norms, and even regular reading of the Bible has become a duty and a task rather than a joy and fulfillment." ("What Shall We Do With the Bible?," *Interpretation*, XXV (Jan. 1971), pp. 95–96.)

17. (Philadelphia: Westminster Press, 1961), pp. 32–33; cf. Langdon Gilkey, *How the Church Can Minister to the World Without Losing Itself* (New York: Harper & Row, 1964), pp. 111–114.

18. Gerhard Ebeling has developed this point persuasively in "The Significance of the Historical-Critical Method for Church and Theology in Protestantism," *Word and Faith* (Philadelphia: Fortress Press, 1960), pp. 17–62.

19. *Systematic Theology*, I (Chicago: University of Chicago Press, 1951), pp. 106–147. Cf. James Barr's very similar sketch of the structure of tradition in *Old and New in Interpretation* (London: SCM, 1966), Ch. I.

20. V. discussions of this by James Barr in *The Bible in the Modern World*, esp. Ch. 1.

21. V., e.g., Robin Scroggs, "Tradition, Freedom, and the Abyss," *New Theology #8* (New York: Macmillan, 1971), ed. Peerman & Marty, pp. 84–104.

Chapter 9

"Authority" and
"Function"

We have been exploring what it is that shapes theologians' decisions about whether to appeal to scripture at all and, if they do, how to construe and use the scripture to which they appeal. We focused the issue by asking in particular whether and how the results of close study of biblical texts shape those decisions. In Chapter 8 our thesis was that while the results of biblical scholarship may well be relevant to making those decisions, they are not decisive. Far more decisive, we suggested, is a logically prior judgment every theologian seems to have to make in which he tries to catch up in a single imaginative characterization the *discrimen* by which his proposals will criticize and reform current churchly forms of speech and action, i.e., the mode in which God's presence among the faithful is conjoined with their uses of scripture. But that discussion was one-sided. It needs now to be balanced by a discussion of how scripture *is* relevant to making those decisions.

It will be useful to begin by exploring in more detail how the discussion thus far raises a serious question whether our analysis of "scripture authority" in *functionalist* terms has not ended up depriving scripture of its *normativity* over against theology, thereby ironically depriving it of its "authority." Then we shall examine, only to reject, the usual way of describing the relation between scripture as "normative" and theology, and, thirdly, propose a better way to

182

describe it, one that reconciles the functionalist terms we have used and scripture's "normativity" for theology. That will put us into a position, fourthly, to show how the results of biblical scholarship are and are not relevant to making these decisions.

LOSS OF "NORMATIVITY?"

One implication of our thesis in the last chapter is this: If a theologian does use the results of historical and literary studies of biblical texts to help determine how he will construe and use scripture, his decision to do so is itself determined by a logically prior imaginative judgment in which he characterizes in one of several different possible ways the basic *discrimen* of any theology that appeals to scripture, i.e., the conjunction of God's presence among the faithful and their uses of scripture. And for that prior decision the only "explanation" that can be given is genetic: It is shaped by the concrete particularities of the way scripture functions in the common life of the Christian community as he has experienced it. The basis for this claim lies in three points we have made in Parts I and II: a) that part of what it means to call a text or set of texts "scripture" is that they are "authoritative"; b) that the concepts "scripture" and "church" are dialectically related; and c) that, given the relevant *general* understanding of the nature and purpose of doing theology, the judgment "Scripture is authority for theology" is analytic in the judgment "Scripture is authority over the common life of the church." Hence, the way in which any particular theologian concretely takes biblical texts as "scripture" and uses them as "authority" in actually doing theology will vary with the way he decides to construe scripture's functioning in the church's common life as the occasion and mode of God's presence.

Now there is an important objection that might be raised to this entire analysis. The analysis seems headed for self-contradiction. On the one hand, it has been shown that part of what it means to call a text or set of texts "scripture" is that they are in some way prescriptive or "normative" for that for which they are authoritative, viz., for the common life of the church, and therefore for "doing theology." On the other hand, the account of what it means to say scripture is "authority" has been cast entirely in functional terms, which might seem purely descriptive. It may be no more than a report about how the texts are in fact used and do in fact function in shaping "Christian identity," both individual and communally. But that would not be an explication of how it is, precisely, *normative*. James Barr has put the worry here well:

> That one's understanding of world and self should be formed by the Bible means the provision of a context within which the basic decisions of faith and life can be made, it does not guarantee that these decisions will be made rightly. In the purely religious influence of the Bible upon man there is, as seen from the viewpoint of Christian faith, an element of ambiguity . . . There have been many examples of religious world-outlooks which have been founded upon the Bible, or supposedly so, but which have, in the judgment of Christians or other groups or of other times, appeared to be manifestly faulty. It is therefore necessary to examine such religious outlooks on self and world, in order to see whether their character really derives from the Bible or from some other cultural source, and to see whether their use of the Bible can be squared with the Bible itself, or with Christian faith itself.[1]

Barr is quite right that it is insufficient to construe scripture's "authority" for either church or theology in terms of its function of providing a "context within which the basic decisions of faith and life can be made." However, our analysis does not make that move. Moreover, the *force* of the sort of worry Barr expresses depends on a widely shared, mainly implicit assumption about the best *general* way to characterize formally the relation between "authoritative scripture" (however that is understood in practice) and "doing theology," (no matter how that is understood). But our analysis shows that assumption seriously misrepresents the ways in which several theologies unquestionably committed to being authorized by scripture actually relate scripture to theological proposals. It calls for another general way to characterize the relation between "scripture" and "theology." If the relation between the two were best described in an utterly formal way by this assumption, Barr's objection would be powerful. But if the relation is given a better purely formal description by our proposal, then it is possible to see how a "functionalist" analysis of the notion of scriptural authority in no way deprives scripture of its "normativeness" *vis à vis* theology.

SCRIPTURE AS "SOURCE"; THEOLOGY AS "TRANSLATION"
Barr's objection rests on the assumption that scripture is "normative" for theology only when it, rather than some other "cultural
source," is that from which theological proposals "derive." That is
to take scripture as "perfect source" for theology. It is part of a
picture that sees theological proposals as "translations" of scripture
as "source." It is this picture that our analysis challenges.

The picture is so common that we may call it the "standard picture" of the relation between scripture and theology. It trades on
"translation" as a metaphor. Scripture is regularly represented as
related to theological proposal as the Hebrew and Greek originals,
say, are to the New English Bible. The metaphor seems to have
been accepted at every point on the spectrum of theological opinion.
Barth, while seeking to understand Bultmann and finding him end-
lessly puzzling, can still agree with him that the message of scripture
must be "translated into other forms, into the language, terminology,
etc. of later ages."[2] Kenneth Hamilton, representing a somewhat
conservative Reformed view of scripture, can assert quite flatly that
"Theology . . . may be described from the perspective of language
as the translation of the gospel into words permitting men to hear
God's Word in the context of their cultural situation . . . ,"[3] while
James Robinson, reflecting the perspective of the "new-herme-
neutic," can defend the thesis "that theology is hermeneutic: the
interpretation of meaning. Such interpretation takes place in language and hence as translation of meaning."[4] Of course "translation"
here is only a metaphor. As Carl Braaten has pointed out, it is not
meant in "the superficial sense of reduplicating the words of one
language into more or less equivalent words of another language,
but in the sense of a radical transference of meaning, a transcultura-
tion of the Word into new words."[5]

There is an important *systematic* theological reason for the nearly
unanimous adoption of this metaphor. In the neo-orthodox period
"revelation" was the cardinal theological topic.[6] In systematic works
it is regularly the first material theological topic addressed. Christian
faith is defined as a response to revelation, the significance of Jesus
Christ is elucidated chiefly in terms of his being the revealer, the
church is said to be founded on revelation. Hence the content of
revelation is the subject matter theology is to explicate. Doctrines

about the Bible and its authority were always developed as part of doctrines of revelation. What is important to note here is the formal patterns according to which theological proposals are inter-related. Despite important material differences in their doctrines of revelation, there is this common pattern running through the writings of almost all theologians of the period: God's self-revelation is the proximate basis of the Bible's authority. The answer to "Why is the Bible authority?" is "Because it provides our one link with God's revelatory act."[7] When that is the context in which the matter is discussed, it necessarily follows that what is important about the Bible is that it somehow preserves the content of revelation. Accordingly, if theology's task is to elucidate the content of revelation, it follows that theological proposals are best seen as "translations" of biblical meanings.

However, our analysis of what it means to say "Scripture is au-thority for theology" shows that this standard picture, despite its impressive theological validation, must be set aside as radically mis-leading. It assumes what our analysis has shown is false: That there is necessarily a kind of conceptual continuity, if not identity, between what scripture says and what theological proposals say. That is, it assumes that when theology is done under the emblem "Let theol-ogy accord with scripture," then "doing theology" is the last mo-ment in a continuous movement in which the *same* "meanings" are stated in different "forms," first in the translation (in the ordinary sense) of Hebrew and Greek texts into, say, English, then exegesis of their "meanings," and finally "translation" (in the special, meta-phorical sense) of those same "meanings" into a contemporary idiom.[8] The difficulty with this assumption can be laid out in three objections: a) The metaphorical use of "translate" stretches the concept into unintelligibility, obscuring the possibility of a *concep-tual discontinuity* that our analysis has exhibited between exeget-ing the "meaning" of a biblical text and explicating a theological proposal authorized by "scripture." b) The metaphorical use of "translate" assumes a continuity of "meaning" between theological proposal and scripture, and that creates a problem from the side of exegesis. It obliges one to assume part of what exegesis is supposed to demonstrate, viz., the "meaningfulness" of the texts. c) The metaphorical use of "translate" creates a problem in our effort to understand the structure of theological positions authorized by scripture. It leads us unwittingly to misrepresent the indirect way many theologians bring scripture to bear on their proposals precisely in order to "authorize" them.

Consider first the concept "translation." Any effort to give an adequate description of what goes on in translating from one language to another raises enormously complicated problems in both linguistics and philosophy of language. Jules L. Moreau has written a study of theology as "translation"[9] that is very sophisticated about these matters and so can serve as a significant instance of the "standard picture."

"Translation," Moreau says, "is a dynamic function . . . which consists of relating two structures each of which has been adequately understood in its own terms by the translator."[10] The theologian is a translator "of the gospel into a secular environment." The "two structures" he is trying to relate are "the mythic structure of the gospel" and "the logical structure of the secular world's thought."[11] "Therefore, *theological* language is always a function of two factors: (1) the semantic structure of the church's religious affirmation as it is most responsibly understood, and (2) the semantic structure of the world addressed by the church."[12] He suggests that "The ante-Nicene church was successful in forging a language for Christian communication with the Hellenistic world because that church *translated* its religious language into a theological language employing the semantic structure of the Greek philosophical vocabulary."[13] Luther and Calvin tried "breaking the hold of the classical Greco-Roman semantic structure upon the mind of the church," but their successors did not grasp what they were up to and the effort aborted.[14] In our day the most effective translators "are not those who render the text afresh but those who have responsibly striven to expound and set forth in some systematic way what is called, for better or for worse, Biblical theology."[15] Moreau later discusses and criticizes Bultmann and Tillich as instances of this, and proposes that "process philosophy" might provide more adequate conceptual resources for translating the "semantic structure" of the gospel into the contemporary world's "semantic structure."[16]

What I want to point out here is not any transgressions this argument may make in the territory of linguistics or philosophy, but its overextended use of "translation" as a metaphor. The difficulties may be brought out by making two quite modest remarks. The first is to note the sheer magnitude of the two things the theologian as translator is obliged to relate to each other. Is there really *a* "semantic structure," e.g., *the* "mythic structure," to the Bible? Is the Bible really a "whole" in that way? Or does it not include quite a variety of kinds of discourse and different "semantic structures"? So too, is there really *a* "semantic structure" or "logical structure" to the world's thought? Is the "secular world" more of a "whole" in that regard than it seems to be in any other respect? Use of "translation" as a metaphor for the relation between Bible and contemporary theology seems to trade on misleading block thinking.

Perhaps, however, the blocks could be demythologized. Then, perhaps, doing theology would consist in making a large number of separate acts of "translation" and the metaphor would hold, but in a more pluralistic way? That calls for a second remark. Recall Moreau's insistence that the best "translators" today set forth the "semantic structure" of the Bible in a *systematic* way. Bultmann and Tillich were cited as major instances. Presumably they are effective for our day because they are doing what the ante-Nicene theologians did for their day: They "translate" the church's language into a "systematic structure" that is the functional equivalent today of "Greek philosophical vocabulary" in the Hellenistic world. As Bultmann himself puts it, they are translating the *kerygma* into a new "conceptuality."

But is that not a contradiction in terms? When one translates a newspaper article, a novel, or a poem from German words, say, into English words, one hopes to be able to preserve several aspects of the original. One hopes, for example, to be able to preserve something of its tone and style, something of its subjective impact on the reader. And one hopes to preserve the same *concepts*. Indeed, one test of the adequacy of a translation is how far it has been able to preserve the same concepts. If that is the case, then it is logically impossible to translate from one conceptuality to another. By definition the move from one conceptuality to another is to *change* the concepts.

The result of a move from one conceptuality to another is not a "translation" but a "redescription." A chemist's technical account of the explosion at the gas works is not a translation into more precise language of an account given in colloquial English by a reliable eyewitness. It is a redescription that uses different concepts at crucial points in the account. My body moves and I give an account of it as *my* action. A team of physiologists and neurologists may give a quite different technical account of the same bodily movement. But the "scientific" account is not a translation of my first-person, ordinary English account. It is a redescription using quite different concepts at crucial points. Writing of Christ's death, Paul may say that "Christ died for us." Bultmann may say that the story of Christ's death brings us the possibility for "authentic existence," and Tillich may say that the story of his death mediates to us the "power of being." But the latter two are not translating what Paul said. They are redescribing it in *different* concepts, and perhaps for very good reasons and to good effect. But nothing is gained by stretching "translation" so far in order to characterize them that the metaphor becomes meaningless.

A systematic statement of the gospel is "systematic" in part because it develops a system of technical terms whose meaning is stipulated to express highly precise and technical concepts. The concepts are defined in mutually referencing ways so that one has to employ the whole set of terms in order to use any of them. The relation of the technical language of English speaking physicists to ordinary English may be, in some respects, like the relation between an English dialect and standard English. But in several respects the relation is not like that at all. The technical language of English speaking physicists may be translated into the technical language of French speaking physicists in ways in which it can never be translated into ordinary English, for the shift into technical French preserves the same concepts whereas the shift into ordinary English calls for a redescription of the phenomena in new concepts. To call the latter a "translation" would be to use the term in ways that go beyond the range of apt usage.

Precisely the same difficulty seems to infect the suggestion that theological proposals set forth in a system of technical terms in English (or German, Greek, or Japanese) are *by definition* "translations" of passages of scripture. Used that way, "translation" is not only stretched beyond the limits of intelligibility, it obscures the fact that there may be a *conceptual discontinuity* between what the biblical texts say and what the theological proposals say. The latter may be redescriptions of what the former describe in a quite different set of concepts, but in that case they are precisely *not* "translation."

A second way to state the difficulty with the standard picture: Its assumption of a conceptual continuity between the "meaning" of the texts as ascertained by exegesis and the "meanings" explicated in theological proposals obliges one to assume something that exegesis must rather demonstrate. D. E. Nineham has pointed out that, given its logical home in a doctrine of revelation, the translation picture brings with it the assumption that in discovering the meaning of a passage of scripture one is "dealing with a word of God, part of God's self-disclosure to the situation in which the words were originally written and spoken." And that necessarily entails the "*assumption* that the word of God would also prove to have contemporary meaning, and that the exegete's task was not completed till he had discovered what it was." But, Nineham objects, "Many statements in ancient texts have *no* meaning today in any normal sense of the word 'meaning.' No doubt if you reflect long enough over any ancient statement—even, let us say, an historical inaccuracy in some ancient Egyptian annals—interesting reflections of some sort will occur to you . . ." But that is quite different from explicating " '*the* meaning' (for today) of a short biblical passage."[17] To adopt the "translation" picture of the relation of theology to scripture begs the range of questions Nineham is raising.

The problem is created because the translation picture wrongly assumes that "meaning" has only one meaning. By suggesting that theological proposals express the same "meaning" as the biblical texts that authorize them, it obliges one to assume that the texts do have some sort of meaning. After all, it is perfectly intelligible to say that through exegesis one explicates the "meaning" of a text, and to say that a theological proposal expresses the "meaning" of the same text. What the translation picture obscures, however, is that "meaning" may be used here in two different senses. That is, it obscures the possible conceptual discontinuity between text and proposal.[18]

The third way to state the difficulty with the standard picture is to note that "translation" is not an adequate metaphor for the indirect way in which some theologians actually bring scripture to bear on their theological proposals. Recall the seven case studies in Part I. The metaphor of "translation" may fit three of them: Where scripture is authoritative when construed as teaching doctrine, and the theological task is to restate those doctrines (Warfield); and where scripture is construed as proposing concepts, and theology's task is to elucidate the logic of those concepts (Bartsch and Wright). But the metaphor does not fit the other four cases. In each of them scripture is brought to bear on theological proposals only *indirectly*, as it does when scripture directly renders present an agent and gives an identity description of him, and thereby indirectly bears on theological proposals about that agent and the implications of his presence (Barth); or when scripture evokes insight into cosmic process, and thereby bears indirectly on theological proposals about that process (Thornton); or where scripture evokes a certain mode of subjectivity, and thereby bears indirectly on theological proposals about that mode of subjectivity (Bultmann and Tillich). In each of these four cases the theologian preserves some distance between scripture and his own theological proposals. The proposals are in some way *based on* scripture, but they are not direct restatements or "translations" of what scripture says. Even though these theologians too espouse the standard picture in their doctrines about the Bible, it does not in fact describe or validate their own theological practice!

The trouble with the "translation" metaphor in this regard, then, is that it defines the theological task in a tendentious way. It is used as though it were applicable to all theological positions: Theology is the explication of the content of revelation by a translation of the biblical message into contemporary idiom. But in fact it makes some theologians' methods for bringing scripture to bear on theology normative and implicitly invalidates the actual methods of other theologians. If we want to give a *generally applicable* account of what determines theologians' decisions about how to construe and use scripture, we need first to have a general description of the scripture-theology relation that is "theological position neutral," and does not tacitly make certain theologians' methods normative. Without such a term, it is impossible to state fairly what is at issue as between two opposed Christian theological positions.

The question about what our analysis does to scripture's *normativity* for theology centers finally, not on the "functional" terms we have used in the analysis, but on *what* it is in scripture that is normative. To say that scripture is normative for Christian theology is to say that there is something in it *determinate* enough to impose some controls on what theologians may say in the name of elucidating Christian faith and life. The "standard picture" of scripture's relation to theology leads one to assume that it is the determinateness of the biblical texts' conceptual content that makes it normative. As "normative," scripture is "perfect source." So James Barr can say the test of whether scripture has really been normative for a theological proposal is whether the proposal "derives from the Bible or from some other source." But the "standard picture" has turned out to be radically misleading. It is misleading because it misuses "translation" as a metaphor for the relation between biblical texts and all biblically authorized theologies (regardless of their enormous differences) in a way that obscures possible and theologically legitimate conceptual discontinuity between scripture and the theological proposal it authorizes; because it leads one to beg important exegetical questions about biblical texts; and because it misrepresents the way in which some theologians bring scripture to bear on theological proposals. So, while we can agree with Barr's remark that scripture's possible functions are not exhausted by its "providing a context" that shapes understandings of self and world, we must add that neither is it exhausted by being "perfect source" for Christianly apt theological proposals. If one does not state the problem about "normativity" in a way that simply assumes the validity of the "standard picture," it is possible to see how our analysis of its "authority" does in fact preserve scripture's "normativity" for the common life of the church and therewith for theology.

THE NORMATIVITY OF PATTERNS

Surely the issue about scripture's normativity for theology is not *genetic*, that is, not whether scripture was the source from which a theologian originally got his idea, but rather whether the theologian's proposal is Christianly apt. To say that biblical texts taken as Christian scripture are normative for Christian theology is to say that they play a necessary role in passing judgment on the Christian apt-

ness of current churchly forms of life and thought and on theological proposals about how to reform them. As its "authority,"
scripture is "normative" for a proposal's Christian aptness, not for
its origin.

We have tried to show that ultimately theological proposals are
assessed over against a *discrimen*, i.e., a pair of criteria that are
"organically related to one another as reciprocal coefficients," viz.,
the presence of God among the faithful in conjunction with the uses
of scripture in the church's common life. The concrete *locus* of
these two, the place where they are actually accessible to the theologian, is in the concrete details of the common life of the Christian
community as the theologian experiences it by participating in it. He
is able to use them as a *discrimen* in doing theology only as he
catches up the entire complex of ecclesial uses of scripture and divine
presence in an imaginative judgment that construes it all in a "root
metaphor." That is how the *discrimen* as a concretely lived reality
in the life of the church becomes an intellectual tool the theologian
can use in doing theology. The peculiar distinctiveness of each theologian's imaginative characterization of the *discrimen* is thus rooted
in the concrete particularities of the common life of the church
insofar as he is involved in it.

We have also tried to show that what theologians appeal to on
the "scripture" side of the *discrimen* (setting aside for the moment
the "presence of God" side) is some type of *pattern* in biblical texts.
Indeed, we saw that one of the major things that distinguish types
of theology from one another is that in their construals of the scripture side of the *discrimen* they appeal to quite different patterns.
And the patterns in the biblical texts are highly *determinate*. They
express certain beliefs, affective states, attitudes, policies, and the
like, and not others; they solicit and even evoke certain feelings and
attitudes, and not others; they tell certain stories, and not others.
And they do all these things in certain ways and interrelate them in
certain patterns, and not in others. Judgments about them are corrigible by attending to these particularities.

In short: Our analysis suggests that it is the *patterns* in scripture,
not its "content," that make it "normative" for theology. To analyze
scripture's authority in functional terms involves no compromise of
its "normativity" for theology. This is scarcely an original sugges-

tion. It has been made in Christian thought at least as far back as St. Athanasius.[19] To say that biblical texts taken as scripture are "authority" for church and theology is to say that they provide patterns determinate enough to *function* as the basis for assessment of the Christian aptness of current churchly forms of life and speech and of theologians' proposals for reform of that life and speech.

There are two respects in which this way of looking at the matter is superior to the "standard picture" of scripture's relation to theology. In the first place, our proposal is more generally applicable to different kinds of theologies that acknowledge scriptural authority because it is more purely *formal*. There are, we saw, a number of different kinds of patterns in scripture each of which is quite determinate and may serve as norm for theology. By stressing that normativity is a function of the determinateness of patterns as such, rather than the determinateness of some one kind of pattern, say, patterns among doctrines or concepts, we are able to give a purely formal description of the relation of scripture to theology, i.e., a description that does not involve any material judgment about *which* pattern in scripture ought to be taken as normative.

By assuming that to call scripture "authority" necessarily means taking it as "perfect source" for theology, the "standard picture" implicitly made one of the ways in which theologians construe and use scripture normative for them all. Its translation metaphor aptly describes those who take the patterns among doctrines or concepts in scripture as its authoritative aspect and bring it to bear quite directly on its proposals. But it misrepresents those who take other patterns in scripture as its authoritative aspect and bring them to bear on their proposals quite indirectly. If one assumes that to call biblical texts "authoritative scripture" *means* that they function as the perfect source that theological proposals "translate," then it is not hard to show that theologies that appeal to other patterns in scripture and bring them to bear on theological proposals indirectly are not "really" taking scripture as "normative." But that is to beg the root questions about scriptural authority, viz., what "scripture" and "authority" are to mean, how biblical texts are to be construed and used in doing theology.

Our proposal that to call biblical texts "authoritative scripture" is, in part, to say that it provides patterns determinate enough to rule "doing theology" normatively has the advantage that it fairly describes *both* those types of theology that the "standard picture" also describes adequately and those it does not. After all, even those theological arguments, in which scripture *is* used as "perfect source" of which theological proposals are the "translations," take certain *patterns* in biblical texts as normative, viz., patterns among doctrines or concepts. It is the fact that scripture can provide determinate patterns, not that it can serve as perfect source (though, of course, it may do that *also*) that makes it "normative."

Secondly, our *general* description of how scripture relates to all theological proposals authorized by scripture, regardless of important differences among them on other scores, is superior to the "standard picture" in that it more fairly represents the sort of intellectual activity involved in doing theology. A norm as "perfect source" basically calls for conceptual analysis and deductive argument: A proposal that is judged adequate by such a norm is a proposal that retains all the "content" that was present in the "perfect source." Norm as "pattern" also covers this case, although we saw in Chapter 7 how very difficult it is to confine oneself to this method. However, norm as "pattern" can also call for a different sort of intellectual activity in which "reason" and "imagination" are inseparable.

This can be brought out by noting how the authoritativeness of patterns in scripture is like the way a law is authoritative. In a widely-cited essay on "Authority, Reason, and Discretion in the Law," Carl Friedrich argues that an authoritative legal communication is "authoritative" precisely because it "possesses the *potentiality of reasoned elaboration.*"[20] By this proposal "authority" is a potentiality; the texts do not have to have been reasonably elaborated to be "authority." And the extent to which various texts are open to reasoned elaboration is a matter of degree. On this proposal, a law is truly "normative" precisely to the extent that it can be elaborated to meet unforeseen developments and to cover novel legal problems. And that is at once an imaginative and a reasoned act.

What is important is the suggestion that an authority is "normative," not insofar as its content is preserved without change, but insofar as it can serve as the starting point for a process of elaboration over which it exercises control because it is the model for the elaboration. So scripture is authority for theological proposals, not by being the perfect source of the content that they fully preserve, but by providing a pattern by which the proposal's adequacy as elaboration can be assessed. The elaboration of the pattern involves both reasoning and imaginative insight to see just how it may be elaborated to meet new situations and problems faced by the Christian community.

Now, there are three ways in which the determinateness of the patterns in scripture's forms of Christian speech can impose controls on imaginative construals of the mode in which God is present among the faithful.

First, there is a range of biblical patterns that sets *outside limits* to the ways in which God's presence can be construed. The patterns of biblical expression themselves exhibit a variety of ways of construing it. But they clearly exclude certain logically possible construals. For example, they exclude any construal of the mode of God's presence in the forms of speech appropriate to discussion of "the demonic," or "the benign indifference of the universe," or "inexorable moral evolution."

Second, the variety of patterns of biblical expression may be taken to provide a *limited range of determinate possibilities* for construing the mode of God's presence. One can distinguish among forms of expression that are characteristic to Matthew, Mark, or Luke, to John, or Pauline writings, or Hebrews, or to the Pastoral Epistles. Each may be taken as a set of patterns for one kind of authentically Christian speech about theological matters. The collection as a whole, then, can be taken as a set of different but quite determinate patterns any one of which can be reasonedly elaborated in new theological proposals. The determinateness of each would then exercise its own peculiar controls on my theology, depending on which one or ones I adopt as paradigmatic for my forms of expression. In this vein it is sometimes said that if one takes the New Testament as such as "authority" one is acknowledging that its theological diversity exhaustively exhibits the variety of types of theology that are Christianly acceptable.

For those theologians who adopt the concept "canon" as a technical theological term, there is a third way in which the determinateness of patterns and scripture imposes controls on the theological imagination. To take scripture as "canon," we said, is to take it as a "whole" constituted by the way in which the use of each of its "parts" in the common life of the church is related to the use made of the other "parts." The concept "canon" thus brings with it the judgment that the patterns characteristic of one "part" of the canon stand in *some* determinate relationship to the paradigmatic forms of speech characteristic of each of its other "parts." Imaginative construal of the mode in which God is present would then be subject to controls imposed, not simply by the determinateness of individual scriptural paradigms, but more importantly by the determinateness of the way those paradigms are related one to another within the canon taken as a "whole." Of course, the particular way in which they *are* related will vary from theologian to theologian, depending on the sort of "wholeness" each *concretely* ascribes to scripture. We saw in Chapter 8 that that can vary a great deal. Each theologian decides it for himself in the way he imaginatively construes the mode of God's presence.

Perhaps the clearest illustration of this comes in the case we drew in Part II from Barth's discussion of the "Royal Man": What controls Barth's construal of the mode of God's presence as the Risen Lord is not simply a variegated set of biblical expressions about Jesus as "human" and others about Jesus as "divine," but rather the way in which stories about Jesus' enacting human intentions are consistently related *in certain patterns within the context of the canon* to stories about how he enacted divine intentions. In cases like this, biblical patterns not only set the outside limits to what can count as apt imaginative construal of the mode of God's presence, not only provide the exhaustive array of Christianly apt ways to construe it; beyond all that they specify determinate ways in which various aspects of the construal are to be related to one another.

"EXEGESIS" AND THEOLOGY

This has some implications for the sense in which it may be said that the results of biblical study *are* relevant (though not decisive) to the decisions theologians make about how to construe and use the scripture. The determinate patterns in the biblical texts are open to close study. Any claim that a particular theological proposal is a reasoned elaboration of a particular pattern is corrigible by close study of the pattern to which appeal is made.

However, it does not necessarily follow from this that the results of biblical exegesis provide "controls" over the making of theological proposals. For there are several different types of activity that can legitimately be called "exegesis." Their results impose quite different kinds of possible controls on theology. And which kinds of "control" they may actually impose depends on decisions that neither exegesis nor the declaration that biblical texts are authoritative scripture can of themselves settle.

To begin with, one has to decide whether in doing exegesis one is studying biblical texts as *texts* or as *scripture*. To exegete the texts simply as texts is to engage in one of at least two different kinds of historical inquiry. (i) One may study a biblical text taken as a historical source that itself has historical sources. "Exegesis" in this sense is part of the historian's craft wherein the history of the text is reconstructed, or a part of ancient history is reconstructed using the text as a source of validating evidence. (ii) One may study a biblical text simply as it stands. This enterprise differs from the first because its goal is different. The aim of the inquiry is not so much to discover the sources out of which the text came, but rather what interests shaped the work of the one who put it into its present state and how it would have been understood by its original audience in its original context. One seeks to understand "what it meant" as used in its present form in its original setting. Both of these yield historical judgments. Of course, the results of either may be useful in achieving results in the other. (iii) One may, however, study a biblical text taken as Christian scripture. Such an exegesis would result in judgments about it precisely as used in certain rulish and normative ways in the church's common life to help nurture and reform her self-identity. Taken that way, an exegetical judgment is part of the theological task. It is guided in important ways by theological judgments about the nature of the church's task and about just how scripture ought to be used in the church's common life to help keep her faithful to that task. In particular, it involves a judgment about which of several patterns in scripture are normative for doing theology and ought therefore to be the principal subject of the exegesis. And those judgments, I have been arguing, are decisively shaped by an imaginative judgment about the mode in which God makes himself present in and through those uses of scripture, a judgment that is logically prior to any exegetical judgments about the text.

The results of these different kinds of exegesis bear on the doing of theology in quite different ways. Let us call them respectively "exegesis$_1$,""exegesis$_2$," and "exegesis$_3$." By definition, exegesis$_1$ and exegesis$_2$ cannot of themselves help scripture function normatively in doing theology, for they are studies of biblical texts as texts and precisely not as "scripture." However, they do exercise other sorts of control over a theologian's uses of his imagination. Strictly speaking, only the results of exegesis$_3$ function normatively in theology. Moreover, under certain circumstances, the results of exegesis$_3$ may include the results of exegesis$_2$ and that way the latter (and sometimes the results of exegesis$_1$, for that matter, when they are necessary to doing exegesis$_2$) also bear normatively on doing theology. However, *whether* the results of exegesis$_2$ are relevant, and *what* patterns in scripture are studied in exegesis$_3$ depend on a logically prior and imaginative decision about how to construe "scripture" which is not itself corrigible by the results of any kind of biblical study. We shall develop each of these points in turn.

Exegesis$_1$ and exegesis$_2$ appear historically to have exercised a certain amount of psychological influence on theologians' imaginative and reasoned elaborations of biblical patterns. Exegesis in the historical and literary modes has been an important aid to transcending the *status quo* opinions prevalent in a Christian community at any particular time. We noted that in order to be truly "critical," theology must transcend that *status quo* in order to see ways in which it needs to be reformed. Otherwise its proposals, far from being critical of how the church engages in her mission, simply celebrate her current practices. One of the important features of historical and critical study of biblical writings is that they force close attention to the determinateness, the details, of the texts. It is frequently pointed out that such painstaking attention to small details of wording and structure have repeatedly prompted major new imaginative construals of Christianity's "central reality" and with it major reforms in the church's common life. One thinks of Augustine, Luther, and Barth wrestling with Romans under quite different circumstances and to different ends, but with the common result that they inaugurated major changes in forms of speech and action in the church. It is also the case that their imaginative and influential insights seem to subsequent historical exegesis to be seriously in error.[21] That suggests that the controls laid on the theological imagination in this way by historical and literary exegesis are more important for their psychological than their conceptual results.

There is a second way in which $exegesis_1$ and $exegesis_2$ impose controls on theology. They figure in part of what we called in Chapter 8 the conditions for reasoned elaboration. The results of $exegesis_1$ and $exegesis_2$ set limits to what may be asserted historically and literarily about biblical passages. We saw in Part II that theological arguments are "field encompassing." They may include a variety of logically diverse claims from a variety of fields of study. Hence historical and literary claims about scripture may play some role in arguments made on behalf of theological proposals. If they are made, they have to conform to what can be established by normal methods of historical or literary-critical argument. This is a necessary condition for reasoned argument. Theologians enjoy no exemptions from ordinary canons of rationality that would permit them to acknowledge a historical or literary claim about some part of the Bible in a non-theological context and yet assert something inconsistent with it in the course of an argument in support of a theological proposal.

Neither of these is a way in which the results of exegesis function normatively in doing theology; only $exegesis_3$ can provide that. Only $exegesis_3$ is a study of biblical texts taken as scripture. But that means that it is study of scripture done within the context of a certain construal of the text: studying it in regard to certain patterns which are taken to be authoritative, and not in regard to others, as filling certain kinds of functions in the common life of the church, and not others, as having certain kinds of logical force, and not others.

Thus, *what* is studied in $exegesis_3$ depends on a prior decision about how to construe and use the texts; and that, we argued in Chapter 8, is grounded in an imaginative construal of the basic *discrimen* of Christian theology, a construal itself rooted in the concrete particularities and peculiarities of the church's common life as the theologian participates in it.

So too, *whether* the results of exegesis$_2$ come to function normatively in doing theology depends on the same imaginative act.
Given certain construals of the mode of God's presence, it may be
decided that the way the passage should be construed in theology
now is identical with "what it meant" as used in its original setting.
In that case, the actual results of exegesis$_3$ would be identical with
the results of exegesis$_2$. But that may not be the case. It depends on
a theological and not on an exegetical judgment. The point is especially important in connection with these theological positions in
which "church" is understood in dialectical relation, not just with
"scripture," but with scripture as "canon." For in that case an
exegetical judgment of a particular passage is necessarily incomplete
until it is explicitly interrelated with exegetical judgments about the
original meaning of passages from the other "parts" of the canon
whose dialectical relationship constitute the canon a "whole."[22] That
is, "exegesis" is then necessarily exegesis "within the canon."[23]

Thus the results of "exegesis" of biblical texts *taken as scripture*
do function in normative ways in doing theology by making as precise as possible a theologian's grasp of the patterns in the biblical
texts that he identifies as their authoritative aspect. However, while
the results of this biblical scholarship are clearly *relevant* to doing
theology, they are not ultimately *decisive*. They are themselves
shaped by a prior imaginative theological characterization of theology's *discrimen*. It dictates *which* patterns will be studied, and it
dictates in respect to *which uses* of the patterns (e.g., in present
church only, or in certain more ancient periods of the church, or
in the texts' original settings) it will be studied.

NOTES

1. James Barr, *The Bible in the Modern World* (London: SCM, 1973), p. 101.
2. Karl Barth, "Rudolph Bultmann—An Attempt to Understand Him,"
Kerygma and Myth II, ed. Hans-Werner Bartsch, tr. Reginald H. Fuller
(London: S.P.C.K., 1962), p. 87.
3. Kenneth Hamilton, *Words and the Word* (Grand Rapids: Eerdmans,
1971), p. 10; cf. p. 104.
4. James Robinson, "Theology as Translation," *Theology Today*, XX (Jan.
1964), p. 518. Robert Funk suggests that this even goes on *all through* the
Bible: ". . . Paul found it necessary to translate the gospel into theology . . ."

[*Language, Hermeneutics and Word of God* (New York: Harper and Row, 1966), p. 132].

5. *History and Hermeneutics* (Philadelphia: Westminster, 1966), p. 39.

6. V. Braaten, Ch. 3 ("The Idea of Revelation Through History") for an excellent, brief historical sketch of how this came about.

7. Examples of this abound in studies of theologians undertaken from such diverse perspectives as Gustaf Wingren in *Theology in Conflict*, esp. pp. 79–83, and Hermann Diem in *Dogmatics*, tr. Harold Knight (Edinburgh: Oliver and Boyd, 1959), esp. Chapters 2–4.

8. This assumption provides the common framework, for example, for the theological disagreements that drive a discussion moving from Karl Barth's proposals in *Church Dogmatics*, Vol. I, Pt. 1. [trans. G. T. Thomson and Pt. 2. trans. G. T. Thomson and Harold Knight (Edinburgh: T & T Clark, 1936, 1956)] through Heinrich Ott's *Theology and Preaching,* [tr. Harold Knight (Philadelphia: Westminster Press, 1965)] and Gerhard Ebeling's *Theology and Proclamation,* [tr. John Riches (Philadelphia: Fortress Press, 1966)] both of them written at least in part in dialogue with Rudolf Bultmann; to Hans-Dieter Bastian's essay "From the Word to the Words," written with an eye to recent communications studies; *Theology of the Liberating Word,* ed. Frederick Herzog (Nashville: Abingdon Press, 1971), pp. 46–76.

9. *Language and Religious Language* (Philadelphia: Westminster, 1961).

10. Moreau, pp. 193–4.

11. Moreau, p. 158.

12. Moreau, p. 185.

13. Moreau, p. 192.

14. Moreau, p. 190.

15. Moreau, p. 148.

16. Moreau, pp. 158–180.

17. "The Use of the Bible in Modern Theology," pp. 180–181.

18. This is the important logical point implicit in Krister Stendahl's controversial distinction between asking of scripture "what it means" and asking "what it meant." ["Biblical Theology, Contemporary," *The Interpreter's Dictionary of the Bible* (New York: Abingdon, 1962), Vol. I, pp. 418–432.] Stendahl suggests that the theologian's task is to explicate "what it means"; the task of the student of scripture is to ask "what it meant." The logical point is that the basic theological judgment ("what it means") may be conceptually discontinuous with the historical and interpretive judgment ("what it meant"). Stendahl's way of putting the distinction has the advantage of allowing us to specify at least four quite different ways in which the two might be related to each other: (i) A theologian might decide that "what it means" is simply identical with "what it meant," by whatever methods of historical inquiry that is established. (ii) He might decide that "what it means" is a systematic elaboration of all the mutually coherent propositions that can be shown to be contained in "what it meant," even though those implications may never have occurred to the original authors and might have been rejected by them. "Contained" may be construed in any of several ways. It might mean "are logically entailed in"; it might be "are encoded in, and may be decoded from by using the following code-key" (cf. allergorical, numerological, etc. explications of "what it means"). (iii) He might decide

that "what it means" is a redescription in contemporary terms of the same phenomena of which "what it meant" was an earlier and now archaic description, unuseable now no matter how well suited it may have been to its own time and culture. This assumes that the theologian has access to the phenomena independent of scripture and "what it meant," so that he can check the archaic description and have a basis for his own. [Clearly, while (ii) may be "translation," (iii) is "redescription."] (iv) He may decide that "what it means" is simply the way the biblical texts are used in contemporary Christian communities, just as "what it meant" is simply the way they were used in an ancient community. In that case the only connection between "what it meant" and "what it means" is genetic: The text of "what it meant" is the direct historical ancestor of the text of "what it means." None of these decisions can itself be either validated or invalidated by exegetical studies of the text, for what is at issue is precisely how exegetical study is related to doing theology.

Criticism of Stendahl's distinction on the grounds that it implies that interpretation of scripture is not the same as "doing theology" begs the issue. It tacitly assumes the validity of one of these four ways (the first) of relating "what it meant" to "what it means." That may be a justified view. Nevertheless, *it is a theological judgment in its own right*, grounded in a construal of the church's "central reality" in a certain way, and is not a historical or hermeneutical judgment. The question of what it means for scripture to be *authority for theology* (i.e., how "what it meant" *bears on* "what it means") cannot be identified with the question how best to *interpret* the biblical texts. Once one has interpreted the texts, especially when their intelligible meaning is clearly "relevant" to men's lives today, one still has not yet decided how "what it meant" should be brought to bear on "what it means." What is more, one does not thereby even have in hand the grounds for deciding the matter. Those grounds are provided by a logically quite different sort of judgment, an imaginative, "holistic" construal of the mode in which God is present among the faithful.

19. Athanasius called them "paradigms." The term had, of course, been used by Plato to refer to the eternally fixed and wholly ideal types of which particular material things are resemblances. "Athanasius came to reserve the term *paradeigma* for those images, like that of 'light' and 'radiance' in which the Bible spoke to reveal the way and will of God to man. Here as elsewhere in the history of Christian thought," Jaroslav Pelikan points out, "a term ... originally borrowed from metaphysics, came eventually to acquire connotations that were more specifically exegetical." *The Light of the World* (New York: Harpers, 1962), pp. 26–27.

20. *Authority* (Cambridge: Harvard University Press, 1958), ed. C. Friedrich, cf. pp. 35–38.

21. Cf. Krister Stendahl's discussion of the mistakenness of Augustine's and Luther's interpretations of Romans, "The Apostle Paul and the Introspective Conscience of the West," *Harvard Theological Review*, Vol. 56, (1963), pp. 199–215. Rudolf Bultmann's findings seem to agree with some aspects of what Stendahl thinks Paul was saying in contradistinction to what Augustine and Luther took him to be saying; cf. "Romans 7 and the Anthropology of Paul," *Existence and Faith* (New York: Meridian Books, 1960), ed. S. Ogden, pp. 147–158.

22. Cf. our discussion of "canon" as a "whole" of "parts" in Chapter 5, pp. 106–107.

23. For a self-conscious illustration of this, *v.* Brevard Childs, *Biblical Theology in Crisis*, Part III.

Chapter 10

Some Morals for Doctrines
of Scripture.
A Review

Each of the last two chapters has sketched one side of a circular relation between scripture and theology. It shows that scripture bears on the making of theological proposals in two ways that are very important but not by themselves decisive. In some ways the circle has formal similarity to the celebrated "hermeneutical circle." First, the concrete ways in which biblical texts are used as scripture in the church's common life helps shape a theologian's imaginative construal of the way that use is conjoined with God's presence among the faithful. The determinate patterns in scripture suggest a range of images from which he may select or construct a root metaphor for that *discrimen.* The particularities of the concrete use of scripture peculiar to the common life of the church as he experiences it will shape which images strike him as most apt. Then, secondly, we showed that it is that imaginative characterization of the central reality of Christianity, "what it is finally all about," that *is* decisive for the way the theologian actually construes and uses biblical texts as scripture in the course of doing theology. Thus this imaginative construal of the *discrimen* fills the function that the "life-relation" or "preunderstanding" of the text is said to fill in accounts of the hermeneutical circle: It decisively determines how one will take the text, what sorts of questions one will assume are

appropriate to ask. Scripture is *relevant* to the making of that imaginative judgment because it shapes the context in which it is done
and provides the range of materials out of which it is made. But
scripture is not *decisive* precisely because the judgment is imaginative, free, creative.

So too, scripture is relevant but not decisive for the *way* it is
construed and used in doing theology. Determinate patterns in it
set limits to the range of ways in which it may be construed. And
particular theological proposals are corrigible by check against biblical texts insofar as they make historical, literary, or theological
claims about the texts. But just how a theologian does finally construe and use scripture is decisively determined, not by the texts as
texts, nor by the texts as scripture, but by that logically prior imaginative judgment. For it yields something like a "gestalt" of the
richly complex but utterly singular mode in which God is present
among the faithful as they use scripture in certain ways. And that
"gestalt" determines what he takes theological proposals to be about,
how that "subject matter" is related to scripture, and therewith how
scripture is to be construed and used.

If we need a substitute for "translation" as a metaphor for the
relation of theology to scripture, we may return to our earlier liken-
ing of "theological positions" to Alexander Calder's mobiles, although not much hangs on this metaphor and it cannot be pushed
very far. It fits to this extent: Individual theological proposals have
their meaning in their use in the context of a "theological position."
"Theological positions" are best seen, not as complex overall arguments, but as imaginative structures in which individual theological
proposals dealing with various theological *loci* are balanced off one
another in different arrangements. The "position" may be taken as a
whole as the expression of a particular vision of the basic character
of Christianity, "what it's all about." The actual way in which any
particular "position" is structured is largely shaped by a root construal of the central reality in Christianity, the mode in which God
is present. Like other works of the imagination, a "theological position" thus solicits critical analysis of its structure and of the roles
played within it of its constituent parts, i.e., theological proposals.
Scripture's bearing on theological proposals must then be analyzed
first in terms of its bearing on the imaginative vision that gives a

position its peculiar shape as a "whole," and then on the way it is construed and used in each of the proposals and clusters of proposals that comprise the various parts of the "whole."

This yields an entirely formal concept of "theology." It does not define theology in terms of a proper subject matter, whether in terms of an ideational reality like a set of true doctrines, or a concrete actuality like a present agent, or an ideal possibility like the transition from inauthentic to authentic existence. Nor does it specify which of the traditional theological topics a contemporary theology ought to treat and which it may ignore. It is a concept of "theology" congruent with our equally formal examination of what "authority of scripture for theology" means in the context of theologians' actual practice of theology, not in their doctrines about scripture.

It is important to repeat here at the end of this study a point on which I insisted at the outset: This is not itself a theological "programmatic essay" making proposals about any theological *locus*, not even the doctrine of scripture.

However, there are some purely formal morals to be drawn from this analysis for certain types of doctrines about scripture. It is appropriate to note them here as a kind of postscript, and to use this as an occasion to review some of the main themes developed in our analysis. We shall do it in two steps corresponding to the two stages in the circle between theology and scripture.

AUTHORITY IN CHURCH AND
WHERE TO TALK ABOUT SCRIPTURE

Both "scripture" and "authority" are best understood in functional terms. Since scripture's authority specifically for theology is a function of its authority for the common life of the church, it is best to review *first* how scripture's "normativeness" for the *church's life* may be understood in functional terms. We noted that to call a set of writings the "church's scripture" is by definition to say that they are "authority" for the church. It is to say that they are the writings that, given certain views of "church," *ought* to be *used* in her common life to nurture and correct her forms of speech and action so that she remains faithful to her task. They are "normative" precisely in that they are to be used in the context of self-critical reflection in which the church tests the forms of her common life and seeks to correct them where the need for that is apparent. In this use scripture is taken as having some kind of "logical force." That is, it is taken as *doing* something that decisively shapes the community's identity, whether teaching doctrine, proposing concepts, rendering an agent, expressing and occasioning saving events, etc. However, each different imaginative construal of the *discrimen,* i.e., the conjunction of God's presence and certain uses of scripture in the church, brings an importantly different sense of "authority." We saw that the differences can be noted (i) by attending to the different sorts of response each solicits (*belief* of doctrines taught, personal *appropriation* of concepts proposed, existential *encounter* with a present agent, quasi-*aesthetic response* to imagistic or symbolic "expressions" of the occurrence of saving events), (ii) by noting the different ranges of phenomena in relation to which each claims to be authoritative (beliefs, concepts, an agent's identity, modes of subjectivity), and, (iii) by distinguishing the various kinds of proximate basis for authority each assumes (something in the ideational mode, or in the mode of a concrete actuality, or in the mode of an ideal possibility).

This functionalist analysis of "scriptural authority over the church" brings with it an important implication concerning the conceptual home of some doctrines of scripture in some theological positions. Scripture's authority specifically for theology, we said, is a function of its authority for the common life of the church. Its authority for the church's common life consists in its being used in certain rulish and normative ways so that it helps to nurture and reform the community's self-identity and the personal identities of her members. Moreover, "theology" is charged with critical examination of the forms of the church's speech and action to see that they remain faithful to her "task." Hence the "authority of scripture" has the status of a *postulate* assumed in the doing of theology in the context of the practice of the common life of a Christian community in which "church" is understood in a certain way. In short, the doctrine of "scripture and its authority" is a postulate of practical theology. Therefore, the least misleading conceptual home of this sort of theological discussion of scripture's authority, i.e., doctrines about biblical authority, would be as part of the elaboration of doctrines about the shaping of Christian existence, both communal and individual, i.e., a part of doctrines of "sanctification" and "ecclesiology."

This would involve a departure from the standard location of doctrines about scripture in theological positions developed in the neo-orthodox period. There doctrines about scripture were consistently developed as part of doctrines of "revelation," rather than as part of doctrines about the shaping of Christian existence. It was regularly suggested that scripture is "authority" because it preserves for us in one form a "content" that has been revealed in the past and must be restated in new forms by contemporary theology.

There are two important objections to this way of giving a *theological* account of scripture's "authority." For one thing, as we have shown at length, explicating scripture's "authority" in terms set by a doctrine of "revelation" misrepresents the way many of the theologians who do so actually use scripture to help authorize their own proposals. It requires the "translation" picture of theology, in which scripture is brought to bear on theological proposals very directly, whereas many of these theologians actually bring scripture to bear on their proposals quite indirectly.

Secondly, there is a convergence of critical judgment from otherwise quite different theological perspectives that the allegedly "biblical" doctrines of "revelation" developed in the neo-orthodox era were conceptually incoherent. To begin with, it has been argued persuasively that there is no one biblical concept "revelation." Moreover, the variety of biblical ways of speaking about God's modes of communication with man cannot be fit together coherently under any synthesis of biblical concepts. So too, it has been argued that the concepts of "revelation" employed by many theologians in the neo-orthodox period not only cannot pass muster as syntheses of biblical concepts of "revelation," but are in their own right conceptually incoherent and are incapable of ordering the variety of theological claims that have been subsumed under them.[1]

The suggestion that it would be less misleading if many doctrines about scripture were set into the context of theological discussions of the shaping of Christian existence rather than in doctrines of revelation does not presuppose that these critiques of the concept "revelation" in many "neo-orthodox" theologies are incontrovertible. Rather, it is grounded in a concern to keep that question open. It ought not to be prejudged by the way the logically independent issue of how to organize theological proposals is settled.

Nor does it imply that claims about the reality of "revelation," in any of several possible senses of that term, must be denied, or that the concept "revelation" should be dropped from Christian theology. On the contrary, it suggests that such claims might be less misleading if they were not all pulled under a conceptual umbrella called "*the* concept of 'revelation' " and were, instead, scattered out among discussions of other theological *loci*. The proposal in no way denies claims about the cognitive aspect of the life of faith. "Identity," both that of the community and that of her individual members, may be shaped by coming to have new beliefs, just as it is shaped by coming to have new attitudes, policies, and affective states. It may include holding a set of beliefs, truth claims about man and the world in which he lives, and God in whose presence he lives, which may be said to be "revealed" or based on "revelation." Locating discussions about the nature and authority of the Bible in the context of discussions of "Christian existence" rather than in the context of a "doctrine of revelation" would not logically invalidate any such claims. On the contrary, it would have the advantage of allowing each sense of "revealed" to be discussed on its own terms. When all the senses in which quite different kinds of things (not only beliefs, but also attitudes, policies, affective states, etc.) that are said to be based on "revelation" are ordered under some one overarching concept "revelation," as happens in conventional doctrines of revelation, then they are all assimilated to the logical tyranny of the overarching concept of which they are said to be "instances," and the nuances distinguishing them from one another are lost.

Nor does the proposal that theologians develop their doctrines about scripture in the context of discussions of "Christian existence" imply a denial of claims about scripture's "inspiration." Doctrines about the inspiration of scripture often provide the major content of doctrines about the Bible. For that reason it has played no role in this essay. We have been concerned with how theologians actually use scripture, rather than with their doctrines about it. However, the proposal does draw attention to a logical point: A doctrine about scripture's "inspiration" is not identical with a doctrine about its "authority." "Authority" cannot *mean* "divinely inspired." "Inspiration" is a property of texts, while "authority," we have argued, is a relational term. To say a writing is "inspired" tells one nothing about *how* it is to be construed, nor does it give reasons for using it one way rather than another to help authorize a theological proposal. Rather, to say a set of writings is "inspired by God" is to begin to give an explanation, not for why they are to be construed or used in certain ways, but for why they function effectively when they *are* so construed and used. It is, the explanations all say in one way or another, the work of God the Holy Spirit. And the work of the Holy Spirit is largely discussed in terms of his relation to the nurturing and reforming of the identity of the Christian community and the personal identities of her members, especially those members called "prophets" and "apostles." Thus, doctrines of the "inspiration of scripture" are second-order doctrines: Given a doctrine of scripture's "authority," i.e., how scripture ought concretely to be used and construed in the common life of the church and in doing theology, a doctrine of "inspiration" gives a theological explanation of why, when scripture is used that way, certain results sometimes follow.

Far from implying an *a priori* negative judgment on doctrines of inspiration, our proposal that doctrines about the Bible ought to be developed in the context of discussions of "Christian existence" is logically congruent with a *variety* of doctrines about the divine inspiration of scripture. It can be used to state the traditional view that it is the texts themselves that are inspired so that, as Sanday put it, "the Bible as a whole and in all its parts was the Word of God, and as such that it was endowed with all the perfections of that Word . . . so that all parts of it are equally authoritative, and in history as well as in doctrine it was exempt from error."[2] It can be used equally fairly to state the nineteenth century "liberal" attempts to derive the "inspiration" not of the texts, but of their authors from an examination of their "religious experience" as that was shaped by their involvement in an evolutionary process of "progressive revelation" in history.[3] And it can be used to state just as fairly Barth's proposal that "inspiration" refers neither to a property of the texts nor to an experience of their authors, but to the promise of God the Holy Spirit to be present among the faithful when these writings are used in the common life of the church.[4]

AUTHORITY IN THEOLOGY AND
HOW TO TALK ABOUT SCRIPTURE

As our analysis showed that "scripture" and "authority" in the church are best understood in functional terms without compromise to their "normativity," so too they can best be understood in regard to "doing theology" in functional terms without loss to their "normativity." Theology is "done" as one of the activities compromising the life of the Christian community. Hence, given certain concepts of "church," it necessarily uses scripture to help authorize its proposals. We suggested that scripture fills the function of "authorizing"a particular theological proposal when it is used to fill some role in an argument designed to make a case for the proposal in the face of objections to it. Since there are several logically quite distinct roles (data, warrant, backing, conditions of rebuttal, etc.), there are several different senses in which scripture can help "authorize" a proposal. There are several different senses of "authority." At the same time, we saw, there are several logically distinct ways in which the scripture that is used can be construed. Each different construal consists in taking as authoritative the determinate pattern of relationships among some one determinate aspect of scripture (the doctrines it teaches, the concepts it proposes, the narratives by which it gives a description of an agent's identity, the images or symbols through which it expresses the occurrence of a saving event, etc.). It is the determinateness of these patterns and of their mutual relations that allows the scripture used in theological arguments to function *normatively* to authorize a proposal.

However, scripture functions this way, we saw, only in the context of a tacit agreement to construe it this way, and not that, and to use it in argument in this way, and not in that. And that agreement rests on a shared imaginative construal of Christianity's "central reality," the mode in which God is present among the faithful. Differences in judgment about how to construe and use scripture in theological arguments are grounded, we tried to show, in different construals of this *discrimen* by which theologies are finally assessed. Each such construal is an act of the imagination, but scripture functions normatively to rule them too. Scripture's patterns, we showed, can suggest "root metaphors" on which to construe Christianity's "central reality" which are patient of reasoned elaboration through arguments in support of particular theological proposals. Further, we suggested how the very determinateness of the patterns in scripture can be relied on to set outside limits to the range of ways in which the "central reality" can be construed; or they can provide a range of acceptable models on which to construe it; or, if scripture is taken as "canon," the pattern of the mutual relations that constitute them a "whole" can dictate the basic patterns in which the *discrimen* is construed.

There are a couple of morals to be drawn from this for the way in which theological proposals about scripture are put. For one thing, it suggests a revision in the usual way in which "Word of God" is used as a technical theological term for scripture. Usually in theologies developed in the neo-orthodox period, to call biblical texts "Word of God" suggests that they are "authority" for theology because they preserve for us in one "form," a "content" that has been revealed in the past and must be restated in new "forms" by contemporary theologians. It suggests that the theologian's task is not to answer the question, "What does the Bible say?" but rather, in Leonard Hodgson's phrase, "What is God using the Bible to say?"[5] But our analysis has shown that when theologians construe and use scripture in the actual practice of theology to help authorize their proposals they do not always or necessarily take it as a means by which God is *asserting* or *proposing* something. They sometimes take it as a means by which he does other sorts of things than teach. When it is used as a technical theological term, "Word of God" must be used with care so that the full *diversity* of ways in which scripture may be construed precisely as authority for theology is not compromised. Our analysis of how "scripture" is "authority" in the context of actual theological practice suggests that it would be less misleading and more fruitful of insight into how he is actually going to construe and use scripture if a theologian made it explicitly clear when he uses "Word of God" in his doctrine about scripture that it is a way of drawing attention, not to "what God is using the Bible to *say*," but to "what God is using the Bible *for*," viz., shaping Christian existence.

The point is this: It may be perfectly correct to say, in a *theological* proposal, that one of the things God is "using" the Bible for is to "say" certain things to men. But that is at most only *one* sort of thing Christians have tended to say God is "doing" with the Bible. Although it is logically possible to construe all the different things one might be inclined to say he is "doing" with the Bible as various ways in which God "tells" men something, it is seriously misleading to do so. It makes "revelation" the cardinal theological topic. It implies that scripture's importance rests on its preserving the "content" of "revelation," and requires us to think of "theology" as the translation into an accessible language of *the* "meaning" of what God is "telling" or "revealing" through the Bible's archaic language. And that, we have been arguing, seriously misrepresents what a number of important modern theologians have in fact been doing and how they use scripture in the course of doing it. Therefore, instead of taking "God saying" as the overarching image for all the various things Christians are inclined to say God "does" with the Bible, we have proposed "shaping identity": Speaking *theologically*, God "uses" the church's various uses of scripture in her common life to nurture and reform the self-identity both of the community and of the individual persons who comprise it. Theological proposals are to elucidate what that identity is and ought to be, and what reforms are called for and why. However, "shaping" is abstract. Every actual set of theological proposals (i.e., every "theological position") is given its peculiar shape by some concrete construal of the mode in which that "shaping" takes place. And that, we have suggested, is an imaginative act, not an exegesis of the "meaning" of what God "says" through the Bible.

There is a second moral to be drawn from our analysis of how "scripture" is "authority" in the practice of theology for the *way* in which doctrines about scripture are put. The analysis suggests the importance of stressing the limits of what such a doctrine can accomplish. The idea of scriptural "authority" is sometimes stated in terms of scripture's power to "control" theological proposals. This is supposed to make a doctrine about scripture of crucial importance to the developing of an adequately Christian theological position. Only if one gets quite straight on how scripture is authority can one be sure of developing theological proposals that are *truly* in accord with scripture, and so, aptly Christian. Our analysis of how "scripture" is "authority" in the doing of theology suggests that this lays too high an expectation on any doctrine of scripture.

We have stressed that theological proposals are finally to be assessed over against a *discrimen*: The uses of scripture in the common life of the Christian community and the active presence of God taken together as criteria that are "organically related to one another as reciprocal coefficients." That is possible in practice only as the entire complex of ecclesial uses of scripture and divine presence is caught up in an imaginative judgment that construes it in all its complexity and singularity in a "root metaphor." In actual practice, it is that imaginative construal that is the basis of assessments of theological proposals and the "theological positions" they comprise.

Discussions of the "authority of scripture" are necessarily abstractions from this *discrimen*. They deal only with one side of it, viz., the use of scripture in the common life of the church. In the nature of the case the other side of the *discrimen*, viz., the work of God the Holy Spirit, is not patient to systematic mapping. The same must be true of "second order" analyses like this essay that reflect on what is at issue as between opposed concepts of the authority of scripture and propose terms in which to state the issues and opposed views fairly; they too deal only with the uses of scripture abstracted from the complex of the concrete *discrimen*.

Accordingly, it is utterly unrealistic to expect either a doctrine about scripture or second-order discussions of scripture and theology like this essay to identify *the* way in which scripture can "control" theology so as to keep it Christianly apt. "Control" is simply a misleading term to use. It surely cannot be supposed that to call scripture "authority" means that properly employed it could "guarantee" the correctness of our proposals, if only we could figure out how to employ it properly. No "hermeneutic" and no doctrine of the authority of scripture could hope to discover the key to that perfect employment. Surely, Christianly speaking, it would be improper even to hope for that. For the full *discrimen* by which theological proposals are finally to be assessed includes the active presence of God. No "theological position" would presume to tell us how to use scripture so as to "guarantee" that God will be present to illumine and correct us. Theological proposals are concerned with what God is now using scripture to do, and no degree of sophistication in theological methodology can hope to anticipate that!

NOTES

1. Cf. discussions by Gerald Downing, *Has Christianity a Revelation?* (London: SCM, 1964), Chs. 2 and 3, essays by Wolfhart Pannenberg, Rolf Rendtorff, and Ulrich Wilkins in *Revelation as History* (New York: Macmillan, 1968), tr. David Granskou, Chs. I, II, and III.
2. W. Sanday, *Inspiration* (New York: Longmans, Green, 1896), p. 392.
3. Cf. Sanday, *Inspiration* and *The Oracles of God* (London: Longmans, Green, 1891); also Charles Gore, *The Doctrine of the Infallible Book* (New York: Doran, n.d.). For a useful survey of this view see Alan Richardson, *The Bible in the Age of Science* (Philadelphia: Westminster, 1961), Ch. 3.
4. Karl Barth, *Church Dogmatics*, I/2 (Edinburgh: T. & T. Clark, 1956), tr. G. T. Thomson & H. Knight, pp. 514–526.
5. "God and the Bible," in L. Hodgson, et al., *On the Authority of the Bible* (London: SPCK, 1960), p. 8.

BIBLIOGRAPHY
AND INDEX

Bibliography

1. BOOKS

Aland, K., *The Problem of the New Testament Canon* (London: Mowbray, 1962)

Barr, J., *The Bible in the Modern World* (London: SCM, 1973)

————, *Old and New in Interpretation* (London: SCM, 1966)

————, *The Semantics of Biblical Language* (London: Oxford University Press, 1961)

Barth, K., *Church Dogmatics* (Edinburgh: T. & T. Clark, 1936), Vols. I, Pts. 1 and 2; II, Pt. 1; III, Pt. 1; IV, Pts. 1–3.

Bartsch, H.-W., *Kerygma and Myth*, Vols. I, II (London: SPCK, 1962)

Bauer, W., *Orthodoxy and Heresy in Earliest Christianity* (Philadelphia: Fortress, 1971)

Boman, T., *Hebrew Thought Compared With Greek* (London: SCM, 1960)

Braaten, C., *History and Hermeneutics* (Philadelphia: Westminster, 1966)

Bright, J., *The Authority of the Old Testament* (Nashville: Abingdon, 1967)

Bruce, F. F., *Tradition Old and New* (Grand Rapids: Zondervan, 1970)

Bryant, R., *The Bible's Authority Today* (Minneapolis: Augsburg, 1968)

Bultmann, R., *Jesus Christ and Mythology* (New York: Scribners, 1958)

————, *Theology of the New Testament*, 2 Vols. (New York: Scribners, 1955)

von Campenhausen, H., *The Formation of the Christian Bible* (Philadelphia: Fortress, 1972)

Childs, B., *Biblical Theology in Crisis* (Philadelphia: Westminster, 1970)

Congar, Y.-M., *Tradition and the Traditions* (London: Burnes & Oates, 1966)

Cullmann, O., *Christ and Time* (Philadelphia: Westminster, 1954)

Diem, H., *Dogmatics* (Edinburgh: Oliver & Boyd, 1959)

————, *Das Problem des Schriftcanons* (Zurich: Evangelisher Verlag, 1952)

————, *Was heisst Schriftgemäss?* (Neukirchen, Kreis Moers, 1958)

Dodd, C., *The Authority of the Bible* (London: Fontana, 1956)

Downing, G., *Has Christianity a Revelation?* (London: SCM, 1964)

Ebeling, G., *The Nature of Faith* (Philadelphia: Fortress, 1961)

————, *The Problem of Historicity* (Philadelphia: Fortress, 1967)

————, *Theology and Proclamation* (Philadelphia: Fortress, 1966)

Evans, C., *Is 'Holy Scripture' Christian? and other questions* (London: SCM, 1971)

Evans, D., *The Logic of Self-Involvement* (London: SCM, 1963)

Farley, E., *Requiem For a Lost Piety* (Philadelphia: Westminster, 1961)

Florovsky, G., *Bible, Church, Tradition: An Eastern Orthodox View* (Belmont: Norland, 1972)

Forsyth, P., *The Principle of Authority* (London: Independent, 1952)

Frei, H. W., *The Eclipse of Biblical Narrative* (New Haven: Yale, 1974)

————, *The Identity of Jesus Christ* (Philadelphia: Fortress, 1975)

Fuchs, E., *Studies of the Historical Jesus* (London: SCM, 1964)

Funk, R., *Language, Hermeneutic, and Word of God* (New York: Harper & Row, 1966)

Gilkey, L., *How the Church Can Minister to the World Without Losing Itself* (New York: Harper & Row, 1964)

————, *Naming the Whirlwind: The Renewal of God-Language* (Indianapolis: Bobbs-Merrill, 1969)

Gore, C., *The Doctrine of the Infallible Book* (New York: Doran, n.d.)

Hamilton, K., *Words and The Word* (Grand Rapids: Eerdmans, 1971)

Hartt, J., *A Christian Critique of American Culture* (New York: Harper & Row, 1967)

Harvey, V., *The Historian and the Believer* (New York: Macmillan, 1966)

Henry, C., *Revelation and the Bible* (Grand Rapids: Baker, 1958)

Heppe, H., *Reformed Dogmatics* (London: Allen & Unwin, 1950)

Jenkins, D., *Tradition, Freedom and the Spirit* (Philadelphia: Westminster, 1951)

Johnson, F. E., *Religious Symbolism* (New York: Harper, 1955)

Johnson, R., *Authority in Protestant Theology* (Philadelphia: Westminster, 1959)

Jowett, B., *The Interpretation of Scripture and Other Essays* (London: Routledge & Sons, n.d.)

Keck, L., *Taking the Bible Seriously* (Nashville: Abingdon, 1962)

Kelsey, D., *The Fabric of Paul Tillich's Theology* (New Haven: Yale University Press, 1967)

Kierkegaard, S., *On Authority and Revelation* (New York: Harper, 1966)

Lindbeck, G., *The Future of Roman Catholic Theology* (Philadelphia: Fortress, 1970)

Machen, J. G., *Christianity and Liberalism* (Grand Rapids: Eerdmans, 1923)

Mackey, J., *The Modern Theology of Tradition* (New York: Herder & Herder, 1963)

Marxsen, W., *The New Testament as the Church's Book* (Philadelphia: Fortress, 1972)

Moltmann, J., *The Theology of Hope* (London: SCM, 1967)

Moreau, J., *Language and Religious Language* (Philadelphia: Westminster, 1961)

Outler, A., *The Christian Tradition and the Unity We Seek* (New York: Oxford, 1957)

Pannenberg, W., ed., *Revelation as History* (New York: Macmillan, 1968)

Pelikan, J., *The Light of the World* (New York: Harper & Row, 1962)

Rahner, K., *Inspiration in the Bible* (New York: Herder & Herder, 1964)

Rahner, K. and Ratzinger, J., *Revelation and Tradition* (New York: Herder & Herder, 1966)

Reid, J., *The Authority of Scripture* (London: Methuen, 1957)

Richardson, A., ed., *Biblical Authority for Today* (Philadelphia: Westminster, 1951)

————, *The Bible in the Age of Science* (Philadelphia: Westminster, 1961)

Robinson, J. and Cobb, J., eds., *The Later Heidegger and Theology* (New York: Harper & Row, 1963)

————, *The New Hermeneutic* (New York: Harper & Row, 1964)

Rowley, H. H., *The Unity of the Bible* (New York: Meridian, 1957)

Sanday, W., *Inspiration* (New York: Longmans, Green, 1896)

————, *The Oracles of God* (London: Longmans, Green, 1891)

Sanders, J., *Torah and Canon* (Philadelphia: Fortress, 1972)

Simon, Y., *The Nature and Functions of Authority* (Milwaukee: Marquette University Press, 1940)

Smart, J., *The Interpretation of Scripture* (Philadelphia: Westminster, 1961)

————, *The Strange Silence of the Bible in the Church* (Philadelphia: Westminster, 1970)

Sundberg, A., *The Old Testament of the Early Church* (Cambridge: Harvard University Press, 1964)

Tavard, G., *Holy Writ or Holy Church* (London: Burnes & Oates, 1959)

Thornton, L., *The Dominion of Christ* (London: Dacre, 1952)

Tillich, P., *Systematic Theology*, 3 Vols. (Chicago: University of Chicago Press, 1963)

Toulmin, S., *The Uses of Argument* (Cambridge: Cambridge University Press, 1963)

Warfield, B. B., *The Inspiration and Authority of the Bible* (Philadelphia: The Presbyterian and Reformed Publishing Co., 1948)

Williams, R., *Authority in the Apostolic Age* (London: SCM, 1950)

Wingren, G., *Theology in Conflict* (Philadelphia: Muhlenberg, 1958)

Wright, G. E., *God Who Acts* (London: SCM, 1952)

————, *The Old Testament and Theology* (New York: Harper & Row, 1969)

2. ARTICLES AND CHAPTERS OF BOOKS

Aland, K., "The Problem of Anonymity and Pseudonymity in Christian Literature of the First Two Centuries," in *The Authority and Integrity of the New Testament* (London: SPCK, 1965), ed. K. Aland, pp. 1–14.

Arendt, H., "What Was Authority?" in *Authority*, ed. C. J. Friedrich, Jr., (Cambridge: Harvard University Press, 1958), pp. 81–113.

Barr, J., "The Authority of the Bible: A Study Outline," *The Ecumenical Review*, 21 (1969), pp. 135–166.

————, "The Old Testament and the New Crisis of Biblical Authority," *Interpretation*, XXV, 1 (Ja 1971), pp. 24–40.

————, "Revelation Through History in the Old Testament and in Modern Theology," in *New Theology #1* (New York: Macmillan, 1964), ed. Peerman and Marty, pp. 60–75.

Barth, K., "Rudolf Bultmann—An Attempt to Understand Him," in *Kerygma and Myth*, II (London: SPCK, 1962), ed. R. H. Fuller, pp. 83–133.

————, "The Strange New World Within the Bible," *The Word of God and The Word of Man* (London: Hodder & Staughton, 1928), ch. II.

Bartsch, H.-W., "Begriff der Versöhnung im Neuen Testament—Die biblische Botschaft vom Frieden," unpublished manuscript in "Minutes of the Conference on God's Reconciling Work Among the Nations Today," 28th June—3rd July, 1965, Ecumenical Institute, Bossey, Switzerland.

Beker, J. C., "The Function of the Bible Today," in *Commitment Without Ideology* (Boston: Pilgrim, 1973), ed. Batson, Beker, Clark.

Bouyer, L., "Holy Scripture and Tradition as Seen by the Fathers," *Eastern Churches Quarterly*, II (1947), Supplemental Issue, pp. 2–16.

Bratsiotis, P., "The Fundamental Principles and Main Characteristics of the Orthodox Church," *The Ecumenical Review*, 12 (Ja 1960), pp. 154–163.

Bultmann, R., "Is Exegesis Without Presuppositions Possible?", in *Existence and Faith* (New York: Meridian, 1960), ed. S. Ogden, pp. 289–297.

————, "The Problem of Hermeneutics," *Essays* (New York: Macmillan, 1955), pp. 234–262.

————, "Prophecy and Fulfillment," in *Essays in Old Testament Hermeneutics* (Richmond: John Knox, 1964), ed. C. Westermann, pp. 50–76.

————, "The Significance of the Old Testament for the Christian Faith," in *The Old Testament and Christian Faith* (New York: Harper & Row, 1963), ed. B. Anderson, pp. 8–36.

Chapman, G. C., "Ernst Käsemann, Hermann Diem, and the New Testament Canon," *Journal of the American Academy of Religion*, XXXVI, 1 (Mar 1968), pp. 3–13.

————, "The Proclamation-History: Hermann Diem and the Historical Theological Problem," *Interpretation*, 18 (1965), pp. 329–345.

Cullmann, O., "The Tradition," in *The Early Church* (Philadelphia: Westminster, 1956), ed. A.J.B. Higgins, pp. 59–105.

Diem, H., "Die Einheit der Schrift," *Evangelische Theologie*, XIII (1953), pp. 385–405.

Dulles, A., "Paul Tillich and the Bible," in *Revelation and the Quest for Unity* (Washington: Corpus, 1968), pp. 220–245.

————, "Reflections on Sola Scriptura," in *Revelation and the Quest for Unity* (Washington: Corpus, 1968) pp. 65–82.

Ebeling, G., "The New Testament and the Multiplicity of Confessions," in *The Word of God and Tradition* (Philadelphia: Fortress, 1968), pp. 148–160.

————, "The Significance of the Critical Method for Church and Theology in Protestantism," in *Word and Faith* (Philadelphia: Fortress, 1960), pp. 17–62.

————, " 'Sola Scriptura' and Tradition," in *The Word of God and Tradition* (Philadelphia: Fortress, 1964), pp. 102–148.

Florovsky, G., "The Ethos of the Orthodox Church," *The Ecumenical Review*, 12 (Ja 1960), pp. 183–198.

Frei, H., "Theological Reflections on the Gospel Accounts of Jesus' Death and Resurrection," *The Christian Scholar*, XLIX, 4 (Winter, 1966), pp. 263–306.

————, "The Mystery of the Presence of Jesus Christ," *Crossroads*, 17, 2 & 3 (Ja.-Mar. & Apr.-June, 1967).

Friedrich, C., "Authority, Reason, and Discretion," in *Authority* (Cambridge: Harvard University Press, 1958), C. Friedrich ed., pp. 28–49.

Gilkey, L., "Cosmology, Ontology, and the Travail of Biblical Language," *Journal of Religion*, 41 (1961), pp. 194–205.

Gore, C., "The Holy Spirit and Inspiration," in *Lux Mundi* (New York: United States Book Co., n.d.)

Hodgson, L., "God and the Bible," in *On The Authority of the Bible* (London: SPCK, 1960), L. Hodgson *et. al.*

de Jouvenel, B., "Authority: The Efficient Imparative" in *Authority*

(Cambridge: Harvard University Press, 1958), ed. C. Friedrich, pp. 159–170.

Käsemann, E., "The New Testament Canon and the Unity of the Church," in *Essays on New Testament Themes* (London: SCM, 1964), pp. 95–107.

Kaufman, G., "Ground of Biblical Authority: Six Theses," *Journal of Bible and Religion*, 24 (Ja 1956), pp. 25–30.

———, "On the Meaning of 'Act of God'," in *God: The Problem* (Cambridge: Harvard University Press, 1972), pp. 119–148.

———, "What Shall We Do With the Bible?," *Interpretation*, XXV, 1 (Ja 1971), pp. 95–112.

Kelsey, D., "Appeals to Scripture in Theology," Journal of Religion 48, 1 (Ja 1968), pp. 1–21.

Konstantinidis, C., "The Significance of the Eastern and Western Traditions Within Christendom," *The Ecumenical Review*, 12 (Ja 1960), pp. 143–153.

Küng, H., " 'Early Catholicism' in the New Testament," in *The Council in Action* (New York: Sheed & Ward, 1963), pp. 159–195.

Lampe, G., "The Authority of Scripture and Tradition," in *Authority and the Church* (London: SPCK, 1965), ed. R. R. Williams, pp. 3–20.

Nineham, D., "The Use of the Bible in Modern Theology," *Bulletin of the John Rylands Library,* 52, 1 (Autumn, 1969), pp. 178–199.

Novak, M., "Culture and Imagination," *Journal of Ecumenical Studies*, 10 (Winter, 1973), pp. 128–140.

Ogden, S., "What Sense Does It Make to Say 'God Acts in History'?" in *The Reality of God* (New York: Harper & Row, 1966), pp. 164–188.

Outler, A., "Traditions in Transit," in *The Old and the New in the Church* (Minneapolis: Augsburg, 1961), ed. P. Minear.

Pannenberg, W., "The Revelation of God in Jesus of Nazareth," in *Theology as History* (New York: Harper & Row, 1967), ed. S. Ogden and J. Cobb, pp. 101–135.

Pelikan, J., "Overcoming History by History," in *The Old and the New in the Church* (Minneapolis: Augsburg, 1961) ed. P. Minear.

Rahner, K., "What is a Dogmatic Statement?," in *Theological Investigations* V (Baltimore: Helicon, 1966), pp. 42–67.

Ramsey, I., "The Authority of the Church Today," in *Authority and the Church* (London: SPCK, 1965), ed. R. R. Williams, pp. 61–83.

Robinson, J. M., "Theology as Translation," *Theology Today,* 20 (Ja 1964), pp. 518–527.

Schlink, E., "The Significance of the Eastern and Western Traditions for the Christian Church," *The Ecumenical Review,* 12 (JA 1960), pp. 133–142.

Schutz, J., "Apostolic Authority and the Control of Tradition: I Cor. xv," *New Testament Studies*, 15, pp. 439–457.

Scroggs, R., "Tradition, Freedom, and the Abyss," in *New Theology #8* (New York: Macmillan, 1971), pp. 84–104.

Skydsgaard, K., "Scripture and Tradition," in *Challenge and Response* (Minneapolis: Augsburg, 1966), ed. W. Quanbeck, pp. 25–59.

————, "Scripture and Tradition," *Scottish Journal of Theology*, 9 (1956), pp. 337–358.

————, "Tradition as an Issue in Contemporary Theology," in *The Old and the New in the Church* (Minneapolis: Augsburg, 1961), ed. P. Minear, pp. 20–36.

Stendahl, K., "The Apostle Paul and the Introspective Conscience of the West," *Harvard Theological Review*, 56 (1963), pp. 199–215.

————, "Biblical Theology, Contemporary," in *Interpreter's Dictionary of the Bible* (Nashville: Abingdon, 1962), pp. 418–432.

Tavard, G., "Scripture, Tradition, and History," *Downside Review*, 72, pp. 234 ff.

Index